THE
RENEWAL
OF MYSTICAL
THEOLOGY

THE
RENEWAL
OF MYSTICAL
THEOLOGY

Essays in Memory of
John N. Jones (1964–2012)

Edited by
Bernard McGinn

A Herder & Herder Book
The Crossroad Publishing Company
New York

A Herder & Herder Book
The Crossroad Publishing Company
www.CrossroadPublishing.com

Book design by The HK Scriptorium

Library of Congress Cataloging-in-Publication Data
available from the Library of Congress.

ISBN 978-0-8245-2231-5

Books published by The Crossroad Publishing Company may be purchased at special quantity discount rates for classes and institutional use. For information, please e-mail sales@CrossroadPublishing.com.

Contents

Contributors   vii

Foreword
Gwendolin Herder, Publisher of
   The Crossroad Publishing Company   ix

Introduction
Bernard McGinn   xiii

"Poem. For John, with Gratitude"
Matthew Lickona   xvii

Part I
Historical Perspectives on Mystical Theology

1. The Eschatological Consciousness of the Christian Mystics
   Harvey D. Egan, S.J.   3

2. Comprehending the Incomprehensible:
   John Scottus Eriugena as Mystic
   Bernard McGinn   25

3. From the Radically Apophatic to the Radically
   Kataphatic: From Meister Eckhart to Jacob Boehme
   Cyril O'Regan   47

4. Showings to Share: The Mystical Theology
   of Julian of Norwich
   Marilyn McCord Adams   88

5. The Ignatian Mystic
   Phyllis Zagano   109

6. Teresa of Avila on the Song of Songs
   Lawrence S. Cunningham   131

7. Is Darkness a Psychological or a Theological Category
   in the Thought of John of the Cross?
   Edward Howells   140

8. The Contemplative Turn in Ficino and Traherne
   Mark A. McIntosh   162

Part II
Contemporary Issues in Mystical Theology

9. When Mysticism Is Outlawed: The Case of Said Nursi
   Margaret Benefiel   179

10. Being as *Símbolo*: A Latino Reading of
    Dionysian Aesthetics
    Peter J. Casarella   189

11. In Christ: Theosis and the Preferential Option for the Poor
    Roberto S. Goizueta   219

12. The Christocentric Mystagogy of
    Joseph Ratzinger/Benedict XVI
    Robert P. Imbelli   238

13. Contemplative Ecology: A Mystical Horizon
    for the Twenty-First Century
    Diarmuid O'Murchu, MSC   263

Contributors

MARILYN MCCORD ADAMS
  Philosophy of Religion Center, Rutgers University
MARGARET BENEFIEL
  Executive Director, Shalem Institute for Spiritual Formation, Washington, DC
PETER J. CASARELLA
  Department of Theology, University of Notre Dame
LAWRENCE S. CUNNINGHAM
  Department of Theology, University of Notre Dame
HARVEY D. EGAN, S.J.
  Department of Theology, Boston College
ROBERTO S. GOIZUETA
  Department of Theology, Boston College
EDWARD HOWELLS
  Department of Theology, Heythrop College
ROBERT P. IMBELLI
  Department of Theology, Boston College
MATTHEW LICKONA
  La Mesa, CA
BERNARD MCGINN
  Divinity School, University of Chicago
MARK A. MCINTOSH
  Department of Theology, Loyola University, Chicago
DIARMUID O'MURCHU, MSC
  Dublin, Ireland
CYRIL O'REGAN
  Department of Theology, University of Notre Dame
PHYLLIS ZAGANO
  Senior Research Associate-in-Residence, Hofstra University

Foreword

Gwendolin Herder
Publisher of The Crossroad Publishing Company

The world of study and publishing has much for which to thank John N. Jones, as Bernard McGinn explains in the following introduction. At The Crossroad Publishing Company, with its imprints Crossroad and Herder & Herder, we were given the great blessing to be with John day-in, day-out for twelve precious years.

Born in Richfield, Utah, on May 22, 1964, John graduated summa cum laude with a degree in Religion from Claremont McKenna College in 1986. But he began his collegiate career at a community college so that he could be close to his recently widowed mother. That happy blend of intellectual excellence and personal generosity was to become a hallmark of John's life.

Following his undergraduate studies, he traveled to Spain on a Thomas J. Watson Fellowship to pursue his interest in Spanish mysticism. John later earned a master's degree in Theological Studies at Harvard, an M.A. at Yale, and—with the successful defense of his dissertation on the Trinitarian theology of Pseudo-Dionysius—a Ph.D. from Yale University in 1997.

Dr. John Norman Jones arrived at our office, manuscript in hand, hoping to talk to an editor. We took him out to lunch, and by the end of the meal in a noisy Manhattan restaurant, somewhat surprisingly, John had accepted the position of Marketing Manager for the Herder & Herder theological program. We were that impressed with his learning, his kindness, and his obvious dedication to craftsmanship, and we hoped he would be able to use those gifts to sustain and enhance the Herder family's 200-year tradition of publishing. We were not disappointed. John brought excellence as he brought friendship.

As our Editorial Director, John quietly did much to help shape the direction of Crossroad and Herder & Herder. He built long-term relationships with both established authors and new voices. He worked on important books by writers such as Meister Eckhart, Bernard McGinn, Francis Cardinal George, Christoph Cardinal Schonborn, Timothy Gallagher, Ronald Rolheiser, George Weigel, Gregory Popcak, Rowan Greer, Paula D'Arcy, Richard Rohr, Brian Robinette, Phyllis Zagano, and many others. But he also conceived and ran the Herder & Herder Young Theologians program. He worked hard to develop the manuscripts of first-time authors, though he rarely accepted credit for the role he played in the finished book. Instead, his focus was on the author and the work—the way it might help the author to grow as a thinker and writer, energize the theological debates of the day, and bring the reader further along in the search for truth, as well as the pursuit of hope.

Like a true mystic, John held his own life lightly even as he took it seriously. He owned little, and he spent long hours in meditation. Though an accomplished poet and scholar in his own right, he chose instead to work as an editor, placing his considerable gifts in service to the thought and writing of others. In both his personal and his professional life, he sought the comfort and happiness of those around him, making sure their concerns were understood and addressed. But his worldly detachment and self-effacing manner were not an attempt to retreat from life. Rather, they enabled him to better engage it: to push forward without seizing the spotlight, to practice justice swathed in kindness.

A writer by nature, John worked hard on refining his impressive public speaking skills. John cared deeply about communicating authentically with others. With John, one felt truly understood and always supported. Only after his early death did we learn just how many people he accompanied in his kindness and wisdom. That illness impeded his ability to speak added immense pain to his time of passion.

On the night of October 8, 2012, John Jones passed away peacefully after a courageous battle with oral cancer. John met the illness—and the deep suffering it brought—with characteristic grace, a grace informed by the profound sense of hope he cultivated over decades spent studying mystical traditions and applying the wisdom he found there. All of us who surrounded him during his last weeks experienced it as a grace. As death approached, John's goodness and graciousness shone ever more brightly. He used what ability he had left to concern himself with others' well-being, and actively attached himself to a hope so strong it never left him while he labored to leave the earth—a powerful testament to his beautiful character and a lasting gift to those near him. John's life was consummate in its simple coherence of thought and practice.

Even today, every time I leave the office I double check my keys—John used to be right there in case I would not have them with me. Then I remember him reviewing my letters or marketing texts, gently suggesting, "Can we put the word *hopeful* in."

We would like to thank Professor Bernard McGinn, who conceived and initiated this volume, and also did much of the work for it. Thanks to every contributor for writing a special chapter for John. Thanks also for the poetry of Matthew Lickona, who understood John, and to David Ciampichini for giving us the beautiful portrait for the cover. — Then, there is all that hope that John will enjoy the book.

Introduction

Bernard McGinn

Some of those who have contributed to this volume of studies in memory of John N. Jones are old enough to remember the days when mystics and mystical theology were considered marginal to the church, inhabitants of the stranger shores of religion. For Catholics, mystics were those "rare birds" (*rarae aves*) whose unusual, often bizarre graces (visions, locutions, ecstasies, stigmata, elevations, etc.), demonstrated that God was really more on the side of those suspicious of mystics, although a few of the mystical birds had been approved by ecclesiastical authority after long examination. In any case, the birds were meant for admiration rather than imitation. For many Protestant Christians, the very word "mysticism" conjured up a nonevangelical, ersatz form of Christianity, more dependent on Greek philosophical religion than the gospel. All that has changed within living memory.

The emergence of the mystical element from the fringes of respectability to the central role it now enjoys in Christian faith is evident, even if the causes and ultimate significance of this movement of the Spirit still remain somewhat hidden. Nonetheless, the change has been real, as shown by the fact that fifty years ago only a handful of the major mystical texts of Western Christianity were readily available to those hungry to drink from the authentic sources of this tradition. Today, devoted seekers (and even curious readers) have access to more of the solid food of deep spirituality and mystical piety than perhaps at any time in the history of Christianity. This revival has nurtured a renewed attention to the theological study of mysticism, as a host of articles, books, and conferences of the past decades has amply demonstrated.

The renewal of mystical theology has involved the efforts of devoted people from many walks of life—not only mystics themselves but also scholars and students, teachers and preachers, retreat givers, seekers after spiritual wisdom, and (yes) editors and publishers convinced of the importance of making the riches of the mystical tradition available to a new generation of readers and willing to devote their efforts to this endeavor. This is where the late John N. Jones, Editorial Director of the Crossroad Publishing Company for many years, comes in for special remembrance. Taken from us all too soon, John was a major figure in the renewal of mystical theology in the contemporary world, partly through his own writings, but especially through his generous help and sagacious care in soliciting, editing, and producing a wide range of books on spirituality and mysticism during his time at Crossroad-Herder. John was an academic, trained in the critical study of religion at Yale University, where he defended a dissertation on the mystical theology of Pseudo-Dionysius in 1998. John's life, however, took a different turn after he began working for Crossroad-Herder in 2000. Although he published important essays on Dionysius, John's real vocation as a nurturer of the revival of interest in mystical theology emerged during his years at the press. Gwendolin Herder, the Publisher of Crossroad-Herder, speaks to the impact he had on his friends and coworkers at the press in the Foreword she kindly wrote for this volume, and all the contributors to this book could testify to what John meant to them and their professional work. Some have done so in the essays that follow; all have shown their eagerness to honor John, as a friend, colleague, and consummate editor. This is a signal mark of the affection and respect we all had for John N. Jones.

A brief word about my own contact with John, which inspired me to put this volume together. In the late 1990s John sent me a copy of his dissertation. I thought that it was an original and provocative work, one that deserved publication as an important contribution to the renewed interest in Dionysius. John, however, soon began working for Crossroad-Herder as what I would call their "Editor for Mysticism," though I realize he did much more for the press over the years he worked there. Ever on the lookout for good new scholarship on mystical topics, John and I consulted over the years about promising dissertations, submitted manuscripts, and the like, although he was very much his own best judge about these matters. I had the opportunity to work closely with him in the editing and production of the two most recent volumes of my ongoing history of Christian mysticism under the general title *The Presence of God*. John was a superb editor, one with a discriminating sense of when to offer help and when to leave the author to make his or her own mistakes (which might be later corrected). What most impressed me about him was the tact and the generosity he extended to new authors, meticulously working with them to refine their manuscripts for publication. In all his work as an editor he demonstrated rare dedication and superb intelligence.

I considered John a friend and colleague, although our contacts were not frequent. Over the months of his final illness in 2012, as I was finishing the page proofs for *The Varieties of Vernacular Mysticism* (Crossroad-Herder, 2013), we had a number of e-mail exchanges, but, fitting his self-effacing nature, John said nothing about his health problems and I was absorbed with many projects. Receiving an e-mail from the press about his death in October 2012 was a tremendous shock for me. In subsequent weeks and months, the more I thought about John's tragic early death, the more I became convinced that some memorial to such an extraordinary human being, one who did so much for the renewal of mystical theology, was a fitting, if insufficient, tribute to a person who dealt with others with such gentleness, helpfulness, and generosity.

With the encouragement of Gwendolin Herder, I began to develop plans for this volume. My intention was to ask for contributions from authors who had worked with John at Crossroad-Herder, or who had had close contact with him over the years. The staff at the press provided me with a helpful list of such persons, many known to me, others not. All those I contacted were invariably enthusiastic about the idea of honoring John, but, given the obligations of the academic life today, some possible contributors were regretfully not able to commit to writing an essay for the volume. Nonetheless, the reader should be aware that, along with the thirteen essays contained in this volume, there is "a cloud of witnesses" hovering over this tribute.

The essays in this collection vary greatly. Some are detailed studies with abundant scholarly apparatus; others are more general surveys. This is as it should be, because the renewal of mystical theology is being pursued in many ways today. I have divided the contributions into two broad sections: (I) Historical Resources for the Renewal of Mystical Theology; and

(II) Contemporary Issues in Mystical Theology. It is an artificial division: When was history not important for current discussion, especially in spirituality and mysticism? When were contemporary issues not imbued with historical implications? Nonetheless, the distinction is helpful for differentiating between the essays that are primarily directed to investigating major mystical texts of the Christian tradition and those that analyze what the tradition may bring to bear on current concerns. The eight essays of part I are organized in chronological fashion, beginning with a broad piece on a key issue in Christian mysticism ranging over many centuries and figures. The next seven essays feature original analyses of key mystics in the Christian tradition between the ninth and the seventeenth centuries—John Scottus Eriugena; Meister Eckhart and Jacob Boehme; Julian of Norwich; Ignatius of Loyola; Teresa of Avila; John of the Cross; and Marsilio Ficino and Thomas Traherne. The five essays of part II feature fresh perspectives on crucial contemporary issues in the study of mysticism, one dealing with a crisis in modern Islamic mysticism, three concerning issues in Catholic mysticism, and a final essay returning to a broad perspective, that is, the relation of mysticism to ecology.

Some introductions to volumes of collected essays feature detailed descriptions of the contents of the volume, summarizing the purpose and content of each piece. I would like to spare the reader this editorial intrusion, confident that anyone who picks up this book is well able to read the titles and will need no intermediary for the experience of plunging into the essays themselves. What I do want to say before closing this brief introduction, however, is a sincere word of thanks to each of the distinguished authors who agreed to contribute to this memorial volume—all of whom have expressed their personal debt to our friend, John N. Jones. I am also immensely grateful to Gwendolin Herder and the other members of the staff at Crossroad–Herder who encouraged this volume from the start and whose many efforts have brought it to fruition. John's memory will live on, not only in the many authors whose works he nurtured into print but also among all who are concerned with the renewal of mystical theology that is so evident in the essays in this memorial volume. In the communion of saints we pray: *Requiescat in pace.*

Chicago, July 2015

For John, with Gratitude

Matthew Lickona

Of course the devil grabbed your tongue
You fool, you wagged it oft enough,
And let it drip with scorn for rough-
made words that chapped and stung
the chilly soul; to nudge it toward despair;
preferring gentle speech that played
like sunlight cross your cell, strayed
to laughter, and singed with devil's hair.
Of course your flesh is wasting now
you monk, so rarely you indulged it.
(Or if you did, so rarely you divulged it.)
Eschewing fatted calf for sacred cow,
retreating from your matter into mind
til now your Brother Ass begins to buck
against its weightless load, no truck
'twixt soul and what gets left behind
for now. And now of course you walk the path
that all men walk, but I still fear to tread,
believing more than I the rising from the dead
and God whose love has vanquished all his wrath.
Your flickering tongue, your flashing eye
Your bearded wit and naked grin
Your boyish faith that love will win
These will endure, and only death will die.

(October 3, 2012)

Part I

HISTORICAL RESOURCES FOR THE RENEWAL OF MYSTICAL THEOLOGY

1

The Eschatological Consciousness of the Christian Mystics

Harvey D. Egan, S.J.

Karl Rahner maintained that biblical texts about the afterlife are not a preview or advanced coverage of coming events but statements about a person's *present* existence before God. In his view, knowledge of the last things comes from an etiological anticipation of what we know here and now about ourselves as graced sinners in relation to God.[1]

The Christian mystics fascinated Rahner because he appreciated that from them one "hears the views of the person who himself experiences most clearly and with the least distortion the relationship which exists between the human subject and . . . God."[2] Moreover, because "the characteristic piety of a mystic is given a special depth and power by the specifically mystical element of his piety,"[3] Rahner highlighted the mystic as someone for whom the often barely audible and frequently distorted experience of God found in everyone has been purified and amplified—and with no deformation. In short, the mystics are the true loudspeakers of the redeemed sinner's standing before God.

On the basis of Rahner's theology, I claim that what one finds in the lives of the Christian mystics can prove useful for a deeper theology of death, purgatory, hell, and heaven. These realities are not only merited in this life but also, to some extent, begin and are experienced here. Mystical death, for example, sheds some light on the mystery of actual death. I also contend that the intense sensitivity of the Christian mystics to the presence of the least resistance in their relation to God's love causes purgatorial and even hellish states that can be viewed as a paradigm of postmortem purgatory and hell. In addition, when purged of their sins,

3

even the remnants of sin (their least disorder), the mystics by God's grace are capable of an extraordinary ability to love more selflessly; that is, they experience a foretaste of eternal life. Thus, the mystical journey foreshadows physical death, postmortem purification, damnation, and eternal life.

MYSTICAL DEATH CONSCIOUSNESS

When the apostle Paul wrote, "I know a man in Christ who fourteen years ago was caught up to the third heaven. Whether it was in the body or out of the body, I do not know—God knows. And I know that this man—whether in the body or apart from the body, I do not know, but God knows—was caught up to paradise" (2 Cor. 12:2–4), he was the first person in the Christian tradition to attest to the experience of mystical death. And because of his transformation into Christ, he confessed that it was no longer he who lived but Christ living in him (Gal. 2:20)—yet another aspect of his mystical death.

Instances of mystical death abound in the history of Christianity. For example, the Franciscan ecstatic mystic Giles of Assisi (ca. 1190–1262) asserted that during his many mystical raptures—some lasting for weeks—he felt as if the soul were being wrenched away from his body and his body dying. These God-given experiences empowered him to contemplate the beauty of his own soul, to learn divine secrets, and to labor more diligently in God's service. Mystically married to God, Giles became a parent of transcendental life for others. When asked if he desired martyrdom, he claimed that mystical death—that is, contemplation—was the better death.[4]

Bonaventure (ca. 1217–1274) placed Christ at the beginning, in the middle, and at the end of his famous work *The Soul's Journey into God*, to underscore Jesus' major role in the soul's mystical ascent into God. This treatise focused, however, on Christ, the soul's bridegroom, the God-Man who is the gateway and door to mystical contemplation, to "ecstatic anointings" that produce the "learned ignorance" so dear to many mystics. Thus, the mystical Christ, the very life of the soul's life, the Christ who heals and transforms the soul's spiritual senses and then plunges it into its deepest depths, dominates the *Journey*. Bonaventure urged, "Let us, then, die and enter into this darkness. Let us impose silence upon all our cares, our desires, and our imaginings." With Christ crucified, who as a dark fire "that totally inflames and carries us into God by ecstatic unctions and burning affections," one "passes out of this world" in mystical death to the Father. Moreover, "whoever loves this death can see God."[5]

At the age of twenty-three, Catherine of Siena (1347–1380) experienced her "mystical death," a four-hour God-given ecstasy in which her body seemed to be dead.[6] The classic statement on mystical death, however, is found in *The Spiritual Canticle* by John of the Cross (1542–1591). He wrote, "How do you endure, O Life, not living where you live, and being brought near death by the arrows you receive from that which you conceive of your Beloved."[7] John, therefore, is paradigmatic of those mystics who view contemplation as a type of mystical death, that is, not living on earth because, during contemplation, one lives in heaven.

In addition to the delightful raptures of contemplation—that is, mystical death in the usual sense—there is also a dark rapture with all the psycho-physical marks of ecstasy that is brought about by an intense and painful concentration on God's absence, an abrupt invasion of a wild and unbearable desire for God, an acute sense of the loss of the self's former fervor, and a seeming loss of all meaning, except hanging and dying on the cross with Christ. I would ascribe this type of mystical death to the mysticism of the suffering servant or victim soul.

The urban anchoress Margaret the Cripple (d. ca. 1265)[8] exemplifies this form of dark mystical death. Margaret embodied the profound mystery of suffering and dying with Christ crucified. Mystics of her tenor are not those who experience the cross as the setbacks encountered in great apostolic undertakings but rather those who manifest God's hand even in life's apparent absurdities: natural failings, physical defects, sickness, suffering, old age, and death. More important, they have also grasped the redemptive value of suffering, that Christ redeemed the world through his undergoing loneliness and isolation, not only by his death on the cross; they have learned how even hidden, sacrificial love is apostolic. The victim-soul mystic is the prime example of the person who allows God alone to determine who and what one is. By focusing on suffering as the way to God, Margaret indirectly criticized the fascination of her age with rapturous consolations.

Mother Teresa of Calcutta (1910–1997) was once called "the most powerful woman in the world" by the former Secretary General of the United Nations, Javier Pérez de Cuéllar. This hyperbole notwithstanding, it can be said of this Albanian peasant "Saint of the Gutters," the saint of God's thirst to love and be loved by humanity, that she is history's best-known nun. Appreciated primarily for her service to the "poorest of the poor"—and honored for it through a Nobel Prize—Mother Teresa's extraordinary holiness and mystical depths came to light only a few years ago because of the publication of her private correspondence. Early in her life as a nun, Mother Teresa took an exceptional private vow to consider even the smallest voluntary refusal to submit to God's will to be a "mortal sin." Writing later to her spiritual director, she informed him that she often begged Jesus for the grace to do promptly whatever he asked her, however small, and that she would "rather die" than refuse him. This private vow was the motivation behind all that she did and one of "her greatest secrets."

Mother Teresa's writings contain only a brief statement about the 1946–1947 honeymoon period of her mystical life, during which she experienced so much "union—love—faith—trust—prayer—sacrifice."[9] Reflecting back on this stage of her life, she felt much nostalgia for the intimacy she had experienced with Christ: "The sweetness and consolation and union of those six months passed by too soon."[10] There were also "oasis moments" of "joy untold" that punctuated her long bouts of darkness, loneliness, and pain of loss. Her spiritual directors later stated that she was on the brink of transforming union.

Mother Teresa's writings, however, are replete with references to desolation, spiritual darkness, interior suffering, spiritual dryness, deep loneliness, an "icy cold" interior, acute feelings of emptiness and of her own nothingness ("What are you doing, God, to one so small?"). Her feelings of love for God, for Christ, and for others—as well as any experience of faith, hope, and love—simply vanished. The bone-marrow sense of God's absence, of God's rejection, of fear that her soul, Jesus, and heaven were illusions, and of a radical longing for God became her "inner hell" for more than half a century. Mother Teresa's account of her severe trials surpasses even the classical description of the dark night of the soul found in the writings of John of the Cross—whom she had read, but about whom she had remarked only about his deep sense of

God. The exceptionally long fifty-five-year period of interior dereliction—exceeding even the prolonged years of suffering of Paul of the Cross—is unique in the Christian mystical tradition. Her state of mystical martyrdom, of the dark mystical death, serves as a counter-balance to the popular view of mysticism as consisting of ecstatic experiences and states of rapture.

It is remarkable that under these circumstances Mother Teresa never wavered in her resolve to live for "God alone, God everywhere, God in everybody and in everything, God always."[11] Experiencing that God was destroying everything in her to fill her with himself, she came to the realization that this darkness—which she called "her greatest secret" (even her closest collaborators knew nothing about it)—allowed her to identify more closely with the poor. "It often happens," she wrote, "that those who spend their time giving light to others, remain in darkness themselves."[12] The true nature of Christ's early and repeated call to her, "*Come, Come, carry Me into the holes of the poor. Come be My light,*"[13] led to her peaceful acceptance and love of her extraordinary interior darkness as an instrument through which she brought Christ's light to others. In one of the most powerful statements of suffering-servant mysticism ever written, Mother Teresa prophesied, "If I ever become a saint—I will surely be one of darkness. I will continually be absent from heaven—to light the light of those in darkness on earth."[14]

One discovers another anomaly in Mother Teresa's writings: an almost complete absence of references to sin and disorder. For this reason, I see much more in her mystical dereliction than what is classically called the dark night of the spirit. Her freedom from sinfulness, from disorder, and her total fidelity to God's will indicate a person totally open and offering no resistance to God's workings. Her mystical death consciousness is a reparative, redemptive, expiatory death consciousness—a suffering for the salvation of others. The suffering-servant mysticism of the "saint of darkness" is a lived commentary on three Pauline texts. In 2 Corinthians 5:21, the apostle speaks of the sinless Christ who became sin for our salvation; in Colossians 1:24, Paul rejoices that he is filling up what is lacking in Christ's sufferings. Mother Teresa knew that she, her nuns, and all Christians, were called to be "the spirit, mind, heart, mouth, eyes, ears, hands, and feet of Christ," that is, to be the God-forsaken man on the cross for the redemption and salvation of others. In this way, she took upon herself the darkness and sufferings of others—even the pain of resisting the temptations that plagued those she saved.

Mother Teresa lived what the apostle Paul said about himself in Galatians 2:20: "I have been crucified with Christ; it is no longer I who live, but Christ who lives in me." "When outside," she wrote, "in the work—or meeting people—there is a presence—of somebody living very close—in very me."[15] Although she understood that she and her sisters must "more and more be His Light—His Way—His life—His Love in the slums,"[16] she found the hungry, thirsty, naked, sick, and unwanted Christ "in His distressing disguise"[17] in the slums.

Mother Teresa's spirituality and mysticism are utterly simple: mad, passionate, total love of Jesus Christ. "From childhood," she wrote, "the Heart of Jesus has been my first love."[18] One might add that he was her only love: Christ in the poor and the poor in Christ. Mass and the Real Presence of Christ in the Blessed Sacrament dominated her life. She spoke of herself as leading a eucharistic life, a Calvary life. Despite years of crucifying darkness, she affirmed that an "unbroken union" with Christ existed because her entire being was centered on him. "I have loved him blindly, totally, only," she wrote. "I use every power in me—in spite of my feelings—to make Him loved personally by the Sisters and people. I will let him have a free Hand with and in me."[19] She spoke of herself and of her nuns not as social workers—whose work she valued—but as contemplatives who are "twenty-four hours a day with Jesus."[20] And what a wonderful grace and blessing to be able to say at the end of one's life: "Jesus, I have never refused you anything."[21]

PURGATORIAL MYSTICAL CONSCIOUSNESS

The anonymous fourteenth-century author of the classic *The Cloud of Unknowing* provides an unusually clear and concise paradigm for understanding postmortem purgation, or purgatory.[22] Writing specifically for those "who feel the mysterious action of the Spirit in their inmost being stirring them to love" and have resolved to "follow Christ perfectly . . . into the inmost depths of contemplation,"[23] the anonymous monk instructed the contemplative tyro to create a "cloud of forgetting" between oneself and all created things. Because only love, not thought, can reach God, the novice must forget everything and "firmly reject all clear ideas however pious and delightful for they are more hindrance than help" (*Cloud*, chap. 9).

This practice, aided by the repetition of a short, meaningful word, such as "God" or "Christ," causes a "cloud of unknowing" to arise between the contemplative and God. Because thinking has stopped, the contemplative must learn to be at home in the darkness caused by the absence of knowledge and to direct what the monk calls a "dart of blind desire" toward God. Only blind and naked contemplation, that is, one shorn of all thought and images—but filled with love—can penetrate the cloud between God and the contemplative and allow the person to rest quietly in the loving awareness of God's very being.

This blind, loving contemplation is initially easy, consoling, and joyful but quickly turns into a deeply purgative flame. By creating the clouds of forgetting and unknowing, distractions soon arise to become the person's "purgatory" (*Cloud*, chap. 23). Deprived of their natural activity, imagination and reason rebel, which creates a purgative state filled with "great storms" and "temptations." The purging period intensifies when the person loses the contemplative desire, suffers from its loss, cannot return to regular meditation, and is tempted either to strain spiritually or to give up and return to an ignoble or lukewarm Christian life.

Moreover, as the blind stirring of love roots itself more deeply in the soul, it causes all past sins to arise and torture the person (*Cloud*, chap. 69). The monk wrote, "No evil thought, word, or deed remains hidden. . . . At times the sight is as terrible as a glimpse of hell and he is tempted to despair of ever being healed and relieved of his sore burden" (ibid.).[24] If he perseveres in the cloud of unknowing, however, he will be rewarded with the experience of his past sins being healed. "Slowly he begins to realize that the sufferings he endures are not really hell at all, but his purgatory" (ibid.). This is a clear statement of the hellish and purgatorial consciousness of many Christian mystics.

Once the naked dart of mystical love heals the remnants of personal sins, the contemplative suffers greatly from experiencing self as a "lump of sin." The root unity of one's sinfulness, that is, original sin, now shows itself for the evil it is. "This foul, wretched lump called sin," the monk penned, "is none other than yourself" (*Cloud,* chaps. 43, 69). Instructive is his observation that the "cloud of unknowing" causes this profound, holistic tasting of one's sinfulness, which is both hellish and purging.

According to the anonymous author, not only sinfulness but also human existence itself separates us from God. The contemplative comes to the excruciating realization that a great chasm exists between self and God. The painful inability to forget self during contemplation causes an even deeper purification. The monk taught that the "elemental sense of your own blind being will remain between you and your God" (*Privy Counseling,* chap. 13). The "simple awareness of my being," the "cross of self," "the painful burden of self . . . makes my heart break with weeping because I experience only self and not God" (ibid., chap. 14). This purgative experience, however, eventually sets the contemplative "on fire with the loving desire to experience God as he really is" (ibid.).

Employing the typology of his day, the author presents Mary Magdalene, sitting lovingly at Jesus' feet, as the ideal contemplative (*Cloud,* chaps. 16–17). (It was actually Mary of Bethany.) She is the one who reveals the most intense kind of contemplative suffering. Never ceasing to feel an abiding sorrow for the sins that she carried like a great secret burden in her heart all her life, Mary's greatest pain came from her inability to love as much as she was loved. "Sick from her failure to love," the anonymous writer emphasized, "for this she languished with painful longing and sorrow almost to the point of death" (ibid., chap. 16). The more one experiences contemplative love, the greater will be the desire to return this love in full. At the zenith of what is often called the dark night of the spirit, love itself is the contemplative's healing and transforming torture, earthly purgatory. This perceptive monk stressed that the God-given blind stirring of love causes this purgatory only because of the person's resistance and inability to love as much as he or she is loved.

Another example of an earthly purgatory can be found in *The Relation of 1654,* the spiritual autobiography of Marie of the Incarnation (1599–1672), a French Ursuline mystic and the first woman missionary to the New World.[25] The autobiography gives convincing evidence that only someone who has passed through all the stages of the mystical life and attained spiritual maturity could have written it. Marie's explanation of the thirteen states of prayer do not fit the classical pattern of mystical ascent as purgation, illumination, and union. Moreover, when she was in her forties—long after mystical marriage, filled with "so gentle and sweet a fire"[26]—she suffered yet another eight years of mystical purgation, an anomaly because transformative union is usually recognized as the summit of the mystical life.[27]

The slumbering disorders of Marie's lower nature reawakened and brutally assaulted her. Temptations to blasphemy, immodesty, and pride—coupled with a strong sense of being the vilest and most debased of God's creatures—surprised and humiliated her. Debilitating lassitude, anger toward community members, and fear that past blessings were only diabolical delusions encouraged suicidal inclinations.[28] All the faults and imperfections committed since mystical union, which before "seemed like nothing to me now seemed horrible in light of the infinite purity of God who demanded exact reparation for all I had experienced."[29] One evening she felt an evil spirit penetrating her "very marrow and nerves to destroy and annihilate [her],"[30] which she vanquished by her graced humble submission to God's will. Even confidence in her most trusted spiritual directors and confessors vanished—one of the classic signs of the dark night of the spirit.

The Holy Spirit revealed how cunning Marie's corrupt human nature was in hiding her sins and imperfections. She came to realize that only God's light could illuminate the skewed nooks and crannies of her soul to purify, heal, and transform her. Just as the author of the *Cloud of Unknowing* had experienced contemplative love as a two-edged sword, Marie now found that the Spirit's presence—which previously had been one of embracing love—became "a sword that divides and cuts with subtle sharpness,"[31] which Marie called a "honing purgatory." "This is a purgatory," she emphasized, "more penetrating than lightning—a sword that divides and cuts with subtle sharpness."[32] Yet the Spirit's "subtle" and "penetrating" thrusts into her spirit never reached the soul's center, where God is master. However, the experience of God leaving this center for a while hurled her into an "intolerable void," in which "are born those despairs which would like to throw body and soul into hell."[33]

Paradoxically, this spiritual dereliction was experienced only as a "punishment" to be endured, not as something that ensnared and led to immoral conduct. Except for brief periods of God's seeming absence, Marie always experienced an intimate peace in the soul's center. "What I was suffering," she wrote, "was contrary to the state that his divine Majesty maintained at the center of my soul."[34] The trials ended, the "garment of darkness" vanished, and peace came flooding into her soul—at the great price of a veritable purgatory on earth.

Mystical purgatory is also a salient feature in the writings of the thirteenth-century Beguine Mechthild of Magdeburg. When she asked the triune God what was expected of her, she was commanded "to lay herself in utter nakedness" so that when God "flows," she "shall become wet. . . . But when you love, we two become one being."[35] Complying, Mechthild became a "naked soul" and experienced the quiescence of the mutual surrender of God and the soul. Employing poetic hyperbole to express her overpowering experience of love, she made light of even the Virgin Mary's love of God, the blood of martyrs, the counsel of confessors, the wisdom of the apostles, the austerity of John the Baptist, the dandling of and giving suck to the divine infant.

Mechthild proclaimed herself a "full-grown bride" who belonged at her Lover's side. But she realized that this intimacy could not "last long. When two lovers meet secretly, they must often part from one another inseparably."[36] The way of true love, however, consisted not only in ecstasies but also in hanging on "the cross of love in the pure air of the Holy Spirit, turned towards the Son of the living Godhead, oblivious of all earthly things."[37] She was taught to love "nothingness" and to flee "somethingness." The paradox: if one truly desires to love, then one must leave it. "Sinking humility" led her to embrace not only "Lady Pain," but also the "most blessed Estrangement from God," which plunged her first into purgatory and then even "under Lucifer's tail," into hell itself. "Thy SELF must go."[38] She was instructed, if she wished, to drink the "unmingled wine." As with others in the mystical tradition, Mechthild experienced that "the deeper I sink, the sweeter I drink."[39]

God instructed Mechthild that her mystical life comprised three stages: "Your childhood was a playmate of my Holy Spirit. Your youth was a bride of my humanity. Your old age is now a housewife of my Godhead."[40] Tenderness first marked her mystical journey, then sublime intimacy, and finally intense affliction and dereliction. Strikingly enough, Mechthild much preferred the state of "blessed Estrangement from God" to the states of tenderness and intimacy.

HELLISH MYSTICAL CONSCIOUSNESS[41]

Pseudo-Macarius, a late-fourth-century Mesopotamian monk, emphasized a mysticism of fire and light based on Christ's transformation on Mount Tabor, the disciples' Pentecost experience, and the light of God's glory that shines forth from the face of Christ (2 Cor. 4:6). The heavenly fire and light that Christians receive into their hearts bursts forth upon the body's dissolution but also brings about the resurrection. Because of sin, however, Satan has made some people a "hell, a sepulcher, and a tomb dead to God."[42] In descending into hell, Christ also descends into their hell-hearts and conquers Satan there.

The majestic but until recently neglected thirteenth-century mystical Beguine Hadewijch stands out as one of the most sublime exponents of love mysticism in the Western mystical tradition. To her, Love is everything and, therefore, the very meaning of existence. Love is the trinitarian life permeating all reality and one's life. She wrote, "I will tell you without beating about the bush: Be satisfied with nothing less than Love."[43] Hadewijch also confessed that she had nothing else to live on except Love, and she urged her readers to live—not for self-satisfaction—but solely for holy Love, out of pure love, and only to "content Love."

In Hadewijch's Sixteenth Poem in Couplets, she writes of Love's seven names. Love is a "chain" that binds, driving the one bound with madness to devour the Beloved and to be devoured and experience far beyond one's dreams "the Godhead and the Manhood."[44] Love is a "light" that enlightens reason as to how to love the God-Man. "Live coal" is yet another name, because Love burns to death and consumes "man's desire and God's refusal."[45] "Fire" is a name for Love, because it burns to death everything it ever touches so that both blessings and damnation no longer matter. "Dew" is the name under which Love works to impart the kisses that pertain to love, that same kiss that unites the Three Persons in the one God. "Living Spring" is Love's sixth name, because Love is nothing less than Life which gives life to our life, a spring that flows forth but also returns to itself. "Hell," however, is Love's highest name. No grace exists there because this Love engulfs and damns everything. Hadewijch claimed that she was burned to ashes by the fire of this impenetrable, "insurmountable darkness of Love."

Perhaps a more poignant statement of mystical dereliction cannot be found in the Christian tradition.

Hadewijch confessed that Love had been more cruel to her than the devil ever was because the evil one could never stop her from loving God, but Love had taken this away from her. Paradoxically, she valued the hellish cruelty of divine Love more than her youthful raptures and joys. As an "old and wise lover" (a salient feature of her mysticism), she understood that one must forsake love for Love. Love's "highest voice," in her view, was to deny Love with humility. In line with an older tradition, Hadewijch experienced and taught an *epektasis* view of Love, that "inseparable satiety and hunger are the apanage of lavish Love, as is ever well known by those whom Love has touched."[46]

The Dominican preacher John Tauler (ca. 1300–1361) also testifies to hellish mystical consciousness. In one of his sermons he instructs his listeners in the three stages of the mystical life. The first stage focuses on a life of spirituality and virtue that brings one closer to God. The second stage consists of spiritual poverty, "when in a strange way God withdraws Himself from the soul, leaving it anguished and denuded."[47] In the third stage, God divinizes the soul by uniting the created spirit to God's uncreated Spirit.

The second stage is Tauler's depiction of the dark night of the spirit and a paradigm of earthly hell. Deprived of all previous God-given favors, the person is brought into such desolation and "strange affliction" that he wonders if God even exists. Unable to experience anything of God or to find satisfaction in created things, "he feels himself hemmed in between two walls with a sword behind him and a sharp spear in front. What is he to do? Both ways are blocked. . . . To love and to be denied the object of one's love surely would seem worse than any hell, if there could be one on earth. . . . The stronger his experience of God was before, the stronger and more intolerable is now the bitterness and pain of loss."[48]

Some of the most captivating passages in the Christian tradition on purgative and hellish consciousness flow from the mystical wisdom of Catherine of Genoa (1447–1510). "The things that I speak about," she dictated to her spiritual guide, "work within me in secret and with great power."[49] During a Lenten confession, Catherine experienced God as pure love so suddenly and overwhelmingly that she rejoiced: "If, of that which this heart of mine is feeling, one drop were to fall into hell, hell itself would become all eternal life."[50] In her view, hell is precisely obduracy in the face of pure love, the unwillingness to submit to the purging action of God's love, wanting, rather, to remain trapped in the tortures of self love.

Catherine judged her own self as the "very opposite of God"—thus, her worst enemy. The slightest deviation from pure love caused her intense suffering. Moreover, God had revealed to her that self-will was so subtle and deeply rooted that it obeyed only itself—no matter how hard she tried to outwit it. The penetrating awareness of her spiritual corruption became so intense at times that she would have despaired and died, had God not lessened the duration of this experience.[51]

Catherine came to understand that God's fiery love could annihilate the immortal soul. As it is being drawn upward, the soul feels itself melting in the fire of that love of its sweet God.[52] The "rays of lightning" from God's fiery love annihilate all resistance to God, that is, the "impediments" from the "rust of sin." Mixing images, Catherine taught that only these obstacles cause the sufferings of those in purgatory and the soul "feels within it a fire like that of hell." Of course, for the unregenerate—which was not her case—this love is not transformative. Again, the heightened consciousness of the mystic experiences his or her sinful self as an earthly hell, a paradigm of sufferings of the damned.

One of the most fascinating mystical autobiographies ever written, *The Spiritual Life,* flowed from the pen of the Italian mystic nun Camilla Battista da Varano (1458–1524).[53] The inner sufferings that had consumed her for three years compelled her to write her book, the final chapters of which (XVII–XIX) contain one of the most profound depictions of the hellish state of mystical dereliction ever written. While being submerged in what she described as God's deep and profound sea, she became conscious of three paradoxes that left her in despair and drove her to the bottom of a hell filled with the "envenomed dragon of the abyss." Her teaching was that God *is* hell to sinful human beings. As seen in Hadewijch, however, Love itself can be experienced as hell, even for those highly advanced in the mystical life.

Teresa of Avila (1515–1582) described her own form of hellish mystical consciousness, the apogee of which was the excruciating vision of her place in hell—a tiny hole at the end of a long, narrow passageway, filled with vermin and sewage. In this hell-hole, she experienced "the blackest darkness," suffocation, and bodily pains more severe than anything on earth. Worst of all, however, was the spiritual suffering: the soul's suffocation, its constriction, the feeling that it was being wrested from the body; the soul tearing itself to pieces, unhappiness, and despair. To be burned on earth was minor when compared to being burned in this hellhole. "I felt myself burning and crumbling," she averred, "and, I repeat, the worst was that interior fire and despair." She maintained that what she described "can hardly be exaggerated."[54]

John of the Cross (1542–1591) taught that infused contemplation is "nothing else than a secret and peaceful and loving inflow of God, which, *if not hampered*, fires the soul in the spirit of love" (*Dark Night* 1.10.6).[55] The Holy Spirit's love flooding the soul, in John's view, is "the fire and thirst of love" (2.13.4),[56] which seeks only to heal and transform persons so that they "may reach out divinely to the enjoyment of all earthly and heavenly things, with a general freedom of spirit in them all" (2.9.1).[57] Yet, what should be experienced as a "gentle and delightful burning" of the soul in the Holy Spirit is transformed into mystical dereliction, a hell, because of the contemplative's disorder, sinfulness, and miserly love (2.9.11).[58] John wrote, "When this purgative contemplation oppresses a soul, it feels very vividly the shadow of death, the sighs of death, and the sorrows of hell, all of which reflect the feeling of God's absence, of being chastised and rejected by him, and of being unworthy of him, as well as the object of his anger" (2.6.2).[59]

In his instructions concerning the divine light flooding the soul, John taught that "the darkness and evils the soul experiences when this light strikes are not the darkness and evils of the light but of the soul itself" (*Dark Night* 2.13.10).[60] Through these sufferings the contemplative sometimes comes close to death, which "so disentangles and dissolves the spiritual substance—absorbing it in a profound darkness—that the soul at the sight of its miseries feels that it is melting away and being undone by a cruel spiritual death" (2.6.1).[61] It is as if the contemplative were experiencing the very pains of hell, although this is, in fact, an extremely meritorious, earthly purgatory (2.6.6).[62]

BEATIFYING MYSTICAL CONSCIOUSNESS

Many in the Christian mystical tradition viewed Adam as the contemplative prototype because of his supposed direct and immediate consciousness of God that he enjoyed until he sinned. Abraham, Jacob, Moses, Samuel, and other patriarchs are also presented in the Hebrew Scriptures as having a special God-consciousness. Moses and Jacob, for example, claimed face-to-face meetings with God—with some qualifications as to how directly they gazed upon his face (Gen. 32:30; Exod. 33:11, 23; Num. 12:7; Deut. 34:10). Jacob wrestled with God, survived, and was left with an overwhelming sense of God's holiness (Gen. 32:24–25). Because Job saw God (Job 42:5), his agonizing questions ceased, and he repented "in dust and ashes." Because the prophets had "stood in the council of the Lord" (Jer. 23:18), they were authenticated as mystics in action to speak forth God's word. Moreover, according to many in the Christian tradition, if these figures of the Hebrew Scriptures had foreshadowings of the beatific vision, Paul the apostle certainly must also have experienced this.

Perhaps the boldest and most intriguing Christian claim ever made for a beatifying mystical consciousness is attributed to the ecstatic Franciscan mystic Giles of Assisi (ca. 1190–1262), who professed that he saw God so clearly that "he lost all faith."[63] Second in line may come from the pen of the Third Order Franciscan mystic Angela of Foligno (ca. 1248–1309), who claimed to have experienced in this life some form of the beatific vision. She wrote of a divine working in her soul that was "so deep and ineffable an abyss that this presence of God alone . . . is the good that the saints enjoy in eternal life" (*Memorial* IX).[64] In her view, however, the least saint in heaven has more of what can be given to any soul before death.

On three separate occasions Angela found herself in a most exalted and ineffable way "standing or lying in the Trinity" (*Memorial* IX),[65] and she saw the "All Good" in darkness. She comprehended that the thicker the darkness, the more profound the experience. In this darkness, her soul saw "everything and nothing at once" (ibid.).[66] When the Trinity plunged her into this "extremely deep abyss," all fear was removed from the soul and God secured it firmly in faith and hope. Incapable of describing this experience, she cried out: "Whatever I say about it is blasphemy" (ibid.).[67] Concomitant with this experience, Angela discovered in her soul "a chamber into which there enters no sort of grief or joy of any virtue whatsoever, nor anything else that can be named or expressed. But into it there enters that greatest Good, and in that manifestation of God (which I do blaspheme in thus naming it, seeing that I have no word wherewith to speak of it perfectly) is the whole truth."[68]

Third in this line, I would place the Beguine mystic Hadewijch, who daringly wrote that she had looked upon the face of God. She maintained that, in a vision, a seraph had raised her to heaven and said, "Behold, this is Love, whom you see in the midst of the Countenance of God's nature; she has never yet been shown here to a created being"[69]—a "Countenance" that Hadewijch was to see numerous times. Moreover, Christ himself had granted her personally a glimpse of his eternal glory: "And he took me out of the spirit in that highest fruition of wonder beyond reason; there I had fruition of him as I shall eternally."[70]

Less audacious claims are found in the writings of one of the great guides of Western monasticism, John Cassian (ca. 365–ca. 435). He taught that the goal of the monastic life is the partial restoration of Adam's prelapsarian contemplative oneness with God. Cassian wrote of "pure prayer" as the essence of perfection and a foretaste of heaven. "This prayer," the monk stressed, "centers on no contemplation of some image or other. It is masked by no attendant sounds or words. It is a fiery outbreak, an indescribable exaltation, an insatiable thrust of the soul. Free of what is sensed and seen, ineffable in its groans and sighs, the soul pours itself out to God."[71]

Cassian also advocated the Eastern monastic *monologistos* prayer, that is, prayer in one formula. Although the Jesus prayer is perhaps the most famous example, Cassian may well be the first to give full articulation to the continuous repetition of an evocative verse, in this case, Psalm 69:2, "O God, come to my assistance, Lord make haste to help me." For him, this psalm verse "carries within it all the feelings of which human nature is capable."[72] Moreover, perseverance in this prayer "will lead you on to the contemplation of the unseen and heavenly, and to that fiery urgency of prayer which is indescribable and which is experienced by very few."[73] Guarded by angels, one is ecstatically lifted up to silent prayer and becomes absorbed in the loving union that binds the three trinitarian Persons, a powerful foreshadowing of eternal life.

In agreement with John Cassian is Isaac the Syrian (d. ca. 700), a mystic and thinker of unusual clarity and richness, who wrote to guide his monks in reaching the ecstatic contemplation of God, which fore-shadows the glories of heaven. He described a "prayer of no prayer,"[74] which is attained only by a single person in generations. Because what is genuinely spiritual, in his view, must be free of all movement, in the "prayer of no prayer," every motion of the tongue, intellect, will, imag-ination, and heart ceases. Only through the "prayer of no prayer" does a person gain entrance into the heart's secret chamber where stillness and silence reign. There is no prayer there, no weeping, no desire, no exterior or interior movement at all, and even no free will—only the "prayer of no prayer."

Awe, wonder, ravishing, self-forgetfulness, divine vision, and, para-doxically, no vision follow in the wake of the "prayer of no prayer." One is conscious only of the light of the Holy Spirit, which seizes the inner and outer person, producing a profound spiritual inebriation. Engulfed by the Holy Spirit, the prayer of no prayer forces the spirit above itself to gaze ecstatically into the incomprehensible silence and bestows an unknowing more sublime than knowledge, a learned ignorance. This paradise-like prayer may be transitory, but it is indeed an actual fore-taste of the resurrected life. Isaac's homilies underscore, however, that all prayer—even the highest state of "no prayer"—is inextricably connected with psalmody and liturgy, especially the Eucharist.

Bernard of Clairvaux (1090–1153) is also a prime example of those mystics who understood contemplation as a type of ecstatic dying to the world and a foretaste of heaven.[75] Through contemplation, God con-summates his marriage with the errant person, illuminating the intellect so that it becomes rational, prudent, and wise. Because God is a vio-lent Lover who is loved violently by the bride, the human will becomes forceful, powerful, and even fierce. In a statement that was to have great resonance in the later mystical tradition, Bernard taught, "If the soul knows this—or because it knows this—is it any wonder that this soul, this bride, boasts that that great majesty cares for her alone as though he had no others to care for."[76]

Finally, the theological mystic Thomas Aquinas (1224/25–1274) taught that, although no one in this earthly life can return to the condition that Adam enjoyed before his sin,[77] contemplation as a state is not only close to that of the prelapsarian Adam but is also ordered to the beatifying vision of God in heaven: "In contemplation," he wrote, "God is seen through the medium of the light of wisdom that elevates the mind to behold divine things. It is not that the divine essence itself is seen in an immediate way, but this is the way God is seen through grace by a contemplative after the state of sin, though it was realized more perfectly before the Fall."[78]

CONCLUDING SUMMARY

Many more examples of a delightful or of a dark mystical death consciousness, of a purgatorial and hellish consciousness, and of a beatifying mystical consciousness can be found in the fecund Christian mystical tradition. I have selected mystics who especially appealed to me and whose writings indicate that the teachings of the mystics can and should be used as a theological source. Both the delightful and the dark mystical deaths of the mystics can and do point to a deeper understanding of earthly joy, suffering, and death in conjunction with a heightened experience of God and a deeper assimilation of the mystery of Christ's life, death, and resurrection. I have never lost the conviction that purgatorial consciousness and hellish mystical consciousness are not only stages in the mystical journey to full union with God but are also paradigmatic of postmortem purgatorial sufferings and the terrifying and obdurate narcissism of the damned, if there are any damned. These stages consist of a deepened sense of one's individual sins, of one's root sinfulness, of creaturely nothingness, and of the inability to love sufficiently. The mystical tasting of one's disorder and sin—in the face of the Holy—is itself an incipient purgatory and hell. To paraphrase Meister Eckhart: only the *Nît* (No) to Love in one's being burns.[79] When one is cleansed of sin, as well as the remnants of sin and disorder, and when God has so enlarged a person's ability to love as much as one is loved—then beatifying mystical consciousness is indeed a foretaste of heaven's delights.

Notes

1. Karl Rahner, *Foundations of Christian Faith: An Introduction to the Idea of Christianity*, trans. William V. Dych (New York: Seabury, 1978), 431–33; idem, "The Hermeneutics of Eschatological Assertions," in *Theological Investigations,* vol. 4, *More Recent Writings,* trans. Kevin Smyth (Baltimore: Helicon, 1966), 323–46. See also Karl Rahner and Herbert Vorgrimler, "Hell," *Dictionary of Theology*, 2nd ed., trans. Richard Strachan, David Smith, Robert Nowell, and Sarah O'Brien Twohig (New York: Crossroad, 1981), 205.

2. Karl Rahner, "Mystical Experience and Mystical Theology," in *Theological Investigations,* vol. 17, *Jesus, Man, and the Church,* trans. Margaret Kohl (New York: Crossroad, 1981), 92.

3. Karl Rahner, "The Ignatian Mysticism of Joy in the World," in *Theological Investigations,* vol. 3, *Theology of the Spiritual Life,* trans. Karl–H. Kruger and Boniface Kruger (Baltimore: Helicon, 1967), 280–81.

4. See Harvey D. Egan, S.J., *Soundings in the Christian Mystical Tradition* (Collegeville, MN: Liturgical Press, 2010), 101–2.

5. *The Soul's Journey into God,* in *Bonaventure—The Soul's Journey into God, The Tree of Life, The Life of St. Francis,* trans. Ewert Cousins, Classics of Western Spirituality (New York: Paulist, 1978), VII, no. 6, 115–16.

6. Egan, *Soundings*, 209.

7. *The Collected Works of St. John of the Cross,* trans. Kieran Kavanaugh and Otilio Rodriguez, rev. ed. (Washington: Institute of Carmelite Studies, 1991), 45, *The Spiritual Canticle,* no. 8.

8. Egan, *Soundings*, 107–8.

9. *Mother Teresa: Come Be My Light; The Private Writings of the "Saint of Calcutta,"* ed. Brian Kolodiejchuk (New York: Doubleday, 2007), 83, undated letter to Lawrence Trevor Picachy, S.J., between 1957 and 1960. All references to Mother Teresa are to this volume.

10. *Mother Teresa*, 83, letter to Joseph Neuner, S.J., April 1961.

11. *Mother Teresa*, 168, letter of Archbishop Ferdinand Périer, S.J., to Mother Teresa, July 29, 1956.

12. *Mother Teresa*, 248, letter to Missionaries of Charity Superiors, November 17, 1964.

13. *Mother Teresa*, 44, notes of "the copy of the Voice since September 1946."

14. *Mother Teresa*, 230, letter to Joseph Neuner, S.J., May 6, 1962.

15. *Mother Teresa*, 211, letter to Joseph Neuner, S.J., probably April 1961.

16. *Mother Teresa*, 262, letter to Patty and Warren Kump, December 1, 1967.

17. *Mother Teresa*, 266, letter to Archbishop Lawrence Trevor Picachy, S.J., December 21, 1969.

18. *Mother Teresa*, 14, letter to Joseph Neuner, S.J., July 14, 1967.

19. *Mother Teresa*, 195, 351, retreat notes.

20. *Mother Teresa,* 286, speech at Regina Mundi Institute, Rome, 20 December 1979.

21. *Mother Teresa,* 331, testimony of Sister Margaret Mary.

22. *The Cloud of Unknowing and the Book of Privy Counseling,* new ed., introduction by William Johnston (Garden City, NY: Doubleday-Image, 1976). What follows is a revised portion from my article, "In Purgatory We Shall All Be Mystics," *Theological Studies* 73 (December 2012): 870–89.

23. *Cloud of Unknowing*; see also the foreword.

24. Shortly after his conversion, Ignatius of Loyola's scruples over past sins—which he confessed again and again—caused such pain and self-hatred that he contemplated suicide. See *St. Ignatius' Own Story,* trans. William J. Young, S.J. (Chicago: Loyola University Press, 1956), nos. 19–25.

25. Marie of the Incarnation, "The Relation of 1654," in *Marie of the Incarnation: Selected Writings,* ed. and trans. Irene Mahoney, Sources of American Spirituality (New York: Paulist, 1989), 41–178. All subsequent references to Marie are to the "Relation." She writes of thirteen states of prayer; I refer to them by the ordinal number followed by the chapter number and page number in *Selected Writings.*

26. *Marie of the Incarnation,* Seventh State, XXII, 82.

27. A fourteenth-century Beguine, Marguerite Porete, wrote that there are "two other stages . . . which God gives that are greater and more noble than this [mystical marriage]" (Marguerite Porete, *The Mirror of Simple Souls* [New York: Paulist, 1993], 190–91, chap. 118). Even Porete, however, does not teach of dark nights after transforming union.

28. *Marie of the Incarnation,* Eighth State, XXXV, 103.

29. *Marie of the Incarnation,* Twelfth State, LII, 142.

30. *Marie of the Incarnation,* Eighth State, XXXV, 105.

31. *Marie of the Incarnation,* Twelfth State, LII, 142.

32. *Marie of the Incarnation,* Twelfth State, LII, 142.

33. *Marie of the Incarnation,* Twelfth State, LII, 143.

34. *Marie of the Incarnation,* Thirteenth State, LVIII, 156.

35. *Mechthild of Magdeburg: The Flowing Light of the Godhead,* trans. Frank Tobin (New York: Paulist Press, 1998), 76, book II, no. 6, 76. Referred to as Tobin translation.

36. Tobin translation, 62, book I, no. 44.

37. *Revelations of Mechthild of Magdeburg* or *The Flowing Light of the Godhead,* trans. Lucy Menzies (London: Longmans, Green, 1953), 79, book III, no. 10. Referred to as Menzies translation.

38. Menzies translation, 25, book II, no. 44.

39. Tobin translation, 156, book VI, no. 12.

40. Tobin translation, 277, book VII, no. 3.

41. For an overview of theologies of hell, see Harvey D. Egan, S.J., "Hell: The Mystery of Eternal Love and Eternal Obduracy," *Theological Studies* 75 (2014): 52–73.

42. *Pseudo-Macarius: The Fifty Spiritual Homilies and The Great Letter,* ed. and trans. George A. Maloney, Classics of Western Spirituality (New York: Paulist, 1992). See Homily 1, no. 2, 37; Homily 11, no. 1 and 11, 90 and 95; Homily 25, no. 9, 163.

43. *Hadewijch: The Complete Works,* trans. Mother Columba Hart, O.S.B., Classics of Western Spirituality (New York: Paulist, 1980), 108, letter 24.

44. *Hadewijch,* 353, Poems in Couplets 16, no. 45.

45. *Hadewijch,* 354, Poems in Couplets 16, no. 85.

46. *Hadewijch,* 222, Poems in Stanza 33, no. 25.

47. *Johannes Tauler: Sermons,* trans. Maria Shrady, Classics of Western Spirituality (New York: Paulist, 1985), 141, sermon 40, *Carissimi, estote unanimes in oratione.*

48. *Tauler,* 143, sermon 40.

49. Catherine of Genoa, *Purgation and Purgatory; The Spiritual Dialogue,* trans. and notes Serge Hughes, introduction by Benedict J. Groeschel; preface by Catherine De Hueck Doherty, Classics of Western Spirituality (New York: Paulist, 1979), 86.

50. Catherine of Genoa, *Vita,* quoted by Friedrich von Hügel, *The Mystical Element of Religion as Studied in Saint Catherine of Genoa and Her Friends*, 2 vols., 2nd ed. (Westminster, MD: Christian Classics, 1961) 1:159.

51. Catherine of Genoa, *Purgation and Purgatory*, 81.

52. Ibid., 79.

53. For what follows, see Bernard McGinn, *The Varieties of Vernacular Mysticism 1350–1550*, vol. 5 of *The Presence of God: A History of Western Christian Mysticism* (New York: Crossroad, 2012), 306–11.

54. *The Collected Works of St. Teresa of Avila*, vol. 1, *The Book of Her Life; Spiritual Testimonies; Soliloquies* (Washington: Institute of Carmelite Studies, 1976), 213–14, chap. 32, nos. 1–3.

55. *The Dark Night*, 1.10.6 in *Collected Works*, 382 (my emphasis).

56. *Collected Works*, 425.

57. Ibid., 412.

58. Ibid., 416.

59. Ibid., 404.

60. Ibid., 427.

61. Ibid., 403–4.

62. Ibid., 406.

63. *Actus Beati Francisci et Sociorum Ejus,* quoted by Martin Buber, in *Ecstatic Confessions*, ed. Paul Mendes-Flohr and trans. Esther Cameron (San Francisco: Harper & Row, 1985), 48.

64. *Angela of Foligno: Complete Works,* trans. Paul Lachance, O.F.M. (New York: Paulist Press, 1993), 213.

65. Ibid., 204.

66. Ibid., 203.

67. Ibid., 205.

68. *Book of Divine Consolation of the Blessed Angela of Foligno*, trans. Mary G. Steegmann (New York: Duffield & Windus, 1909), 191, Vision 8.

69. *Hadewijch: The Complete Works*, 299, Vision 13, no. 97.

70. Ibid., 277, Vision 5, no. 59.

71. John Cassian, *Conferences*, trans. Colm Luibheid, Classics of Western Spirituality (New York: Paulist, 1985), 138, X, no. 11.

72. Ibid., 133. *Conferences*, X, no. 10.

73. Ibid., 136, *Conferences*, X, no. 10.

74. *The Ascetical Homilies of Saint Isaac the Syrian*, trans. The Holy Transfiguration Monastery (Brookline, MA: Holy Transfiguration Monastery, 1984), 122, Homily 23.

75. Bernard of Clairvaux, *On the Song of Songs*, vol. 3, trans. Kilian Walsh and Irene M. Edwards, Cistercian Fathers Series (Kalamazoo, MI: Cistercian Publications, 1979), 49–57, Sermon 52.

76. Bernard of Clairvaux, *On the Song of Songs*, vol. 4, trans. Irene M. Edwards, Cistercian Fathers Series (Kalamazoo, MI Cistercian Publications, 1980), 35, Sermon 69 §8.

77. Aquinas argued, however, that Adam did not enjoy the beatific vision, because he did not contemplate God's essence. But thanks to a mediating spiritual effect issuing in his intellect, he did see God without a medium, not through the medium of reasoning from created realities (*Scriptum super Libros Sententiarum*, Book II, d. 23, q. 2, a. 1, ad 1). In his *Summa* (STh Ia, q. 94, a. 1, ad 3) Thomas wrote, "A medium is twofold: one in which something said to be seen through the medium is itself seen simultaneously, as when a person is seen through a mirror and is seen simultaneously with the mirror; the other medium is the one by knowledge of which we come across something unknown, such as the medium in a demonstration. And God was seen [by Adam] without the latter medium, but not without the former medium." I thank Fr. Louis Roy, O.P., for calling my attention to these texts.

78. Thomas Aquinas, *De Veritate*, q. 18, a. 1, ad 4, quoted by Bernard McGinn, *The Harvest of Mysticism in Medieval Germany*, vol. 4 of *The Presence of God. A History of Western Christian Mysticism*, 31.

79. Meister Eckhart, Sermon 5b: *In hoc apparuit charitas dei in nobis* (German Works) in *Meister Eckhart: The Essential Sermons, Commentaries, Treatises, and Defense*, trans. and intro. Edmund Colledge and Bernard McGinn, Classics of Western Spirituality (New York: Paulist, 1981), 183.

2

Comprehending the Incomprehensible: John Scottus Eriugena as Mystic[1]

Bernard McGinn

A century or more ago, when the modern study of mysticism was in its infancy, John Scottus Eriugena's name did not loom large. In the nineteenth century, Idealist philosophers had rediscovered Eriugena as a major speculative thinker; but Catholic theologians, scared off by the 1225 condemnation of Eriugena's *Periphyseon* by Honorius III, as well as by the fact that the first modern edition of the work by the Anglican scholar Thomas Gale in 1681 had been placed on the Index, had little to say about the Irishman.[2] The first generation of serious writers in English about mysticism had trouble dealing with the enigmatic ninth-century Irish thinker. W. R. Inge, in his 1899 *Christian Mysticism*, devoted several pages to Eriugena.[3] While appreciating Eriugena's speculative originality, Inge contends that he "is a mystic only by his intellectual affinities [i.e., with Neoplatonism]; the warmth of pious aspiration and love which makes Dionysius, amid all his extravagance, still a religious writer, has cooled with Eriugena."[4] Evelyn Underhill published her *Mysticism: A Study in the Nature and Development of Man's Spiritual Consciousness* in 1911, though it is now mostly read in later revisions that stretched into the 1930s. Receiving only brief mentions in the original edition, the later "Appendix" Underhill added on the historical evolution of Western mysticism describes Eriugena as marking "the beginning of a full tradition of

This essay was first given as a talk at University College Dublin in March 2014, at the invitation of Prof. Dermot Moran. I wish to thank him and the members of the audience for their kind reception and valuable suggestions.

mysticism in Western Europe."⁵ Alas, Underhill does not tell us what she meant by this. Finally, the work of Underhill's spiritual director, Friedrich von Hügel, *The Mystical Element of Religion*, first published in 1908 and opposed to the influence of Neoplatonism on Christian mysticism, makes only two brief critical mentions of Eriugena in its massive two volumes. A similar neglect is evident in the many Neoscholastic tomes on mysticism published from the late nineteenth century through the middle of the twentieth century.⁶ These works, largely devoted to exploring the mystical teaching of Teresa of Avila and John of the Cross, as well as to showing the conformity of their teaching with that of Thomas Aquinas, had little use for a thinker as problematic as Eriugena.

Both dogmatic prejudices and narrow views of what constitutes "mysticism," or "the mystical element of religion," as Von Hügel called it, played a role in this neglect. Eriugena was doctrinally suspect, and (as the quotation from Inge shows), he does not seem to be as warm—one might even say "fuzzy"—as mystics are supposed to be. Eriugena's writings, unlike those of Teresa and John and many other mystics, provide no accounts of experiences of God (visions, locutions, paranormal experiences), nor do they spend time discussing such gifts. The experiential fallacy that long restricted mysticism to personal accounts of special experiences, or to the explorations of the psychology of such experiences, ruled out Eriugena as a "true mystic." For all that Evelyn Underhill contributed to the study of mysticism, she aptly summarized this skewed view. Speaking of "our Christian Platonists and mystical philosophers," she allows some usefulness to their theories, but claims that "they are no more mystics than the milestones on the Dover Road are travelers to Calais."⁷ From this perspective, Eriugena's universal, speculative, and largely impersonal analysis (save for a few prayers inserted into the *Periphyseon* and elsewhere) could scarcely be described as mystical.

Times change. What I have called the experiential fallacy, while still powerful in some circles, has been increasingly questioned over the past half century. The false dichotomy between mystical narratives, that is, first-person accounts of deep consciousness of God's transformative presence, on the one hand, and attempts to explore and theorize the preparation for, the attainment of, and the consequences following from such modes of consciousness, on the other, has been largely abandoned. The recognition that purported "autobiographical" accounts of "mystical experiences" form just one of the genres in which mystical consciousness has been expressed—and one that itself is deeply theorized in many ways—has brought a new, broader, more flexible approach to the study of mysticism, however much there is still disagreement about what constitutes the modern category of "mysticism" and how it is best approached. Hence, it is no surprise that John Scottus Eriugena has now been welcomed into the camp of the "mystics," without denying him his status as a major speculative thinker, both in philosophy and theology. The two histories of Western mysticism that have appeared over the past quarter century give considerable attention to the ninth-century Irish savant. The second volume of my ongoing project *The Presence of God*, which appeared in 1994, has a chapter on Eriugena.[8] In 1990, in the first volume of his *Geschichte der abendländische Mystik*, Kurt Ruh also devoted a chapter to Eriugena, in which he says, "Johannes Eriugena was not only a 'speculative thinker' (*Spekulierer*), but also a 'spiritual teacher' (*Spirituale*). That fact forms the decisive presupposition that constitutes the fertile soil of mysticism in the High and Late Middle Ages."[9]

Theoretical Foundations

What do we mean by calling Eriugena a mystic?[10] What contribution did he make to the wider tradition of Western Christian mysticism? The purpose of this paper is to try to give an answer to these questions. I have argued elsewhere that the mystical element or aspect of Christian belief and practice concerns the preparation for, the consciousness of, and the effects of attaining a direct transformative awareness of the presence of God.[11] I argue here that Eriugena's teaching can be said to illustrate all the aspects of this heuristic description. Eriugena's thought can also be called mystical in the etymological meaning of *mysticus*, that is, "hidden," a term domesticated in Christianity as early as the second century C.E., primarily to describe the hidden meaning of the Bible. Mystical thinking desires to explore and uncover, to make manifest, what is hidden under the surface of the scriptural letter. For the first thousand years of its history, Christian mysticism was largely exegetical, and it has remained closely tied to biblical interpretation even after the "book of experience" emerged as a special source for mystical writing in the twelfth century. Eriugena, as recent studies have shown, was one of the masters of mystical exegesis.[12] Like Origen and many other mystics, his exegesis is performative, even transformative—the act of reading the spiritual message hidden under the surface of the biblical letter is itself part of the transformation of consciousness that is the goal of mysticism.

On close examination, the mystical tradition reveals itself to have had a rich and varied development. One size does not fit all. Rather, to borrow a phrase from Hans Urs von Balthasar, the truth of mysticism is symphonic—not a solo instrument, but a whole orchestra. To pursue the metaphor further, Eriugena's mystical teaching represents one version (the founding version in the West) of one of the sections of the orchestra, what I term Christian Neoplatonic dialectical mysticism.

It may seem odd to begin this characterization with the adjective "Christian."[13] I do so because there were pagan forms of Neoplatonic dialectical mysticism, and also because in the past mystics like Dionysius and Eriugena have been accused of "Platonizing rather than Christianizing," as Martin Luther put it. A careful reading of these thinkers, however, reveals that their intention, like that of most other Christian theologians, was to provide an understanding of faith (*intellectus fidei*) that would also lead to deeper and unifying contact with God. The mystical theologies of Gregory of Nyssa, Dionysius, and Maximus the Confessor (Eriugena's main Greek sources), as well as his successors, such as Meister Eckhart and Nicholas of Cusa, appealed to many resources, philosophical and theological; but there is broad agreement that the essential themes of these thinkers are Neoplatonic in the sense that they make use of speculative categories originally worked out by Plotinus (d. 270 C.E.) and developed by later Neoplatonists, especially Proclus (d. 485). Not all forms of Neoplatonism, however, can be said to be "dialectical." Augustine was influenced by Plotinus and Porphyry, but his Christian adaptation of Neoplatonism is scarcely dialectical. By dialectical, I mean a form of speculative discourse that insists that the relation between the hidden divine principle and the manifested reality of the world is best explored by the mutual implications of affirmative (i.e., immanent) and negative (i.e., transcendent) predications whose explosive coincidence forces a movement beyond both saying and unsaying. In a simplified form, it involves thinking of determinations by themselves, simultaneously thinking of contradictory determinations, and exploring, insofar as possible, the meaning of the higher unity of contradictory determinations.[14] The Eriugenean mode of this dialectic is summarized in a text in book 1 of *Periphyseon*, "God is said to be essence, but is properly not essence, because it is opposed to nothing. Therefore, God is *hyperousios*, that is, superessential."[15]

Eriugena has many ways of expressing his dialectical thinking. Among these is the famous four modalities (*species*) of the universal category (*genus*) of *natura*, which comprises all that is and all that is not: (1) the nature that creates and is not created; (2) the nature that is created and also creates; (3) the nature that is created and does not create; and (4) the nature that neither creates nor is created.[16] Also noteworthy is book 3's list of nineteen antitheses setting out the coincidence of negations and affirmations that express the relation between the world as theophany, or manifestation, and the unmanifest source. To cite only the first four of these: "Everything that is understood and sensed is the non-appearing's appearance, the hidden's manifestation, denial's affirmation, incomprehensibility's comprehension. . . ." In terms of my title, we can paraphrase the fourth antithesis as stating that the incomprehensible God cancels out or negates divine incomprehensibility by becoming comprehensible in the world as theophany, while the goal of theophany is to negate or transcend itself by returning to the same divine incomprehensibility. God negates himself in order to create himself, that is, to realize himself as the creative principle of the other.[17] That other, the world and more specifically human nature as made in God's image, is created to affirm theophany (i.e., God as manifested), and then to negate manifestation in order to return to the source that is beyond all affirmation and negation. This is the essence of Eriugena's dialectical mysticism.

In order to understand Eriugena's mysticism we should begin with theophany, that is, the world in which we find ourselves.[18] "Just as we come to understanding through sense knowledge, so the return to God is made through the creature."[19] The universe is God manifested in otherness, and, although Eriugena seems to think that *recta ratio* may retain some power even in fallen humanity to recognize this fact, he believes that in our present state reason needs the aid of that other great theophany, the Bible. The correlation between the two theophanic books is discussed in a passage from the *Homily on John's Prologue,* where the four senses of the intelligible world of the Bible are shown to correspond to the four elements of the visible world: history is like the earth in the middle; ethics corresponds to the waters around the earth; natural science to the air; and theology is "the aether and fiery heat of the empyreum of heaven."[20] The four elements are constitutive of the created universe, just as all four modes of reading are needed in biblical hermeneutics, however much fire and theology surpass the lower aspects of both worlds. The two forms of theophany are the starting points for the return to God, but these theophanies need to be decoded, both positively and negatively.

The decoding process is expressed in many ways, not least by Eriugena's frequent use of the language of light and darkness.[21] "All things that exist are lights,"[22] so that "there is no visible or corporeal thing that is not the symbol of something incorporeal and intelligible."[23] Eriugena's attention to the role of symbols, both similar and dissimilar symbols following the Dionysian model, reveals a strong aesthetic component in his writings, both in prose and poetry. Beautiful images and symbols are meant to lead on to an inner grasp of intelligible realities.[24] Theology itself, he says, "like a form of poetry, shapes sacred scripture with its imaginative creations to the decision of our intellectual soul and [its] withdrawal from external corporeal senses . . . into perfect knowledge of intelligible things. . . ."[25] Light and darkness are symbols or metaphors, as well as categories with a metaphysical density capable of revealing the divine dialectic of hiddenness and manifestation. From the perspective of human thinking, they express the interpenetration of the positive and negative poles of the process of "de-theophanizing," which involves both illuminating and obscuring, a knowing that becomes unknowing without ever losing the need for some kind of knowing. As Werner Beierwaltes put it, "the interaction or the One-Being of thinking and non-thinking is a model for the 'divine metaphor' of a darkness which is light in itself, or a light which must appear dark because of its absoluteness."[26] Hence, the importance of the apophatic element in Eriugena's thinking.

John Scottus is one of the most rigorously apophatic of Christian thinkers. Most Christian theologians, building on passages in both the Old and the New Testaments, insist that God is beyond all knowing and speaking. A key test of the difference between general apophatic theology and the strong apophaticism that characterizes dialectical Neoplatonic thinking is whether God can be spoken of as "Nothing." For Augustine and Thomas Aquinas, for example, the mind can never know the essence of God, but they insist that "nothing" is always a term signifying defect and privation. Eriugena is the first Western thinker to advance a transcendental view of "No-thing" as a way of speaking about the First Principle that is both negatively "not-a-thing" and eminently beyond the world of "all that is and all that is not." He says, "Therefore the Divine Goodness, which is called Nothing for the reason that beyond all the things that are and that are not it is found in no essence, descends from the negation of all essences into the affirmation of the essence of the whole universe, from itself into itself, as though from nothing into something."[27] Variations on such language are found throughout the Eriugenian corpus.

John's negative theology analyzing God as eminent No-thing finds its necessary analogue in his negative anthropology. If humanity alone is described as made to God's image and likeness in Genesis 1:26, there must be a sense in which the deepest meaning of being human is that *homo*, that is, human nature, is also "no-thing," and again, not just in a privative but also in an eminent sense. Apophatic anthropology was not Eriugena's creation; it first appeared in Gregory of Nyssa's treatise *De Imagine*, which the Irish savant translated into Latin. Eriugena, however, gives it a systematic development beyond what we find in Gregory, especially in a long treatment in book 4 of *Periphyseon*.[28] God is not only unknowable to the human mind, God also cannot know himself in the sense of knowing as "defining," that is, setting the limits to a thing. God is not a thing. This does not mean that God is ignorant; rather, as Eriugena puts it, "God's ignorance is ineffable understanding" (*ipsius enim ignorantia ineffabilis est intelligentia*). This is the highest and truest wisdom, God's awareness of the divine eminence beyond all that is and all that is not.[29] So too with humanity. "The human mind both knows itself and does not know itself. It knows that it is; it does not know what it is. And through this . . . the image of God is especially thought to be in humanity. . . . What is more wonderful and more beautiful to those thinking upon themselves and their God is that the human mind is more to be praised in its ignorance than in its knowledge."[30] Hence, there is fourfold negativity in the divine–human epistemological relation according to John: (1) humans do not know God; (2) God does not know God, in the sense of defining; (3) humans do not know human nature; and (4) even God does not know human nature in the sense that the unmanifest aspect of human nature is one with the divine and therefore indefinable. The reciprocity between a strong version of negative theology and an equally strong negative anthropology was something new in Western thought and mysticism.

How do we become aware of this dazzling dark truth? And how does God-made-manifest in creation, especially in humanity, come to express not only the cataphatic, but also apophatic aspects of the Unmanifest in the process of de-theophanization? The answer is found in Wisdom, the Creative Wisdom (*sapientia creatrix*) who became man (*sapientia creata*) in Jesus of Nazareth.[31] According to Eriugena, the role of Creative Wisdom in both emanation and return is the central message of the Bible, but it also can be discerned by "right reason," at least for some. The process of creative emanation, according to the dialectic set out in the four species of the genus *natura*, begins when the "Nature that creates and is not created," that is God as the universal cause, gives rise to the "Nature that is created and creates," that is, the world of the Primordial Causes, the exemplary forms of all that exists in our world of materiality and particularity, that is, the "Nature that is created and does not create." The passage from the first to the second species of *natura* takes place in and through the eternal generation of the Word from the Father,[32] who as the *sapientia creatrix* is the "cause of causes" (*causa causarum*), whose first production is the world of the Primordial Causes. Thus, for Eriugena, "the essence of all things is nothing else but the knowledge of all in Divine Wisdom."[33]

Among the Primordial Causes there is one that manifests the divine light in a unique way by its ability to know. This allows it to serve as the *locus*, or place, where Creative Wisdom unifies the Causes. This is the Primordial Cause *homo*, or humanity, defined in terms of the ideal world of the second species as "a certain intellectual concept formed eternally in the mind of God."[34] If the second Person of the Trinity creates the Primordial Causes and through them the physical universe *causaliter*, as their efficient cause, then humanity as the *sapientia creata* has a correlative role in "creating" the world *effectualiter* in the sense that the world is brought into existence in human knowing.[35] As Dermot Moran puts it, "Man and God are one in that they are dialectically united in the concealing/revealing dynamic of the Word."[36] The necessary bond between Creative Wisdom and Created Wisdom found in the *processio* of all things from the first *species* of *natura* is equally valid for the *reditus*, that is, the return *toward* the fourth species, the "Nature that neither creates nor is created"—God as beyond all affirmation and negation. This return can only be effected in the Word. Eriugena says, "The universal goal of the entire creation is the Word of God. Thus, both the beginning and the end subsist in God's Word, indeed, to speak more plainly, they are the Word itself, for it is the manifold end without end and the beginning without beginning, being without beginning save for the Father."[37] Given the fact that emanation involves both Creative Wisdom and Created Wisdom, it is no surprise that both must also be involved in the return, that is, that Creative Wisdom must unite with Created Wisdom in Jesus Christ who restores all things to God in the ideal human nature in which they were made. "The perfection of man," says Eriugena, "is Christ in whom all things are consummated."[38]

Mystical Living

The mention of the return brings us more specifically to the realm of mysticism insofar as the mystical element of religion centers on how consciousness of God's presence may be realized in this life as a preparation for its completion in the beatific vision.[39] The incarnation of the Word can be said to have been part of the divine plan from the beginning, but the particular form the incarnation took in history, the way that Christ restores humanity and the universe by his birth, his death on the cross, his resurrection from the dead, and his ascension into heaven—the mysteries of salvation history—are dependent on his coming to save *fallen* humanity. Eriugena's notion of paradise and the Fall, set out in great detail in books 4 and 5 of *Periphyseon*,[40] are too complex to be discussed here. The Irish scholar insists that humanity fell from "perfect knowledge both of itself and of its Creator" (P 4 [778BC]). Evil is thus primarily ignorance and illusion, the inability of humans to grasp their true relation to God. The "Fall" is an exteriorization of the true, inner humanity into the material world, where we need to exercise reason carefully in a constant struggle to discern the truth. Although the Fall involves fault on the part of humanity, it had been foreseen by God from the beginning. God had thus foreordained the overcoming of the Fall by the *inhumanatio* in which Creative Wisdom becomes man and begins the reincorporation of all humans back into their original union in the Word.

The Christic restoration involves a reintegration of the intelligible and sensible worlds in Christ as "the incomprehensible harmony" (*incomprehensibilis harmonia* [912D]) of the universe. Eriugena analyzes the stages of the return according to several patterns of vertical and horizontal *reditus* found in the later books of *Periphyseon*.[41] The most important is the horizontal fivefold pattern adapted from Maximus the Confessor, according to which (1) at death the body dissolves into the four elements, (2) the body is restored from the elements at the general resurrection, (3) the body is transmuted into a spiritual and androgynous reality following the model of the resurrected Christ, (4) the whole of human nature as the Primordial Cause *homo* is reintegrated into the second species of *natura*, and finally (5) those who have received Christ's grace "will pass over into God himself and will be one in him and with him."[42]

The universal restitution of all things is demanded by Eriugena's systematic approach to *processio* and *reditus*. It was also the source of many of the objections to his system. Where are hell and damnation, for example? Fully aware of the biblical and ecclesiastical teachings on these issues, Eriugena wrestled with how to square the universality of the return with the existence of hell throughout *Periphyseon*. His solution, crudely put, is that on one level, that of essential reality, all will be one; but on the level of knowledge, minds that willfully persist in perverted imagination and ignorance will never recognize the heaven of unification and therefore prefer remaining in the hell of error. The unification process was begun by Christ's resurrection from the dead, especially because he rose androgynously, both male and female, thus overcoming one of the primary divisions of the Fall (see Gal. 3:28 for a biblical foundation). For Eriugena, therefore, mystical consciousness consists in becoming aware of what was always intended and what is now under way in history since the death and resurrection of Jesus.

In analyzing the *reditus*, Eriugena makes use of many of the traditional categories of Christian mysticism, such as contemplation, deification, and unification. Contemplation (*contemplatio/speculatio/theoria*), that is, undivided mental attention to God, became central to Christian mysticism very early on as a way of understanding the beatitude "Blessed are the pure of heart for they shall see God" (Matt. 5:8). In book 5 of

Periphyseon, Eriugena discusses three kinds of contemplation illustrated in three biblical exemplars: Elijah, Moses, and Christ. Elijah is the type of those who contemplate God while still in the body, Moses of those who are released from the body in rapture during this life; finally, Christ figures those who will enjoy contemplation in the resurrected spiritual body.[43] Eriugena also discusses Paul's rapture (2 Cor. 12:2-3), the most famous biblical account of what tradition considered a "mystical experience,"[44] as well as why the evangelist John's rapture, the source for his Prologue, was an even higher ascent to contemplation of the *causa omnium*, the Word as Creative Wisdom.[45] Eriugena does not preclude the possibility of present contemplative contact with God, but he is traditional in providing biblical models for this, not in describing any contemplative states of himself or his contemporaries.

Deification in both its Latin and Greek forms (*deificatio/theōsis*) appears over a hundred times in Eriugena's writings. Like contemplation, deification is begun in this life but reaches its fulfillment only in the next. This is clear from a passage in the *Exposition on the Celestial Hierarchy*: "We, indeed, still like little children, are being formed into the divine likeness within us by symbols and holy images, so that we may now be deified by this likeness through faith and afterwards will be deified in vision."[46] For Eriugena, deification is a process that is philosophical and theological, because both nature and grace play their role. Another passage from the *Exposition* says, "The Holy Trinity itself is our *theōsis*" (*Expositiones* 1 [ed., 18]). Deification is defined as union, as a text from book 5 of *Periphyseon* makes clear. Noting that the word "deification" is rare among the Latin authors, Eriugena says that *theōsis* is "the term which the Greeks usually employ in the sense of the psychic and bodily transformation of the saints into God so as to become one with him and in him."[47]

Union with God, or unification (*adunatio*) as Eriugena preferred to speak of it, is the goal of the return process. John's discussions of union/unification are objective and general, not autobiographical. He was interested not in describing present states of union but rather in analyzing what the Bible and Christian tradition taught about becoming one with God. Eriugena's treatments of the progressive unification of all things in the Word are no less complex than most aspects of his thought. They can be summarized under four headings. First, unification is necessarily christological, as we have already seen. Second, unification is as ineffable and incomprehensible as the mystery it involves—*adunatio ineffabilis/ unitas ineffabilis* are frequent terms. At the beginning of the *Exposition*, speaking of how all things flow out from God and yet subsist in him, he says, "he brings them together in one ineffable harmony, so that it may be multiplied in its universality through an infinite multiplication, and in it all things may be one in incomprehensible uniting."[48] This means that, third, unification in Christ is a differentiating union, one that makes us one at the same time that it subsumes and preserves multiplicity. Therefore, union is dialectical: it is identity in the sense that we realize more and more that God is the "essence of all things" (*essentia omnium*), but it is also not identity, because God always remains the *nihil* of the fourth genus of *natura*, the hidden nature that neither creates nor is created. Fourth and finally, unification is always theophanic. There is no direct and unmediated vision of the hidden divine essence. The "face-to-face" unifying vision of heaven promised by Paul (1 Cor. 13:12) will still be by theophany, although higher "theophanies of theophanies" that go beyond anything found in this life. As Eriugena says, "'Face to face' means 'the closest theophany to God,' as the Apostle says: 'We now behold as in a mirror darkly but then face to face,' meaning by the word 'face' some appearance comprehensible to the human intellect of the Divine Power which in itself is perceived by no creature."[49]

Everything said thus far about Eriugena's mysticism leaves one question unanswered. The Irishman may have been the initiator of one of the influential strands in the history of Western mystical theory, but did he have anything to say about the practice of living a mystical life, that is, about the activities that foster deepening awareness of the divine presence? To answer this question we can turn to the most neglected aspect of his writing, his poetry. Eriugena's *Carmina*, edited by Michael Herren two decades ago, continues to be little studied, despite the editor's just claim that "poetry was for John a central occupation in which he was engaged for most of his known career."[50] Despite the difficulty of Eriugena's poetry and his somewhat annoying practice of inserting Greek words or whole lines into the *carmina*, many of his poems are aesthetically striking and intellectually impressive additions to his oeuvre. The same can be said for the *Homily on John's Prologue*, which is a kind of prose poem, although I shall not consider it here.[51]

Paul Dutton spoke of Eriugena as a royal poet; he certainly was in the sense that most of the longer poems were commissioned by his patron, Charles the Bald (d. 877).[52] Herren called him both an epic poet and a philosophical poet.[53] We can second these descriptions too, at least for the longer pieces among the twenty-five recognized poems and the sixteen probably authentic shorter pieces. I suggest that the majority of the longer poems can also be characterized as liturgico-mystical in the sense that they propose a program of appropriation of the saving events of Christ's redemptive action realized by participation in the major feasts of the church's liturgical year.[54] Deifying return to God is not just a matter of correctly understanding the depths of the biblical message and of intellectual realization of the nothingness of God and of the self, but also of a deepening unification with Christ present in the liturgy.

While poetry does not play as large a role in Christian mysticism as it does in Islamic mysticism, it is by no means marginal, as the examples of Hadewijch, Mechthild of Magdeburg, Jacopone da Todi, John of the Cross, and Angelus Silesius show. John Scottus Eriugena's name can be added to this list. Eriugena's poems show, perhaps even more than *Periphyseon* and the other prose works,[55] that the historical events of Christ's life made present in the liturgy are integral to the process of *processio* and *reditus*. History is not erased, nor even neglected, in Eriugena's system; rather, its real, but limited, value appears when viewed from the dialectical perspective of concealing and manifesting. The incomprehensible does indeed become comprehensible within the world of time, but without ever losing its eternal incomprehensibility.

John saw his poems as an account of history's true epic tale—Christ's overcoming evil—as is evident from the opening lines of the first poem composed for Charles the Bald probably for Easter of 859: "Homer sang of the Greeks and the Trojans, / Vergil himself told the tale of Romulus's child. / As for us, let us sing the good deeds [*pia facta*] of the King of the Angels, / Whom the rejoicing world lauds in continuous course."[56] The Christ-epic surpasses those of Homer and Vergil, not only because it embraces the whole of history but also because it shows how history is rooted in the timeless celestial and supracelestial realms. Poem 2 in Praise of the Cross says, "O fostering cross, past Seraphim and Cherubim you shine, / All that is being, non-being, beyond-being worships you. / The 'Lord of Creation,' the Virtues and the Powers, / And the middle rank of the angels adore you; . . . / So, too, our Church sends you praise with a fitting hymn; / For through you, O bearer of Christ, it was redeemed."[57]

This universal perspective is evident also in Poem 3 on the Pasch, which gives Christ's Passover a cosmic, as well as a historical perspective, seeing it as the "manifestation of things long concealed" (3.46). The first Pasch was that of nature, when "it is said the whole frame of the world totally passed over out of nothing into its proper forms."[58] The second Pasch was that of Moses when he brought the Israelites out of Egypt (3.25–44). These both were "images of the Christ to come," who effected the true Pasch by defeating the Devil and offering himself to the Father to "cleanse the whole world of crime" and to overcome death (3.45–60). The significance of this universal process of redemptive "passing-over" becomes effective for us in the celebration of the Eucharist seen in an eschatological perspective: "Now we solemnize the sacred symbols [*symbola sacra*] of these acts / When the things first known to the mind appear to the eyes, / When the pious mind and heart can grasp the body of Christ, / The flow of sacred blood, and the price of the world, / When we commemorate the Lord's Supper for all years to come, / While the choir resounds freely with many hymns. / O Christ, deign to feed your Charles at eternal banquets, / which these mystical symbols prefigure."[59]

It is not possible to review the full range of the liturgico-mystical poems of John's corpus here, especially the two most noted, Poem 8 on the Redemptive Incarnation, perhaps the most speculative in its affinities with *Periphyseon*,[60] and Poem 25, the "Aulae sidereae," probably composed for the foundation of Charles's new royal chapel of St. Mary at Compiègne in 870.[61] We can, however, summarize the major themes of the christological and liturgical side of Eriugena's mysticism. First of all, these poems, like John's prose works but in another key, are rooted in Eriugena's dialectic view of the emanation (*processio/exitus*) of all things from their hidden divine source and their destiny to be drawn back into the mystery (*reditus*). In Eriugena's *carmina*, the issuing forth from the hidden divine mystery is often expressed in terms of the procession of the Eternal Word from the Father's bosom as the model for the incarnation (e.g., Poems 5.1-8, 8.25-50, 9.47-50), while the return is seen as a consequence of Christ's rising from the dead at Easter (e.g., 7.15-20). A visual model of ascent and descent is often to the fore, as in Poem

9: "Christ came from above to assume an earthly garment: / Clothed in this raiment and with it he flew upwards / and changed the clothing received from the Virgin into God."[62] In Poem 9, beginning "Si vis ourania sursum," the cycle of emanation and return is expressed in language close to *Periphyseon*: "He is the single principle from which the order of the world devolves / into genus, species, harmonies, time and place, / the things that are and that are not, whether seen by sense or mind, / the things at rest and those that move. . . ."[63] The fundamental intent of the *carmina* is to show how the Word's manifestation of the role of the Trinity in creation and incarnation is the root of the call to believers to see the unmanifest in what has been manifested, to explore the mystical depths of creation and the Bible.[64] The Easter Poem 5, for example, says that "the mystical teachings of the holy fathers" sung through the Holy Spirit and the Word "are now made manifest." What they reveal is the eternal predestination of the incarnation: "The plan preceded creation in time, but not without Christ / for Christ, who is always born, sees all things created."[65]

The second major theme of John's poems is the importance of participation in liturgical celebration. Toward the close of Poem 8, for example, Eriugena offers a prayer: "O Christ, deign to look on your trembling servants, / who keep your feasts and revere the gifts of salvation." The "Aulae sidereae" celebrating the Feast of the Nativity begins with a picture of how the visible cosmos with the sun and stars of the zodiac reveals "That all times and places are filled with God's Word, / That the universe entire bears symbols of Christ's birth" (lines 20–21). It concludes with a portrayal of Charles the Bald's "splendid temple" (*praeclarem aedem*), the house of the liturgy, with the emperor seated in the midst of the rich array. Not grasping the meaning of the liturgy is seen as the source of evil action. In Poem 1 Charles's brother, Louis the German, is upbraided for his attack on his brother in 858: "O Louis, . . . / Why do you strive to break God's laws in this way, / ungrateful for what you have, seeking what is not yours? / What is baptism to you, and the holy rite of the Mass? / Do they wind their way to a heart that is ever dissembling?" (lines 65–72).

The final theme of the poems also picks up on something central to Eriugena's prose works: participation in the saving mysteries of Christ's triumph over death not only gives fitting praise to God but also deifies the worshipers. In Poem 1 Eriugena meditates on the blood and water flowing from Christ's side as described in John 19:34: "The water washes the whole world clean of its sin of old; / the blood makes us mortals divine" (*Sanguis mortales nos facit esse deos*).[66] In the Poem on the Cross (2.58–60) the wave of Christ's blood "in which the altar of the Cross is bathed, / Purges, redeems, releases, leads us back to life / and shows to your elect that they are gods" (*Electisque tuis praestitit esse deos*). Deification, implied and explicit, appears elsewhere in the *carmina*.[67] The Carolingian era has been described by André Vauchez as creating a "liturgical civilization," that is, a socioreligious order based on the celebration of the Mass.[68] John Scottus Eriugena, the foremost thinker of Carolingian times, created a distinctive liturgical mysticism.[69]

The Christian Neoplatonic dialectical mysticism that Eriugena introduced into the West appeared in many forms after him. We know that the Irishman had a circle of like-minded scholars around him in the late ninth century. There was also an "Eriugenean revival" in the twelfth century in which Honorius Augustodunensis played a leading role.[70] When Honorius III banned *Periphyseon* in 1225, he noted that the work was to be found in many monasteries in France. The ban did not put an end to reading the Irish thinker. Large selections from *Periphyseon* were included in the Paris *Corpus Dionysiacum*, where they were available to Albert the Great, Thomas Aquinas, Meister Eckhart, and others. The *Homily on John's Prologue* continued to be widely read, although under the name of Origen. Eckhart and Nicholas of Cusa studied Eriugena, though I would not want to call them Eriugeneans. Eriugena was rarely named but often present.

We are living in the midst of a great Eriugenean revival. Beginning in 1933 with the ground-breaking book of Maïeul Cappuyns,[71] and accelerating especially in the past fifty years, more attention has been given to John Scottus Eriugena than ever before. Much remains to be done, however, because with a thinker of Eriugena's stature there is always a kind of *epektasis*, a further penetration into the riches of his message. On a lower level this is a shadow of John's belief about human destiny as a never-ending plunge into the divine mystery. A text from book 5 of *Periphyseon*, reflecting on the search for the incomprehensible infinite God, puts it well: "it necessarily follows that the quest is unending and . . . it moves forever. And yet although the search is unending, by some miraculous means it finds what it is seeking for; and again it does not find it, for it cannot be found. It finds it through theophanies, but through the contemplation of the divine nature itself it does not find it."[72] Incomprehensibility has the last word.

Notes

1. This oxymoron (*incomprehensibilis comprehensio*) is the fourth of the nineteen self-negating pairs found in Eriugena's *Periphyseon* 3 (633A). I will make use of the edition of Édouard Jeauneau, *Iohannes Scotti seu Eriugenae Periphyseon*, 5 vols., Corpus Christianorum: Continuatio mediaevalis 161–65 (Turnhout: Brepols, 1996–2003), 3:240. I will employ P for *Periphyseon*, and cite according to the standard *Patrologia Latina* column number (e.g., 633A), as well as the volume and page number of the Jeauneau edition (e.g., 3:240). Much has been written about this passage; see especially Werner Beierwaltes, "*Negati affirmatio* or the World as Metaphor: A Foundation for Biblical Aesthetics in the Writings of John Scotus Eriugena," *Dionysius* 1 (1977): 127–59; and James McEvoy, "Biblical and Platonic Measure in John Scottus Eriugena," in *Eriugena East and West*, ed. Bernard McGinn and Willemien Otten (Notre Dame: University of Notre Dame Press, 1994), 153–77.

2. One of the first twentieth-century theologians to give some attention to Eriugena was Hans Urs von Balthasar, who has a section on him in *The Glory of the Lord: A Theological Aesthetics, vol. 4, The Realm of Metaphysics in Antiquity* (San Francisco: Ignatius Press, 1989; German original, 1967), 343–55.

3. W. R. Inge, *Christian Mysticism* (London: Methuen, 1899), 133–38.

4. Ibid., 133.

5. Evelyn Underhill, *Mysticism: A Study in the Nature and Development of Man's Spiritual Consciousness*, 12th ed. (Cleveland and New York: Meridian Books, 1955), 457.

6. I have found no references to Eriugena in Neoscholastic volumes on mysticism by such writers as Augustin-François Poulain, August Saudreau, Albert Farges, Juan-Gonzalez Arintero, Ambrose Gardeil, and Reginald Garrigou-Lagrange.

7. Underhill, *Mysticism*, 83.

8. Bernard McGinn, *The Presence of God: A History of Western Christian Mysticism*, vol. 2, *The Growth of Mysticism: Gregory the Great through the 12th Century* (New York: Crossroad, 1994), chap. 3, "The Entry of Dialectical Mysticism: John Scottus Eriugena."

9. Kurt Ruh, *Geschichte der abendländische Mystik*, Band 1, *Die Grundlegung durch die Kirchenväter und die Mönchstheologie des 12. Jahrhunderts* (Munich: C. H. Beck, 1990), 191.

10. Work on Eriugena's mysticism has continued to grow over the past twenty years. A recent contribution is Willemien Otten, "Le langage de l'union mystique: Le désir et le corps dans l'oeuvre de Jean Scot Érigène et de Maître Eckhart," *Les études philosophiques, Érigène* (Janvier 2013–14): 121–41.

11. Bernard McGinn, *The Presence of God: A History of Western Christian Mysticism*, vol. 1, *The Foundations of Mysticism: Origins to the Fifth Century* (New York: Crossroad, 1991), xiii–xx.

12. The literature is too large to cite fully here; see especially the essays in *Iohannes Scottus Eriugena: The Bible and Hermeneutics*, ed. Gerd Van Riel, Carlos Steel, and James McEvoy (Leuven: University Press, 1996).

13. The following sketch of Eriugena's mystical thought uses material from my presentation of Eriugena in chap. 3 of *The Growth of Mysticism*, but many aspects, especially the attention given to John's *carmina*, are new.

14. These three notes of dialectical thinking are based on Hans Georg Gadamer, *Hegel's Dialectic: Five Hermeneutical Studies* (New Haven: Yale University Press, 1976), 20–22. Gadamer argues that they hold for both ancient and modern forms of dialectical thinking, however much we may want to distinguish between ancient dialectical thinkers and modern Idealist dialectical thought.

15. P 1 (459D). See the whole discussion found in 459D–460B (1:186–90). See also 487B (1:304–5).

16. The four *species* of *natura* are introduced in P 1 (441B–445D; 1:3–8). Although explicit analysis of the four *species* becomes somewhat muted in books 2–5 as Eriugena turns his attention more toward Hexaemeral exegesis, they continue to remain important to the structure and argument of *Periphyseon*.

17. On this, see Beierwaltes, *"Negati affirmatio,"* 140.

18. On Eriugena's notion of theophany, see Hilary Anne-Marie Mooney, *Theophany: The Appearing of God according to the Writings of Johannes Scottus Eriugena*, Beiträge zur historischen Theologie 146 (Tübingen: Mohr Siebeck, 2009).

19. P 3 (723C; 3:616–17).

20. *Jean Scot Érigène: Homélie sur le Prologue de Jean*, ed. Édouard Jeauneau, Sources chrétiennes 151 (Paris: Cerf, 1969), 14 (pp. 270–72). Hereafter *Homilia*.

21. On Eriugena's use of light and darkness, see Werner Beierwaltes, "Eriugena's Platonism," *Hermathena* 109 (1992): 53–72; James McEvoy, "Metaphors of Light and Metaphysics of Light in Eriugena," in *Begriff und Metapher: Sprachform des Denkens bei Eriugena*, ed. Werner Beierwaltes (Heidelberg: Carl Winter, 1990), 149–67; and Deirdre Carabine, "Eriugena's Use of the Symbolism of Light, Cloud, and Darkness in the *Periphyseon*," in McGinn and Otten, *Eriugena East and West*, 141–52.

22. This statement (*omnia quae sunt lumina sunt*) is found at the beginning of Eriugena's *Expositiones in Ierarchiam Coelestem*, ed. J. Barbet, Corpus Christianorum: Continuatio mediaevalis 31 (Turnhout: Brepols, 1975), 1.1

(p. 3). Hereafter *Expositiones*. The illuminative power of created theophanies, of course, is not self-generated but depends on their creation by the "Father of lights" (Jas. 1:17) through the coessential light of the Word. For a study and partial translation of this work, see Paul Rorem, *Eriugena's Commentary on the Dionysian Celestial Hierarchy*, Studies and Texts 150 (Toronto: Pontifical Institute of Mediaeval Studies, 2005).

23. P 5 (866A; 5:10).

24. This is well put in a passage from *Homilia* XI: "Sensu corporeo formas et pulchritudines rerum perspice sensibilium, et in eis intelliges dei uerbum. Et in his omnibus nichil aliud tibi ueritas declarabit praeter ispsum qui fecit omnia" (ed. Jeauneau, 254). See also *Expositiones* 1.3 (ed., p. 15).

25. *Expositiones* 2.1 (p. 24). On this passage and the poetic element in Eriugena, see Peter Dronke, "*Theologia veluti quaedam poetria*: Quelques observations sur la function des images poétiques chez Jean Scot," in *Jean Scot Érigène et l'histoire de la philosophie*, ed. René Roques, Colloques internationaux du Centre national de la recherche scientifique 561 (Paris: Centre national de la recherche scientifique, 1977), 243–52.

26. Beierwaltes, "Eriugena's Platonism," 66.

27. P 3 (681C; 3:444-45). There are a number of studies of the divine nothing in Eriugena; in English, see Donald F. Duclow, "Divine Nothingness and Self-Creation in John Scotus Eriugena," *Journal of Religion* 57 (1977): 109–23; and Wayne Teasdale, "Nihil as the Name of God in John Scottus Eriugena," *Cistercian Studies* 19 (1984): 232–47.

28. On this theme, see Bernard McGinn, "The Negative Element in the Anthropology of John the Scot," in Roques, *Jean Scot Érigène et l'histoire de la philosophie*, 315–25.

29. P 2 (593C-94A; 2:412–13).

30. P 4 (771BC; 4:298–301).

31. Eriugena's Christology has also been the subject of many studies; in English, see, e.g., Donald F. Duclow, "Dialectic and Christology in Eriugena's *Periphyseon*," *Dionysius* 4 (1980): 99–118; and James McEvoy, "'Reditus omnium in superessentialem unitatem': Christ as Universal Saviour in Periphyseon V," in *Giovanni Scoto nel suo tempo: L'organizzazione del sapere in età carolingia* (Spoleto: Centro Italiano di Studi sull'Alto Medioevo, 1989), 365–81.

32. There are a number of discussions of this in book 2 of *Periphyseon*, e.g., 547BC, 551C, 552AB, 554CD, 563B–564A, and especially 556B–562A. See also *Homilia* VII (ed. Jeauneau, 230–36).

33. P 2 (559B; 2:266–67).

34. P 4 (768B; 4:284–85). On Eriugena's anthropology, see especially Dermot Moran, *The Philosophy of John Scottus Eriugena: A Study of Idealism in the Middle Ages* (Cambridge: Cambridge University Press, 1989); and Willemien Otten, *The Anthropology of Johannes Scottus Eriugena*, Brill's Studies in Intellectual History 20 (Leiden: Brill, 1991).

35. See, e.g., P 4 (778D–779D; 4:330–31). See also *Homilia* XIX (ed. Jeauneau, 290–98).

36. Moran, *Philosophy of John Scottus Eriugena*, 172.

37. P 5 (893A; 5:366–67).

38. P 4 (743B; 4:176–77).

39. Eriugena's notion of the *visio beatifica* was different from the standard Western view advanced by Augustine and Aquinas; see Dominic J. O'Meara, "Eriugena and Aquinas on the Beatific Vision," in *Eriugena Redivivus: Zur Wirkungsgeschichte seines Denkens im Mittelalter und im Übergang zur Neuzeit*, ed. Werner Beierwaltes (Heidelberg: Carl Winter, 1987), 214–36.

40. For the discussion of the Fall in Genesis 2–3, see especially P 4 (824B–860C; 4:518–665).

41. For summaries of the different forms and logic of *reditus*, see Stephen Gersh, "The Structure of the Return in Eriugena's *Periphyseon*," in Beierwaltes, *Begriff und Metapher*, 108–25; and Willemien Otten, "The Dialectic of the Return in Eriugena's *Periphyseon*," *Harvard Theological Review* 84 (1991): 399–421.

42. This fivefold pattern, adopted from Maximus the Confessor (see *Ambiguum* 37), is first introduced in P 2 (530A–543B; 2:154–205) and is also discussed in P 5. A more complex analysis involving three general levels of return and seven special levels appears in P 5 (1020AD), where this text is found at 1020C.

43. P 5 (998B–1000B; 5:770–79).

44. E.g., P 5 (887CD, 897B); *Expositiones* 8.2 (ed., 123).

45. See especially *Homilia* IV (ed. Jeauneau, 218–20); also *Expositiones* 2.5 (ed., 50–52).

46. *Expositiones* 7.2 (ed., 105). The two levels also are mentioned in John's *Commentary on the Gospel of John*; see *Jean Scot Érigène, Commentaire sur l'Évangile de Jean*, ed. Édouard Jeauneau, Sources chrétiennes 180 (Paris: Cerf, 1972), 3.5 (ed., 224). Hereafter *Commentarium*.

47. P 5 (1015C; 5:836–39).

48. *Expositiones* 1 (ed., 1).

49. P 5 (926C; 5:496). This is John's constant teaching; see, e.g., P 1 (448C), P 2 (557BC), and P 5 (905CD, 945 CD, 1000BD, 1010 CD). See also *Expositiones* 4.3 and 8.2 (ed., 74–75, 133), as well as *Commentarium* 1.25 (ed., 118–26).

50. *Iohannis Scotti Eriugenae Carmina*, ed. Michael W. Herren, Scriptores Latini Hiberniae XII (Dublin: Dublin Institute for Advanced Studies, 1993), 11. I will use Herren's edition and translations unless otherwise noted.

51. For an analysis of the *Kunstprosa* of the *Homilia in Prologum Iohannis*, see Dronke, "*Theologia sicut quaedam poetria*," 244–50.

52. Paul Edward Dutton, "Eriugena, the Royal Poet," in *Jean Scot Écrivain*, ed. G.-H. Allard (Montreal: Bellarmin; Paris: Vrin, 1986), 51–80.

53. Michael Herren speaks of Eriugena as developing a "Christian epic" ("Johannes Scottus Poeta," in *From Augustine to Eriugena: Essays on Neoplatonism and Christianity in Honor of John O'Meara*, ed. F. X. Martin and J. A. Richmond [Washington, DC: Catholic University Press, 1991], 92–106, here 103); in the "Introduction" to *Iohannis Scotti Eriugenae Carmina*, Herren argues for John as a philosophical poet (p. 42).

54. Herren already noted the liturgical dimension of the poems (*Carmina*, 54–55). Eriugena concentrates on the fundamental saving events commemorated in the church's major feasts: the incarnation as redemption (Poem 8; App. 2); Christmas (Poem 25); the passion and the holy cross (Poems 1, 2); the Harrowing of Hell (Poems 6, 7, 9); Easter as the Pasch (Poems 3, 5).

55. Eriugena's prose works do not neglect the mysteries of Christ's saving work; see, e.g., the comments on the incarnation in *Expositiones* 4.4 (ed., 82), as well as in P 4 (745A–746B; 777BC). The transfiguration and resurrection are noted in *Homilia* XXII (ed. Jeauneau, 308). The resurrection is often treated in *Periphyseon* (e.g., 531C–533A, 537C–539C, 894A–895C, 991C–995B), and the ascension is discussed in P 5 (999B). A summary of the importance of the mysteries of salvation is found in the *Commentarium* 1.32 (ed., 176–78).

56. Herren, *Carmina* 1.1–4 (ed., 58–59).

57. Herren, *Carmina* 2.7–14 (ed., 64–65).

58. Herren, *Carmina* 3.5–6 (ed., 68–69): "Quo machinae mundi cumulatim dicitur esse / in species proprias transitus ex nihilo" (my trans.). The first Pasch is described in 3.2–24.

59. Herren, *Carmina* 3.61–67 (ed., 70–71, trans. slightly altered).

60. Poem 8 is in Herren, *Carmina*, 84–89. Its powerful Hymn to Christ (lines 25–86) is one of the high points of Eriugena's poetic art.

61. The "Aulae sidereae" is found in Herren, *Carmina*, 116–21. It is studied in detail by Herren, who shows that the poem both commemorates Charles's celebration of Christmas at Aachen in 869 and proclaims the foundation of his new Palatine Chapel at Compiègne, begun in 870 but not consecrated until 877 ("Eriugena's *Aulae sidereae*, the 'Codex Aureus,' and the Palatine Church of St. Mary at Compiègne," *Studi Medievali*, 3rd ser., 28 [1987]: 593–608). See also John J. O'Meara, *Eriugena* (Oxford: Clarendon, 1988), 180–90.

62. Herren, *Carmina* 9.25–27 (ed., 90–91). See also the "Aulae sidereae," Poem 25.67–71.

63. Poem 9.13–16 (ed., 84–85). See also lines 30–40 (ed., 86–87).

64. Eriugena uses *mysticus* six times in the poems; *mysteria* occurs three times.

65. Herren, *Carmina* 5.1–8 (ed., 76–77).

66. Herren, *Carmina* 1.27–28 (ed., 58–59).

67. For example, "Aulae sidereae," lines 70–71 literally concern Christ's descent and ascent: "Vt deus aeternus factus caro lapsus ad ima, / Sic caro facta

deus uere leuis euolat alta" (ed., 118); but the ascension is the ground for our own deifying ascent. Poem 9.25–31 (ed., 90) makes the same point explicitly.

68. André Vauchez, *The Spirituality of the Medieval West: The Eighth to the Twelfth Centuries* (Kalamazoo: Cistercian Publications, 1993), 15–19.

69. It is interesting to note, as I am reminded by Willemien Otten, how different Eriugena's liturgical mysticism is from that of Dionysius as set out in the *Ecclesiastical Hierarchies*, despite Eriugena's dependence on Dionysius.

70. See Édouard Jeauneau, "Le renouveau érigénean du XIIe siècle," in Beierwaltes, *Eriugena Redivivus*, 26–46.

71. Maïeul Cappuyns, *Jean Scot Érigène, sa vie, son oeuvre, sa pensée* (Louvain/Paris: Universitas Catholica Lovaniensis, 1933).

72. P 5 (919C; 5:468–69). See also 1010CD; *Expositiones* 6.1 (ed., 87–88); *Commentarium* 1.32 (ed., 182).

3

From the Radically Apophatic to the Radically Kataphatic: From Meister Eckhart to Jacob Boehme

Cyril O'Regan

In and through an examination of two German mystics, Meister Eckhart (ca. 1250–1328) and Jacob Boehme (1575–1624), I explore the movement from a production of a form of apophasis none-greater-than-which-can-be-thought to a correlative counter-movement of an equally radical

---

This essay is written out of the well of affection for John Jones, who left us too soon. I taught John at Yale, directed his dissertation, and enjoyed his friendship then and for years after. John appreciated everything and was rattled by nothing. If there was for him an area of particular intellectual and spiritual delight, it was the area of mystical theology. It was not an accident, then, that he wrote his dissertation on Pseudo-Dionysius. Pseudo-Dionysius fascinated him for a number of reasons, for example, the relation between philosophy and theology, the importance of scripture, the divine names, the importance of the symbolic, and the relation of the self to the superessential Godhead who is also the Triune God. See his "Dionysian Mysticism: A Christian Conversion" (Ph.D. dissertation, Yale University, 1998). See also his article "Sculpting God: The Logic of Dionysian Negative Theology," *Harvard Theological Review* 89 (1996): 355–71. John was also drawn to Spanish mysticism. He loved Teresa of Avila and John of the Cross and almost wrote his dissertation on the Spanish mystic Francisco de Osuna (1472–1540), who influenced Teresa. It was this elective affinity to all things mystical that made Bernard McGinn's project in the history of mysticism so personally as well as professionally compelling. If John had a favorite mystic, it was not Pseudo-Dionysius, as one might have expected, but the German mystic Meister Eckhart (ca. 1260–1328), whose thought is very much shaped by the Dionysian corpus. What was stunning about Eckhart for

form of mysticism that is visionary and aesthetic in character. I do so with the dual aims of demonstrating an intimate relation between two forms of German Christian mysticism, both of which have continued to have influence in philosophy and theology up until the present day,[1] and suggesting that the mysticism of radical apophasis tends dialectically to beget its opposite. To prosecute the case, in addition to knowledge of the texts of both Eckhart and Boehme, knowledge of both the immediate theological and mystical backdrop of both of these thinkers is a desideratum. In the case of Eckhart I will isolate three discourses that influence Eckhart's complex mystical discourse and are identifiable as overlapping strands in his Latin and German writings. In the case of Boehme I will refer to the transmission of Eckhartian language and concepts into the Lutheran environment, as well as comment on the presence of Kabbalistic and alchemical discourses. I would like also to set off these radical forms of mysticism, separated by a period of three hundred years, by benchmarking them against the intervening form of mysticism of the Rhineland School and especially the mystical theology of Jan van Ruusbroec (1293–1381), which illustrates a balance between more apophatic and more kataphatic modes of Christian mysticism and in a prophylactic manner sets limits to apophasis introducing injurious ontological distinctions between the Godhead and Trinity and the Godhead and God.

Importantly, while this essay takes account of historical context and provides a sketch of an important trajectory in Christian mystical

---

John was the freedom with which he used the Bible and the theological and mystical tradition, and the casual way he experimented with the vocabulary and grammar of the mystical tradition. While loving the theological and mystical traditions, and thinking them eminently worthy of respect and honor, John savored the way Eckhart put the received tradition in and through his hyperboles and paradoxes about the Godhead. This might have been expected from someone who had immersed himself in Pseudo-Dionysius, for whom naming the divine is the center of mystical reflection. But for John it was the ability of Eckhart to provoke an experience of detachment and letting go rather than simply talking about it that stood out. *Gelassenheit* did not come trippingly on John's tongue, but this was the center of Eckhart for him, the point of view—or absence of point of view—to see everything and assign each thing its proper weight. In particular, John was enthralled by the way Eckhart approached (or avoided) the problem of evil. Is evil a perception, is death a perception? I have felt it necessary, then, to write an essay in which his hero is foregrounded.

theology, it is not historical after the manner of the best historians of the Christian mystical tradition.[2] I am not, for instance, arguing the case that the mysticism of Eckhart or that of Ruusbroec, which creatively assimilated and adjusted it, bears a causal relation to Boehme's visionary and aesthetic kind of mysticism and thus in some sense explains it. Rather, what I am suggesting is that, relative to the common mystical tradition which, before the sixteenth century, was regulated in the main by Augustinian and Dionysian discourse, relative to their proximate sources, and relative also to our Ruusbroec benchmark, the mystical forms of Eckhart and Boehme are so strikingly radical that we illuminate both by bringing them into conversation with each other. The illumination is in my view at its brightest if we read Boehme's theosophy as essentially constructed by a series of transgressive interpretations of some of the most radical features of the apophatic mysticism of Eckhart, that is, those features that seem to be in excess of the hyperboles and paradoxes standardly deployed in the Christian mystical tradition.

The essay has three parts and a brief conclusion. Part 1 lays out Eckhart's mystical theology against the backdrop of its Augustinian, Thomistic, and Dionysian sources. It argues not only that the dominant strand in Eckhart's mystical theology is Dionysian, but that Eckhart stretches the Dionysian inheritance. While the essay does not take a stand on whether Eckhart's thought is best read as being within or without the mainline Christian tradition, it does suggest that, whether typical or not, Eckhart at points seems to stretch the inherited tradition to the point of breaking. Part 2 provides just enough context for and just enough outline of mystical and esoteric sources to make the strange works of Jacob Boehme intelligible. For the most part, however, the focus is on how Boehme's work is characterized by a complex hermeneutic operation in and through which fundamental priorities in Eckhart's apophatic form of Christian mysticism are systematically inverted and made subject to a form of Christian mysticism, at once rigorously and expansively kataphatic and governed by a developmental ontology. In part 3, I measure our radical apophatic and kataphatic forms of mysticism against the more balanced forms of mysticism to be found in Ruusbroec, who seems to be self-consciously correcting for either actual or possible imbalances in the Eckhartian heritage of negative theology. Benchmarking in this way serves to throw into relief the brazenness of the forms of mystical theology exemplified by Eckhart and Boehme. I will conclude with a summary of what I think has been achieved by the essay and point to the continuing vitality of Christian mystical theology at both its apophatic and kataphatic extremes and the perennial value of a mediating form of mysticism such as that supplied by Ruusbroec.

Meister Eckhart: Toward Radical Apophaticism

Few scholars would deny that Aquinas, Augustine, and Pseudo-Dionysius exercise significant influence on the complex discourse of Meister Eckhart, even if most would equally want to insist on its relatively *sui generis* character, variously manifested in the Latin sermons and Latin exegetical works as well as in the German sermons.[3] It is reasonable to assume on historical and textual grounds that Eckhart is fully aware of the thought of Aquinas, especially his metaphysics, his reflections on our language regarding God, and perhaps his views on the Trinity and Christ and on grace and the virtues.[4] By no means, however, does this imply that Aquinas's thought is constitutive of Eckhart's often more radical thinking. I will indicate in due course the ways in which Eckhart deviates from Aquinas on all of the above subjects, and especially on language regarding God and the way the Trinity should be understood.

Augustine's influence on Eckhart and his presence in Eckhart's texts, especially when he addresses the question of human beings' knowledge of God, the intrinsic difficulties of God-talk, and the anthropology of the image of God, have rightly been affirmed in the secondary literature as an important strand.[5] Once again, however, one has to leave open the possibility that Eckhart either disagrees with Augustine on fundamental points and/or stretches him on others.

The most obvious influence on Eckhart is Pseudo-Dionysius, or at least the Dionysian tradition as mediated through medieval theology, not excluding mediation by Aquinas in his treatment of naming God in the *Summa* as well as his commentary on the *Divine Names*.[6] The specifically Dionysian features include a stringent commitment to apophasis, a high anthropology that takes neither sin nor createdness to present fundamental obstacles to union with the "superessential Godhead,"[7] an affirmation of a form of knowing that transcends sense and the discursive intellect, and finally a view of all reality as having symbolic and sacramental capacity. While, undoubtedly, Eckhart stretches even the thought of Pseudo-Dionysius at times—or at least appears to do so—it is evident that Dionysianism is the determinative strand. Not only does it bind itself to the other two figures in Eckhart's work, it might be thought to bend them in a direction that goes contrary to their natural inclinations.

Before I get to my central topic, which is Eckhart's adoption and adaptation of Dionysianism, I would like to indicate Eckhart's swerves from Aquinas and Augustine that require the kind of Dionysian explanation being tendered. Eckhart adopts and then adapts a number of key Thomistic constructs in the interest of underscoring the unsearchable mysteriousness of God as well as an experience of divine presence for which language is not a match. In some cases the adaptation simply involves a rhetorical amping up or conceptual sharpening. In other cases, however, we may well be dealing with outright subversion of Thomistic principles. Some scholars observe a clear pattern of subversion regarding both the ordering of being (*esse*) and knowing (*intelligere*), on the one hand, and the order of being (*esse*) and God (*Deus*),[8] on the other. A central issue in Eckhart's *Parisian Questions* is whether being (*esse*) and knowing (*intelligere*) are coextensive in God. Eckhart answers resoundingly in the affirmative just as Aquinas had done. However, when Eckhart faces the issue of priority and foundation, a rupture is announced. Whereas Aquinas claims that being is foundational regarding knowing, Eckhart inverts the order and insists that knowing is foundational with respect to being. God is because he knows (*quia intelligit Deus est*).[9] Eckhart is in effect subverting Aquinas's doctrine of analogy by exposing what he deems to be an equivocation in *esse*, which refers to finite and infinite being at once. For Eckhart, if we disambiguate as we ought, then it would be best to have *esse* refer only to finite being. On the face of it, knowing is not in a much better situation than being, since, similar to being, knowing can in principle be predicable of finite and infinite reality. Since, however, *intelligere* seems to be understood outside of its relation to sense perception and abstraction and is more nearly in line with a Neoplatonic construct of a special form of knowing apt for the eternal, disambiguation would mean that its authentic signified is the divine as such.

This inversion supports another. A favorite formula in Aquinas, and one that might rightly be regarded as typical of his metaphysical theology, is the identification of God and being: *Deus est Esse*.[10] Thus, while a major twentieth-century thinker like Heidegger thinks of Aquinas as making the category mistake of mistakes, that is, ontotheology,[11] by identifying God and Being, and seems for the most part to exonerate Eckhart, there is in fact no fundamental distinction between Eckhart and Aquinas on this very general point. This is not to say, however, that there are other truly important differences between the two Dominicans. In the *Parisian Questions*, Eckhart regards being and God as convertible and thus suggests *Esse est Deus* or *Esse Deus est* as a functional equivalent of *Deus est Esse*. It turns out, however, that the act of conversion is far from metaphysically innocent. One mischievous implication of identifying *esse* with God without the further specification, for instance, that God is self-subsistent *esse*, is that Eckhart deprives all created being of a reality—albeit dependent—that is all their own. Departing from Aquinas's view of analogy—the analogy of proportionality rather than attribution—the relative order of beings can be, however, equally identified as nothing (*nihil*). As Tobin rightly points out,[12] Eckhart is not here caught in a contradiction. He is simply drawing the logical consequences from the disruption of Aquinas's view of analogy: Things are to the extent they manifest the divine; and insofar as they do not manifest the divine, they are not. Considered as having value only as theophanic without remainder, entities have no value in themselves. As a category, "being" cannot be stretched to cover both God and world; if it covers the former, it does not cover the latter. And logically, of course, if being does cover the created finite world, it is useless with regard to God. Eckhart does not attend to this logical implication in *Parisian Questions*, nor for that matter in his other Latin works. The logical implication, however, is drawn out clearly in Eckhart's German sermons, where he has no compunction about identifying God and nothing.[13]

Of course, as being in its theophanic register becomes what Eckhart refers to as the fullest and purest being (*plenissimum et purissimum esse*),[14] and gets taken out of circulation regarding created temporal and material being, it becomes more apophatically inflected than *esse* in Aquinas. This is clear in Eckhart's dealing with what Gilson calls Aquinas's metaphysics of Exodus. In the *Parisian Questions*, Eckhart agrees with Aquinas on the importance of the "I am who am" (*ego sum qui sum*) of Exodus 3:14. He makes it clear, however, that by no means does this imply that either being or God is available for inspection. Both, he insists, are hidden. The apophatic inflection of *esse* and God is subtly reinforced in Eckhart's *Commentary on Exodus*.[15] First, Eckhart slants things by discussing being (*esse*) in the context of negative predicates, which are more proper to the divine. In particular, *esse* is paired with the Tetragrammaton, which name, Eckhart admits, is conceptually odd in that it is hidden, secret, and inexpressible.[16] Associated with the Tetragrammaton, *esse* becomes the nameless name (*nomen innominabile*). Since, however, in its theophanic register, *esse* is predicable of all that is, then the nameless name is also the name of all things (*nomen omnium*). At the very least, Aquinas's attempt to achieve balance between positive and negative predication is put under severe pressure, if not entirely upset. As is well known, Aquinas is aware that the language we use to refer to beings in the created order cannot be applied properly to God. So a significant degree of epistemic humility is advised. At the same time, he thinks skepticism or agnosticism regarding God is not prescribed. Famously, Aquinas recommends the way of eminence (*via eminentiae*). With disciplined good judgment we can extend certain terms beyond the created sphere where they are properly deployed. "Good" and "true" are two cases in point. Although these terms have real adequacy only in the created sphere, they can be applied to God provided we insist that God's truth and goodness infinitely surpass all human truth and goodness actual or imaginable. Eckhart is convinced that the way of eminence fails—and fails not only in fact but in principle—because it does not sufficiently respect the infinite ontological difference between God and the world. Eckhart touches on this point in his *Commentary on Exodus*. He makes the point fully explicit, however, in the German sermons, which are more rigorously—sometimes tendentiously—apophatic than their Latin equivalents. In Sermon 9, for example, Eckhart seems to be recalling Aquinas only to refute him. In contrast to Aquinas, Eckhart is not prepared to predicate goodness supereminently of God. Given the radical transcendence of God or the Godhead, he insists that "good" is no more predicable of God than "blackness" is predicable of the sun. [17] Eckhart here is at his most brazenly dialectical and hyperbolical, and for that reason his most constitutively Dionysian.

Before I get to the dominant Dionysian strand in Eckhart's thought, I want to say something about the Augustinian strand in Eckhart's discourse, which, similar to that of Aquinas, is inflected in Eckhart's texts by radical dialectic and apophatic recoding. The most superficial of surveys would show there is much in Augustine that highlights the apophatic when it comes to our knowing of God. There is, of course, the insistence on inadequacy of language and concept vis-à-vis God in *De doctrina christiana* (1.6), the assertion made repeatedly in the sermons that God is known as unknown,[18] as well as the reminder in book 8 of *De trinitate* after a conceptual elucidation of the doctrine of the Trinity to the effect that the Triune God is incomprehensible.[19] Pseudo-Dionysius, then, is not the only source for Eckhart's apophaticism, even if it remains fairly safe to say that he is the main source and, arguably, the point from which Eckhart launches his own apophatic experiments in his German sermons. Eckhart can be understood to negotiate with a number of other Augustinian motifs only to press them in a non-Augustinian direction. Perhaps the motifs most relevant to my discussion of how Augustine is appropriated and moved in a more radically apophatic direction are Eckhart's reflections on the image of God and his view of the noetic capacity of the human being. In the German sermons, Eckhart definitely takes on board Augustine's theology of image as this is articulated in *De trinitate* (bks. 9 and 10). In Augustine's masterpiece, the unity of memory, understanding, and will, which constitutes the definition of image, is not understood to be a finite replica of the Trinity so much as the created capacity to participate in the life of the triune God to the degree possible in this life.[20] The quality and intensity of this co-presence, however, are to be measured by what is possible in the eschatological state (bk. 15). Now, not only does Eckhart ignore in a way Augustine does not the reality of sin and the resulting defacing of the image, but he also seems to abolish the difference posited in Augustine between what is possible for human beings in the pre-eschatological and eschatological states respectively.

Even more importantly, however, Eckhart relativizes Augustine's definition of the image. According to Eckhart, the real image lies at a level deeper than memory, understanding, and will, which together are constrained and modulated by createdness and temporality. In his German sermons, Eckhart refers to the image variously as a "spark" (*Fünklein*) or "castle" of the soul.[21] Unlike memory, understanding, and will, the spark, castle, or ground of the soul is uncreated and atemporal. Because of this, the image can enjoy a participation in the divine that is unimaginable in the Augustinian context. When Eckhart moves in his German sermons from the language of "spark" and "castle" to the "birth of God" (*Gottesgeburt*),[22] he moves from capacity to event, from the image being implicitly trinitarian to its being actually trinitarian. In the deepest stratum of image, the birth of the Son is actualized. The Father gives birth to the Son in the soul, and it is through the generation of the Son that spiration occurs. Although Eckhart could very well be indulging in the kind of hyperbole typical of the Dionysian tradition, much of what he says speaks to his subversion of the analogical structure that is constitutive of Augustine's theology of image. Eckhart is often straightforwardly declarative about the radical nature of his views on the divine birth. When it comes to sonship, he denies that he is speaking in an "as if" mode: not only does the Father give birth to the Son in the soul of the mystic who has opened up to the divine in detachment; the Father does nothing less than give birth to the soul *as* the Son. The birthing of the soul as the Son belongs to the order of generation rather than creation, and thus this birth has no beginning in the way a creature has in Augustine's more standard model. Nor does Eckhart have recourse to the standard Augustinian, indeed, standard mystical, relativizing clauses such as "the greatest possible intimacy given createdness," or the "taking on of divine sonship to the degree possible for a creature who can only be a son by grace and not nature." This brings us to the Dionysian influences in Eckhart, in terms both of language and theological substance, and of the consequent inflection of Eckhart's mystical theology. Whatever the mode of transmission of Dionysian ideas, whether through available manuscripts of Pseudo-Dionysius, through what there is available of Pseudo-Dionysius in the writings of Johannes Scottus Eriugena, or through Aquinas's commentary on Pseudo-Dionysius, it is the case that Pseudo-Dionysius is a dominant presence in the mystical discourses of Meister Eckhart. This is witnessed in Eckhart's predilection to hyperbole and paradox evinced especially in the German sermons, a mystical lexicon that, favoring apophasis, puts to serious work the Latin and German equivalent of both the *alpha* privative and the superlative Greek prefix *hyper-*, a focus on exposure to the radical transcendent divine (even if correlative to radical immanence) in excess of the creator and redeemer God who is for us, and an ambiguity as to whether what is absolutely transcendent is the Trinity or the unitary ground beyond the Trinity and which serves as its basis or ground. I speak briefly to each of these Diony-sian elements in turn, although it is obvious that each of these elements is imbricated with all the others.

The use of paradox and hyperbole is to be seen throughout Eckhart's work, although obviously hyperbole is not entirely separable from the lexical indices with which we will be dealing shortly. If hyperbole is char-acteristic of both the Latin and German works, paradox and dialectic are more evident in the German sermons in which Eckhart employs surprising juxtapositions to get our distracted and customary selves to focus on the astonishing that is at hand. Required for any form of mys-tical understanding is a defamiliarization of the putative divine, which routinely falls foul of conceptual idolatry; experiencing the presence of the divine requires, then, an epistemic shift or conversion. Relative to Pseudo-Dionysius of *The Divine Names* and the *Mystical Theology*, Eckhart's use of paradox functions differently, maybe even uniquely. First, there is the vernacular environment of its operation. Second, the language of paradox is more performative than descriptive in that it is construed not simply as an element in an economy of speech about God but rather as a rhetorical means to induce or at least open up the pros-pect of a direct experience of God in the hearer (or reader). The condi-tion of this experience, of course, is the destruction of the careless ways in which we instrumentalize the divine by our all-too-human tendency to speak univocally of God and the world, thereby fatally compromising divine alterity. Third, as exhibited in the German sermons, the domain of the operation of paradox is significantly different from that found in Pseudo-Dionysius. The tone is considerably less hieratic. Although the German sermons are a form of *lectio divina* and either interpret a biblical passage or at least use it as a prompt for a reflection, this is still a less sacral site than the high liturgical site of paradox in Pseudo-Dionysius.[23] In Eckhart's hands, the authority of the Bible is as much vested in function as in definition, as he focuses on its role in shutting out self-will, thereby creating the possibility of an experience of divine pres-ence. Moreover, Eckhart's intent is to show us that just about anything can serve as a prompt and as a cue to remind us that the experience of the divine is subtle as well as mysterious such that it cannot be rendered straightforwardly. It is also true that paradox functions in a decidedly more democratic way in Eckhart in that it initiates and finds expression in the experience in many more people and not simply a group of clerical or monastic adepts. The horizon of Eckhart's work, then, is antihierarchical.[24] To summarize: with regard to the deployment of paradox and hyperbole, Eckhart both repeats Pseudo-Dionysius and represents a step beyond.

The lexical indications that Eckhart is operating largely in a horizon of Dionysian reflection on God are to be found throughout Eckhart's work. The Latin equivalent of the *alpha* privative is *in* and it abounds in the Latin sermons. Latin adjectives, which have *in-* as a prefix are common: *innominabilis*, *ineffabilis*, *innarrabilis*, *incomprehensibilis* are only a few of the many examples.[25] Much the same list can be extracted from the German sermons in which God is pronounced as "hidden," "ineffable," and beyond name, predication, understanding, and images.[26] And then there is the translation of the Greek superlative *hyper* into the Latin *super*, which, in the case of adjectives, demands the Latin superlative ending *-issimus*, and the German *über*. Of course, Eckhart's exposition of the Godhead, who is beyond God, who is proportionate to the perception of divine acts actually done (creation, preservation, redemption) and acts possible (special graces), is patently Dionysian. Here one operative German equivalent of the *alpha* privative is *ane*, or in modern German *ohne*.[27] Eckhart's *überwesentliche Gottheit* pretty much directly translates Pseudo-Dionysius's *hyperousias thearchia*. Of course, the most striking use of apophatic language concerning the divine is that of "Nothing" (*Nichts*). Although the attribution of "nothing" to the radically transcendent divine—who may also be radically immanent—is not entirely original;[28] its use in mystical theology before Eckhart is rare. Eckhart deploys this most extreme of apophatic terms throughout his German sermons,[29] with a view no doubt to disturbing the conventional expectation of the association of the transcendent divine with being or stand-ins such as being as such, or self-subsistent being. This is in addition to the surprising of the metaphysical tradition, which since Parmenides ruled that only being can be thought and that non-being is not thinkable. Precisely in the environment of late medieval Scholasticism there is a rediscovery of the correlation of nothing and unthinkability. The difference is that now the movement is not from nothing to unthinkability but from unthinkability to nothing. Correlative to this is the discovery that the pair of nothing and unthinkability is the pair of pairs, since nothing is the being of beings to the infinite exponential power and unthinkability and non-knowing signify precisely the form of knowing commensurate with the reality that represents the limit to thought. Arguably, the most determinate reason for the designation of "nothing" is to preserve the incommensurability between the divine ground of all that is and all the particular beings that are or are taken to exist. One form of the contrast in Eckhart is that if God and being are identified, then, given Eckhart's allergy to analogy, all beings who are not identical with God come under the umbrella of "nothing." The other form—and the one relevant here—is that if one ascribes being to entities that are the objective correlative of our percepts and concepts, then it is appropriate to mark off God as the absolute singular and different by the application of the non-name of "nothing," which cannot be thought. When naming God is not a hazardous and fraught affair, it is an odd affair; certainly Eckhart does not mean that as ground or abyss (*Abgrunt*) of reality, the absolutely unnameable God or Godhead is nothing *simpliciter*. Indeed precisely as an unfathomable ground or unground the divine nothing is the *plus ultra* of generativity and creativity.

The elaboration of Eckhart's Dionysian apophaticism naturally brings us to one of the most vexed issues in Eckhart scholarship, that is, whether the ultimate ground of all reality is the Trinity, as it is in Augustine and Aquinas, and probably is in Pseudo-Dionysius despite suggestions to the contrary in the *Mystical Theology*, or whether it lies in a reality anterior to it. Scholars are divided on this topic. Some, like Bernard McGinn and Oliver Davies, argue that the superessential Godhead and the Trinity are substantively coextensive in Eckhart.[30] Advocates of this view, however, often show themselves to be willing to concede that, for rhetorical purposes, Eckhart tends to draw a distinction between them, especially when the conceptualization of the Trinity is so facilely dogmatic that it comes to serve the role of an idol, that is, functions as a valorization of the projections of the self onto a reliable and nameable ground of being. Others, like Reiner Schürmann and John Caputo—and even to an extent Hans Urs von Balthasar[31]—advise that, rhetorical innovation notwithstanding, we should in general be prepared to accept the revolutionary nature of Eckhart's thought, which subverts both the received philosophical and theological traditions. In this view, the distinction between the Godhead as nothing and the Trinity maps the distinction between the Godhead as nothing and the God whom we acknowledge to be our creator and redeemer. Schürmann and Caputo not only avail of Heidegger to interpret Eckhart, but in essence read Eckhart as Heidegger before the fact, a Heidegger who has escaped the ontotheological illusion of having a transcendent in place to leverage human hope and allay human fears.[32]

Given the conflict of interpretation, I leave it open as to whether Eckhart did in fact open an ontological gap between the Godhead and the Trinity, just as he opened up an ontological gap between the Godhead and God. It is sufficient for my purposes to underscore that some of Eckhart's more brazenly worded statements in his German sermons could be interpreted to suggest as much. At the very least, then, it can be said of Eckhart that not only did he continue and develop the Dionysian strain of mystical theology, but he also stretched it significantly, even if we stop short of the conclusion that he broke with it. Eckhart also stretched his Dionysian heritage by articulating an anthropology that compromised the createdness of human beings;[33] and in his German sermons, while he used the term *grace* and the equivalent, he did so in ways that might have appeared to some to have naturalized the process of sanctification.[34] I suggest that certain features of Eckhart's writings encourage the view that his work as a whole represents a step beyond the normative Christian tradition, or a step behind to forms of Neoplatonism that claimed that the ultimate could only be the One so superlatively beyond being and knowing that our union with the divine ground of being is one of absorption. This presence of ambiguity in Eckhart's work is provocative. Not only can it lead to the kind of condemnation of his work of which we have historical evidence;[35] it can also lead to attempts to repair or exploit the kinds of distinction he made for quite contrary purposes. In terms of repair, one has to agree with Louis Dupré that one way of coming to grips with the mystical theology of Ruusbroec is to read him as setting limits to theological dangers that are either present in Eckhart's actual work or at the very least in his reception.[36] In terms of exploiting Eckhart's kind of radical Dionysianism, even if taking it in an entirely kataphatic direction, one might think of the speculative thought of Jacob Boehme. In the next section, I take as my main task to show that Boehme accepts both the lexical and substantive Dionysian radicalization of apophatic theology enacted in Eckhart's work, especially in his German sermons, and submits it to a critique in which Eckhart's preferences appear to be entertained only to be inverted, and his radically apophatic form of Christian mysticism turned into a radically speculative and kataphatic form.

Jacob Boehme. Toward a Radical Kataphaticism[37]

The ideational world of Boehme differs entirely from that of Eckhart. It is decidedly a post-Reformation world in which concerns with God's wrath (*Zorn*) and mercy (*Barmhertzigkeit*) are very much to the fore, but equally a post-Renaissance world in which there is a searching for the key to an encompassing mode of explanation which refuses to discard the mystical, alchemical, and even Kabbalistic sources that are in circulation.[38] As has been well documented by Boehme scholars,[39] the "shoemaker from Gorlitz" was influenced by sixteenth-century Protestant spiritual writers such as Sebastian Franck, Caspar Schwenkfeld, and Valentin Weigel, each of whom was trying to find a way beyond biblical literalism and the constraints exercised by doctrines in general, and the doctrines of "scripture alone" and "justification by faith" in particular. Given the obvious vocabulary borrowings, it is safe to say that Boehme appropriates alchemy not so much as science but as a sapiential and visionary knowledge of the correspondences and antitheses in all of reality.[40] In addition, it is worth noting that precisely because alchemy is a discourse of painful transformation homologous to Christ's cross and resurrection, it can be seen to have theological purchase. Not only can the graphic language of the blackening and whitening of the alchemical retort be used to grip the imagination regarding the cross and resurrection which the Christian subject undergoes,[41] but the language can be used with respect to the agonism at the heart of eternity whereby the divine moves from a wrathful to a more benign constitution.[42] There is also some evidence that Boehme came in contact with the Kabbalah and was attempting to adapt it for Christian purposes as other Christian thinkers had done, including the German Johannes Reuchlin.[43] Certainly, Boehme's Unground (*Ungrund*) reminds us of the *En Sof* of the Kabbalah, and his articulation of divine names, some primarily indicative of the judgment or justice side of God and others indicative of the merciful side, give evidence of being a Christian adaptation of the names or *sephirot* in the late medieval Kabbalah that made its way into Germany in the sixteenth century.[44]

Perhaps most important for our present purposes, possibly through the so-called spiritual reformers, but possibly also through *German Theology* (*Theologia Deutsch*), the great fifteenth-century spiritual classic, Boehme came in contact with the medieval mystical tradition. The *German Theology* was a favorite text of Luther. He edited it first in 1516 as a capstone to his reading of Eckhart and Tauler, and again in 1518.[45] Although difficult to label exactly, perhaps the *German Theology* is more nearly a practical than a contemplative text in that its focus is very much on what closes off human beings and what makes possible intimate union with the transcendent God. While it directs much attention to the overcoming of the self-will (*Eigenwille*), which serves as a structural block to the experience of the transcendent God,[46] it avails of apophatic language to evoke a divine transcendence that exceeds the power of concept and language. Still, the *German Theology* is neither a treatise on the divine names, nor is it primarily motivated as Eckhart's sermons are to avoid conceptual idolatry, even though the avoidance of such idolatry is a necessary condition for union with the divine. It is true that terms such as *Gelassenheit* and *Eigenwille*, which are privileged terms in the text, have Eckhartian ancestry. Nonetheless, in the *German Theology* the interpretation of these terms has none of the speculative boldness of the Dominican. Detachment is not correlated with the trinitarian birth, nor is there any suggestion that in the actualization of intimacy with the divine the created condition of the self is absolved. Nonetheless, even if considerably less adventurous than the German sermons of Eckhart, this small text served as a vehicle for Eckhartian ideas as well as expressions.

Despite the lack of a direct historical connection between Eckhart and Boehme, there is real value to bringing them together in order to illustrate how a radical or radicalizing form of apophasis set the conditions for its transposition into an equally radical kataphatic key. To begin, we can say that Boehme appropriates both the kataphatic and apophatic vocabulary of the Christian mystical tradition with a likely assist from Kabbalah. Limiting myself to two texts of his maturity written in 1623,[47] Boehme's hexaemeron, entitled *Mysterium magnum* (MM), and the *De electione gratiae* (EG),[48] Boehme shows himself ready to speak the language of being when it comes to the transcendent God, even if he gives it a twist by referring to the "being of beings" (*Wesen des Wesens* [MM 1, 2; 1, 6]). This kataphatic attribution, albeit in the mode of the superlative, is supported by similar kataphatic attributions such as goodness (MM 3, 2), oneness and simplicity (MM 1, 2; 1, 6; 29, 1), and the root (*Wurzel*) of all things (MM 1, 8; 60, 38). When it comes to designating the divine as the abyssal ground or Unground of dependent realities, the apophatic register is just as prominent. The Dionysian hyperousiology, which was repeated and refined in Eckhart, finds clear and copious expression in Boehme's major texts: God is beyond nature (MM 60, 38) and essence (MM 1, 6); nameless (*ohne Namen* [MM 1, 8; 60, 38]); inexpressible (MM 60, 38); ungraspable (*unbegreiflich* [MM 60, 38]); absolute hiddenness (*Verborgenheit* [MM 1, 9]). Equally interestingly, the ultimate divine or divine ultimate does not admit real duality or a split into subject–object polarity: Boehme admits just enough division (*Schiedlichkeit* [MM 1, 7; EG 1, 6]) to allow talk of the divine unity possessing a form of knowing.[49] Perhaps the two terms most redolent of the changes rung on Dionysian vocabulary are "Unground" and "Nothing" (MM 1, 2-3; 1, 7; EG 1, 2-3). As noted previously, these were the terms in Eckhart which suggested that the Dominican might be moving Christian mysticism beyond the Christian Neoplatonic coordinates that set the metaphysical and epistemological terms for even the radical brands of Christian mysticism.[50]

In Boehme's mature work, the deployment of apophatic language, whether that common to the mystical tradition or that stretching it such as "non-ground" and "nothing," occurs in the context of a distinction between Godhead and God, which if implicit in the Dionysian tradition, is made explicit by Eckhart.[51] Boehme's criteria of the distinction also seem to be basically Eckhartian in that only God is personal and inscribable within a web of relations, whereas in contrast, the Godhead is impersonal and has no relation to anything other than itself. We judged earlier that in Eckhart there was some ambiguity as to whether he was positing an analytic or real distinction between the Godhead and the Trinity. In the case of Boehme, however, although the Trinity is closely related to the Unground, it is really rather than analytically distinct from it. In *Mysterium magnum* and *De electione gratiae*, one of Boehme's central tasks is explaining how and why the Trinity emerges from the Unground.

Boehme's general answer is that the production of the Trinity is a first expression of the will to manifestation that is a defining feature of the Godhead as nothing (MM 1, 3; 2, 1). Relative to the Unground, the Trinity is an expression of light and above all life. There is nothing accidental about the emphasis on the latter. However the Trinity is to be characterized, it must conform to Luther's notion of the living God. It remains a question for Boehme, however, whether the post-Unground differentiation into the Trinity constitutes a sufficient condition for the bifocal personal divine of wrath and mercy of Luther. In the context of its relation to the Unground, the livingness of the Trinity is fairly inchoate and still within the gravitational pull of the hyperousiological Godhead. Boehme in fact turns what is a positive in Eckhart's and Pseudo-Dionysius's view of superessence into a pejorative: what is superessential is from an ontological point of view not really essential—thus in a sense is in-essential (without essence). Boehme is convinced that there is need of further elaboration of the conditions of livingness at the level of the divine itself. This is necessary in order to square with the experience of the Christian believer, and this in order to square with the sense of the living God rendered in Scripture who condemns and saves.

Boehme can be said, then, to reproduce the two binaries of the Eckhartian tradition, the first asserted, the second perhaps no more than intimated. And, as already suggested, he makes both of these distinctions equivalently real. Effectively, Boehme disambiguates Eckhart: the distinction between the Unground and the Trinity is as real as the distinction between the Godhead and the personal God of Christian faith. This, however, is not the whole story, nor even the most important part of the story. When we put Eckhart and Boehme side by side, a number of extraordinarily interesting transformative operations become apparent:

First and crucially, we witness the devaluation of the ultimate ontological value of the divine nothing or Unground. In Eckhart, the supereminence of the divine Nothing rests on a positive attitude toward divine simplicity, unity, and hiddenness. While in part Eckhart's positive attitude has an experiential basis, crucially it rests on a foundational ontological decision, which is very much in line with the Christian mystical tradition in general and the Dionysian tradition in particular. In Boehme's speculative mystical discourse, the hyperousiological divine is not positively in excess of being or in excess of the personal God of Christian faith.

Rather the Unground is understood privatively: to avail of Boehme's haunting image, the Unground is "thin" (*dun*), therefore, more a lack than a surplus of being. This means also that "nothing" is a derogative rather than a superlative. The Unground is beyond being and is mysterious, but more because of its indeterminacy regarding being than its superdeterminacy, which permits infinite expression.

Second, and relatedly, granted a nontrivial degree of separation between the divine Nothing and the Trinity, Boehme's speculative form of mysticism subverts the relative order of ontological priority intimated in Eckhart at his more Neoplatonic moments, that is, the priority given to simplicity and unity, nonrelationality, and stasis at the level of the superessential Godhead. Boehme often marks the intimate but nonidentical relation between the Trinity and the Unground negatively by insisting that though the Trinity represents an overcoming of stillness, a pluralization of unity, the emergence of the possibility of relation and a start-up of dynamism that will end in livingness, it does not have sufficient energy to break entirely free from the ontological indigence that is its root and source. Still, precisely because of characteristics that would mark it negatively in the henological regime of Neoplatonism, at the same time the Trinity is more real than the divine at its apophatic best, which is the same as its apophatic worst. In Boehme's speculative form of mysticism, duality, plurality, relationality, and becoming all have positive value. Moreover, they have positive value in the order of knowledge as well as being, or in more technical language, gnoseologically as well as ontologically. In fact gnoseology depends on the ontology: the separation into subject and object, which is a fall in the Dionysian regime, presupposes the emergence of a duality in the Unground or the divine nothing which is simple and unity. One could say that what Boehme is dealing with is the emergence of re-presentation at the level of the divine, one that serves as a model for re-presentation at the human level. This mode of divine knowing seems to be related to, yet in subtle respects different from, the kind of knowing or unknowing attributable at the level of the divine Nothing in an Eckhartian or Dionysian apophatic manifold.[52]

Third, the inversion of priorities continues when it comes to the distinction between Godhead and God or, in Boehme's language, the distinction between the Unground and the personal God of Christian faith. In Eckhart, the latter tends to be understood as a human construct calculated to instrumentalize the divine. The Dominican does not seriously entertain the idea that God is wrathful, nor the idea that the divine is ultimately defined by mercy. The latter follows from Eckhart's cavils concerning the attribution of goodness to God. The biblically centered and Lutheranly formed Boehme thinks that the God of revelation is the true God and that this God is more ontologically, gnoseologically, and existentially developed than the divine Nothing, which is a kind of remainder concept arising out of our disciplined search for a God who is irreducibly mysterious. Boehme is also convinced that the living God of the Bible is more developed than the Trinity, which emerges from the Unground. In Boehme's developmental scheme, the Trinity that emerges is a more trinitarian dynamic establishing the conditions of the appearance of the personal God of Christian faith than the tri-personal God of Augustine or Aquinas. Personhood (*Persönlichkeit*) requires that God take on the conditions of personality—what Boehme calls "principles."[53] There are two eternal principles—each constituted by three distinct attributes—imperfectly correlated with wrath (*Zorn*) and mercy (*Barmhertzigkeit*), respectively.[54] The ultimate personality of God is given in the second principle, the principle of light, which effectively sublimates the first principle. This is a way of thinking about the personhood of God that finds antecedents in both the discourses of alchemy and the Kabbalah, and also finds philosophical translation in German Idealism and most famously in Friedrich Schelling's *Freiheit* essay (1809).[55]

These three inversions lead one to ask what holds the above set of revaluations together. The simplest answer is that the speculative mysticism of Boehme implies both (a) a shift of focus away from the human subject who experiences the divine to the divine itself, and (b) a shift of focus to the dynamic constitution of God as the ground of our being but also the ground of our redemption and sanctification.[56] I treat these two points in order. Boehme produces quite a few works that belong to the standard spiritual genre of speaking to what is required from the self and from God if the self is open to God and thus justified and sanctified.[57] Arguably, well over half of Boehme's opus consists of texts of this sort. The main difference between these texts and other spiritual and mystical texts of the Western tradition lies in Boehme's use of language, especially to the extent to which his own locutions recall the language of Paracelsian alchemy.[58] On the second and more important of these two points, it can be said that texts such as *Mysterium magnum* and *De electione gratiae*—although not only these—are crucially concerned with accounting for how and why a divine who is mysterious and beyond attribution, nonetheless, expresses itself as the personal ground of an extra-divine reality. This provides the "speculative" cast of Boehme's mysticism. Boehme wants to lay out in order the conditions that explain why the world appears as it does and how our religious experience is bifocal in that we experience God as both wrathful and merciful. These conditions are laid out on a narrative line from Unground through the immanent Trinity to God as the personal ground of the created, fallen, and redeemed world. As the movement from mystery to manifestation is described, the register changes from the dominantly apophatic to the dominantly kataphatic. Thus, Boehme can be said to produce a developmental ontology that deconstructs Eckhart's entire hierarchy of valuation and in principle the hierarchy of ontological valuation typical of Dionysian mysticism.

The shift away from an ontology of surplus in divine self-expression to a developmental ontology represents a momentous shift not only in mystical focus but also with regard to how the problem of evil is handled. In one sense, in comparison with Augustine and even Aquinas, Eckhart seems remarkably unpreoccupied with the problem of evil or moral failure. In another sense, however, one can read Eckhart as having anticipated and answered the problem of evil implicitly, first, by means of his emphases on the entirely positive fecundity and generativity of the divine; second, and relatedly, by his insistence on the participation of all would-be finite beings in the divine; and third and finally, by his prioritizing the "inbreaking" of illumination, which both compensates for one's distance from the divine and suggests that all distance, whether because of finitude or form of life and behavior, belongs to the order of appearance. Eckhart's nondevelopmental ontology or theo-ontology thus in part provides an answer to the problem of evil, were it to be posed, and in part subverts it by not allowing the question to get off the ground.[59] In contrast, the problem of evil is urgent in Boehme, and is so from the very beginning of his authorship in *Aurora* (1611).[60] Boehme obsessively rehearses the disturbed or perturbed character of the temporal world with its disagreeable toads, snakes, and malodors, as well as the fraught nature of historical existence marked by hunger, war, and death. Although Boehme does not discount a measure of human agency in the phenomenon of malformation, in *Aurora* he argues that malformity seems so ingrained in the order of things that it can be explained only by appeal to a ground in the divine itself. Boehme's subsequent work offers more and more sophisticated answers to the question of why evil,[61] and thus all are involved in the business of articulating a theodicy. When his thought reaches its maturity in *Mysterium magnum* and *De electione gratiae*, Boehme deploys his developmental theo-ontology to account for its emergence. The answer he gives is that, as the conditions of divine personhood are elaborated, it is necessary to suppose that the personal God of Christianity, who is justice and love—but more love than justice—needs a nature or essence in order to be true being and true life. As Boehme elaborates at the beginning of both of his classical texts, an eternal nature (*ewige Natur*) is the ground of God as person. This ground is best imagined as a chaotic surplus of energy directed and configured, or reconfigured, by God who is divine love. It is this reshaping or refiguring that guarantees that God's love is effective and powerful. Boehme sometimes calls eternal nature the first principle, thereby suggesting an association with Manichaeism. This is not his intent, nor does Manichaeism provide a proper descriptor. The major difference is that in Boehme eternal nature, or the first principle, is internal to the personal God who successfully sublimates it. The trouble is that it does not remain internal to all finite beings. Lucifer, for instance, wants to appropriate eternal nature as a source of power rather than operate in terms of the "let-it-be" of the creature; therefore he becomes what he covets. He is deranged; and in consequence so also is the cosmos.[62] Adam repeats in the key of enfleshed spirit the act of Luciferian self-constitution and becomes similarly deranged. The sublimation of the deranged human nature requires Christ, who himself is the exemplar of perfect sublimation.

Before we shift gear to consideration of a more sober intervening brand of mystical theology, it seems apposite once again to indicate what this essay is about and what it is not. It is not comparative in the strict sense. Were that the case, on the one hand, more discussion of Christ, creation, and eschatology would be in order, since these are important themes in both of our German mystics. On the other hand, one would lose the sense of a peculiarly German phenomenon that produces over a period of three hundred years, first, arguably, the most apophatic mystical theology in the entire Christian tradition, and, second, arguably, the most kataphatic mystical theology of the entire Christian tradition. Nor is our investigation historical in the strict sense; we have not focused on the transmission of Eckhart's texts into the seventeenth century and how another German mystic of genius critically appropriates them. With regard to inheritance, it seems safer to report that Boehme had contact with Eckhartian mysticism through mystical sources, in which, if there are Eckhartian ideas, they have been processed and domesticated. While I do deal with historical material, my main aim is to provide a rationale as to how an extremely apophatic form of mystical theology can dialectically generate its opposite. For this purpose, it is not absolutely necessary for a thinker such as Eckhart to have distinguished the Godhead from the Trinity and the Godhead from God, so much as to note that he opened the possibility of distinctions that were real rather than analytic and rhetorical.

Ruusbroec: A Different Kind of Difference

Now the obverse of exacerbating analytic tensions between Godhead and Trinity and Godhead and God into real tensions and inscribing them into a developmental theo-ontological scheme is their containment in and by forms of mystical theology that are sensitive to the dangers of a henological metaphysics both underwriting and undermining Christian mystical discourse. One could without exaggeration say that this is one of the singular achievements of the Rhineland school of mysticism, whose most prominent representatives are Suso, Ruusbroec, and Tauler.[63] A number of scholars have made this point more specific[64] and have pointed especially to Jan van Ruusbroec as responding either to Eckhart himself or his reception; they have commented favorably on Ruusbroec's elaboration of a form of mystical theology that more nearly balances its apophatic and kataphatic dimensions. An important feature of this balance is that, while Ruusbroec acknowledges the probity of distinctions between Godhead and Trinity and Godhead and God, he judges these distinctions to be acceptable if and only if they are understood to be analytical rather than real.

In texts such as *The Sparkling Stone* and *The Adornment of Spiritual Marriage,* Jan van Ruusbroec articulates a form of mystical theology that, if it gives more weight to Christ, church as institution, creation, and the virtues than one finds in Eckhart, nonetheless, recalls in significant respects Eckhart's Dionysian apophaticism as well as his high anthropology.[65] Although Ruusbroec does not fail to sanction the attributions of "light," "wisdom," and even "goodness" with regard to the transcendent divine,[66] union with which is the purpose of human life, his vocabulary is resolutely apophatic. The transcendent divine is available more through unknowing than knowing and is characterized as hidden, abyssal, incomprehensible, nameless, and more appropriately indicated in darkness and stillness or rest.[67] In his use of negative attribution, Ruusbroec inserts himself into the Eckhartian mystical tradition, which in turn recuperates and creatively extends the Dionysian tradition. In his efforts to correct for forms of knowing that would conceptualize the divine without remainder, and thus constitute forms of idolatry, Ruusbroec also deploys paradox. As we saw in the first section, the use of paradox was one of the means used by Eckhart to put the acquisitive self out of action in its thinking and speaking about God. Of course, what is truly distinctive about Eckhart's use of paradox was its pervasiveness and how it did not depend on the standard Dionysian formulas such as "dazzling darkness." In contrast, Ruusbroec dips into the more standard Dionysian cornucopia when he speaks of hidden brightness (*verborghene claerheit*) and incomprehensible light (*een ambegripeliijc licht*).[68]

In Ruusbroec's texts, apophatic language by and large applies unrestrictedly to the radically transcendent God who is not an object of our individual or communal possession. Nonetheless, in what seems to be a recapitulation of an Eckhartian form of thought, select forms of apophatic attribution apply only to the divine essence. The most notable is "modelessness" (*onwise*).[69] The modelessness of the divine essence is groundless (*afgrondighe*),[70] and it is this modelessness that is the origin and end of the triune life. Ruusbroec in fact opens up the gap between divine unity and the Trinity a bit further by suggesting that unity and rest more properly characterize the divine essence in contrast to the generation of the divine persons, which indicates a plurality in unity and is fundamentally characterized by activity.[71] Ruusbroec underscores the dynamic and living quality of the three persons of the Trinity by speaking, after the manner of Eckhart,[72] of divine birth and using metaphors of fertility and fructification. The Father is the source of the persons of the Son and the Spirit, and the Spirit is the return of the pulsating energy of divine generation back to the Father and to the eternal essence itself.[73]

In line with Eckhart, Ruusbroec has no problem drawing a distinction between the Godhead and the trinitarian persons. The interpretive crux is how the distinction is made and how to characterize it. Although Ruusbroec is quite brazen in his contrastive language, the Flemish mystical theologian is careful at all times to avoid giving the appearance that the distinction between divine essence and the three persons of the Trinity is anything more than the standard analytic contrast sanctioned by the magisterial tradition, and thus in no way in tension with Nicaea or contrary to the trinitarian theologies of Augustine or Aquinas. With regard to our language concerning the transcendent God, for Ruusbroec, mystical theology and doctrine are fundamentally complementary rather than competitive. Ruusbroec's writings in fact admit the generalization that this is true right across the theological spectrum. It is as true with regard to Christology and theological anthropology as it is with regard to our reflection on and our language of God.

Importantly, Ruusbroec is careful in a way that Eckhart is not to link the intra-trinitarian dynamic to divine self-expression in the order of creation. In the procession of the Spirit at the immanent level of the Trinity, there is reversion (*regiratio*) to the Father and in a sense to the divine essence,[74] thus describing a circular motion. Nonetheless, the Spirit is also the locus for the dynamism of the persons to move beyond themselves to another. The distinction of direction is ontological in the strict sense. The intra-trinitarian dynamic is essential or natural; not so the movement of the Triune God to the world. The creation of a world is a purely gratuitous act, even if this act expresses who God is. Ruusbroec's view of creation is controlled by the Neoplatonic trope of *bonum diffusivum sui*, which routinely plays the role of a mean between emanation and a purely voluntarist view of the world being brought into being by God's "good pleasure."[75] Given the extravagant claims made by the illuminists in Ruusbroec's own circle and by a certain interpretation of Eckhart,[76] Ruusbroec shows himself anxious to underscore the doctrine of *creatio ex nihilo*, which at once underwrites the gratuity of creation and the distinction in ontological status between created and uncreated being. Time and again in a manner that recalls Augustine and Aquinas, Ruusbroec insists on a distinction that is especially pertinent given Eckhart's talk of the "uncreated" aspect of the soul and the contemporary talk in illuminist circles of a form of radical sanctification that suggests the abolition of the creator–created distinction, and just as importantly the distinction between Christ as image and mirror of the Father and human beings as image and mirror.[77] With Ruusbroec, human beings are asked to become more and more transparent to the divine. Yet he insists on strict limits. Christ is the exemplar as such, and his person is generated and not created. To some extent, as created beings we can become more than ourselves by participation in the image as such: we can, however, never abrogate our createdness. Moreover, given that in Ruusbroec's case he is not simply presenting a grammar of mystical theology but indicating a possibility for each individual to follow the path, we can never abrogate our creatureliness.

Both our createdness and our creatureliness are exemplified and honored in our practical disposition in life and toward others, what Ruusbroec calls the "common life."[78] The affirmation of the "common life" reflects Ruusbroec's commitment to the mainline theological and mystical tradition, while also constituting something of a redress to the perceived antinomianism of the heresy of the Free Spirit.[79] Eckhart's pronouncements on the detached self-transcending moral norms might have been an exaggerated example of a rhetorical bravura, but they definitely could be enlisted into an exuberant spiritualism anxious to cast aside the institutional church as a mediator of morality as well as grace. Perhaps more troubling, because more systemic, was Eckhart's apparent relativization of the entire system of the virtues, both the cardinal virtues (courage, temperance, justice, prudence), as well as the higher theological virtues of faith, hope, and charity.[80] For Ruusbroec, the highest virtue is love,[81] and while from a strictly theological point of view love is a gift and thus received, it expresses itself outwardly in the solicitude and care of others. In the human condition, love undergirds the common life. Love is communitarian: its site is the very community which it creates, and this community is a situated and engendering form of love that understands human vulnerability and moral failure and mindfully extends divine *agapē* abroad, or rather participates in Christ's and the Holy Spirit's sending it abroad. To participate in this sending is precisely what it means to be a Christian and a follower of Christ.

The principle of selection of Ruusbroec for consideration in this essay is not that he is one of the great mystical theologians of the Western tradition—he is that—but rather that he can be read as limiting tendencies in the most radical forms of apophatic theology in two ways: (a) to separate the Godhead from the Trinity, as well as from the personal God of Christian witness, and thereby to introduce or exacerbate a tension between mystical theology and doctrine that was developing in the late medieval period; and (b) more specifically, on the basis of such separations, to set down the conditions for a dialectic reversal that establishes an equally radical kataphatic form of mystical theology. Heuristically, at the very least, this is a good way to read the speculative mysticism of Jacob Boehme, which essentially changes all the ontological and gnoseological values that Eckhart appears to subscribe to in the boldest of his German sermons and places them in a developmental ontology or theo-ontology in which a personal God and creation are the goal of the immanent Trinity, just as the immanent Trinity is the goal of a divine Nothing that wills a measure of self-determination. Ruusbroec's writings allow him to be regarded as the kind of mystical theologian who feels called to relativize distinctions that seem to be in imminent danger of being absolutized. Thus, his mystical theology can be seen to be a theological intervention: the Triune God is merely analytically distinct from the Godhead, and the Triune God is not simply dynamic process[82] but the intercommunication of the divine persons whose defining characteristic is gift. The balance between divine transcendence and divine immanence and between apophasis and kataphasis achieved by Ruusbroec is quite remarkable, precisely since after Eckhart the balance no longer can be taken for granted. Crucially, Ruusbroec's theological intervention forecloses thinking, as Boehme does, of the Godhead, Trinity, and a God turned toward creation as increasing orders of ontological determinacy, and thus as closer and closer approximations to a fully actualized divine personality. In a word, Ruusbroec's intervention puts out of circulation the process of reversal of Eckhartian preferences, and the assumption of Godhead, Trinity, and creation into a developmental ontology. For purposes of telling our communal and individual stories, it may be necessary to distinguish sometimes between Godhead and Trinity, and Godhead and the God for us as creator, redeemer, and sanctifier. Sometimes we want to insist upon God's absolute transcendence, just as on other occasions we might want to declare his intimacy and make note of his operations in the world and in us. But, on Ruusbroec's account, the distinctions cannot be drawn absolutely; nor is the Christian God a story in the strict sense that, like human beings, there is a required developmental process whereby God becomes all that he can be. Ruusbroec then forecloses the return of theogony into Christian thought, which, as Hans Blumenberg insightfully suggests,[83] represses myth which makes a story of reality. At the same time, Ruusbroec's thought represents a practical-spiritual intervention in that his concern is not only with how God and his actions are construed but also with how to define the nature of the Christian life. Is the goal of Christian life to achieve union with God, or is the truly Christian life a life led in care of others? His answer is, once again, a meticulous balance: union with God is both the fruit of the common life and its fructifying source.

Concluding Remarks

Despite its historical surface, the purpose of the essay has not been historical in the strict sense. Its focal concern has been with particular types of mysticism and, more specifically, with how a radically apophatic type of mysticism can be thought to prepare dialectically for its inversion into a radically kataphatic and speculative type of mysticism. This governed my choice of the two German mystics treated here. To be sure, constraints on radicality are to be found in the writings of both. In the case of Eckhart, what is judged to be truly mysterious is sometimes in fact the Triune God and not the Godhead beyond God and the Trinity. While Eckhart startles us when he seems to claim in the German sermons that the soul is the natural rather than adoptive son of God, his theology of image is sometimes sufficiently Augustinian to gain the approval of a theologian as circumspect as Hans Urs von Balthasar. Then there is the general problem of Eckhart's language: Given the hyperboles and paradoxes, how to distinguish between provocation and claim, between an invitation to seeing things aright by seeing them differently and propositions concerning the divine and the divine's relation to self at odds with the theological tradition? Similarly, on the side of Boehme, there are moments when he too restricts the urge to inquire into the deep things of God, confesses ignorance with respect to the self-development of God, and professes his conviction concerning divine mystery and namelessness. Nonetheless, radical tendencies are sufficiently in evidence in both cases that it may not be an exaggeration to say that Eckhart's apophasis and Boehme's kataphasis are both liminal mystical discourses—indeed, mystical discourses that essentially set the limits to the Christian mystical tradition. Now, as I spoke to the movement of dialectical reversal of Eckhart's mystical discourse in Boehme's speculative form, I did not suggest that Boehme came upon Eckhart's discourse in its pure form. Rather, my point is that the radical Eckhartian tendencies function as a latency in more mainline forms of late medieval Christian mysticism to which Boehme has access. This means that they can be excavated and repeated. This means also—and this is my thesis—they can be recalled only to be inverted.

The other question that the essay addressed, which followed upon the first, was the issue of how a radical form of apophatic mystical theology could be regulated such that it would not set the conditions for the generation of its kataphatic contrary. Given my interest at the very least in "history-likeness," I judged it expedient to look at Ruusbroec. What weighed heavily in selecting Ruusbroec as the example were two factors. First, I took seriously prior suggestions in the scholarship on Ruusbroec to the effect that a plausible way of reading him is to consider him as moderating Eckhart's more radical apophatic tendencies by disambiguating tensions in his ontological commitments, thereby realigning Eckhart's magnificent explorations with the common tradition of mystical theology. Ruusbroec's mystical theology doubles as a somewhat less radical form of Eckhart's mystical theology, more measured in its proportion of apophasis and kataphasis, more balanced in its conjugation of the relations between Godhead, Trinity, and the God who creates, redeems, and sanctifies. Second, in selecting both types of German mysticism, I had in mind why in German Idealism and in the nineteenth century in general both of these forms are embraced,[84] while other forms of medieval mysticism, such as those of Suso, Tauler, and Ruusbroec, were rejected. Ruusbroec's name, for example, was brought up by Bishop

Hans Martensen—the redoubtable enemy of Kierkegaard—in the middle of the century, only to be rejected because he is too accommodating to the theological traditions.[85]

It is not a little interesting also that, in twentieth-century philosophy and theology, the two liminal mystics of the Western tradition have received considerably more play than a mystic and mystical theologian such as Ruusbroec. Eckhart has been sponsored by Heidegger and any number of postmodern philosophers and theologians, has become one of the most cited Christian mystics in the enterprise of comparative mysticism,[86] and has functioned as something of a cornerstone of creation spirituality.[87] Similarly, Boehme has been appropriated in large fashion by the philosopher Nicholas Berdyaev,[88] and with some restrictions in the theologies of Paul Tillich and Sergius Bulgakov.[89] Given the nonliminal nature of his discourse, perhaps this should not surprise. Perfect balance between apophasis and kataphasis in a mystical form may make it appear less exciting than the limit forms of Christian mysticism. Still, such a mystical form from time to time strikes a chord for a major thinker. Hans Urs von Balthasar, who rails against the separation of theology and spirituality in the modern period, thinks that in Ruusbroec one finds not only the perfect harmony but exquisitely responsible use of language regarding God, self, and their relation, as well as a meticulously articulated connection between the active and the contemplative life.

Notes

1. Ernst Benz offers a survey of the assimilation of both Eckhart and Boehme in the modern period in his succinct *Les sources mystiques de la philosophie romantique allemande* (Paris: Vrin, 1968). For a synoptic essay on nineteenth-century reception of Eckhart, see Cyril O'Regan, "Eckhart Reception in the 19th Century," in *A Companion to Meister Eckhart*, ed. Jeremiah M. Hackett, Brill's Companions to the Christian Tradition 36 (Leiden: Brill, 2013), 629–67. Heidegger's appropriation of Eckhart is well known and has been carried forward by John Caputo, Reiner Schürmann, and a host of others. See Dermot Moran's synoptic essay, "Meister Eckhart in 20th-century Philosophy," in *Companion to Meister Eckhart*, 669–98. The reception of Boehme in nineteenth- and twentieth-century German philosophy and theology is equally impressive. Hegel's relation to Boehme is a major object of concern in my *The Heterodox Hegel* (Albany: State University of New York Press, 1994). In addition, Robert F.

Brown has written convincingly on the relation between Boehme and Friedrich Schelling. The theologian Paul Tillich wrote extensively on Boehme early in his career. For English translations of two of these works, see *Mysticism and Guilt-Consciousness in Schelling's Philosophical Development*, trans. Victor Nuovo (Lewisburg, PA: Bucknell University Press, 1974); also *The Construction of the History of Religion in Schelling's Positive Philosophy*, trans. Victor Nuovo (Lewisburg, PA: Bucknell University Press, 1974). In my own work on Boehme I pay considerable attention to Boehme's nineteenth- and twentieth-century reception. See Cyril O'Regan, *Gnostic Apocalypse: Jacob Boehme's Haunted Narrative* (Albany: State University of New York Press, 2002).

2. Bernard McGinn is exemplary in this respect. There is nothing comparable to his multivolume series in the history of mysticism in terms of coverage, technical mastery, and the ability to provide historical context and adjudicate between rival interpretations. I will be referring to a number of these volumes in subsequent notes. In addition, McGinn is one of the foremost conveyers and interpreters of Eckhart's work. See his *Meister Eckhart: Teacher and Preacher,* Classics of Western Spirituality (Mahwah, NJ: Paulist, 1986); also his monograph which is the fruit of forty years of reflection, *The Mystical Thought of Meister Eckhart: The Man from Whom God Hid Nothing* (New York: Crossroad, 2003).

3. I will refer from time to time to Frank Tobin's translation of some of the more important German Sermons in McGinn et al., *Meister Eckhart: Teacher and Preacher*. Tobin translates twenty-four sermons. In the main I will reference the translation of the entire set of ninety-seven German sermons by M. O' C. Walshe. See *The Complete Mystical Works of Meister Eckhart* (New York: Crossroad, 2009). This constitutes an updated version of the two-volume edition published by Element Press in England. Since Walshe's number scheme does not match up with the numbers in the German critical edition by Josef Quint, I will provide the Quint edition number in parentheses. See J. Quint, ed., *Meister Eckhart: Die deutschen und lateinischen Werke* (Stuttgart: W. Kohlhammer, 1936–).

4. I will focus on the so-called *Parisian Questions* together with the Prologues to the *Opus Tripartitum*. For a convenient English translation, see *Parisian Questions and Prologues*, trans. Armand A. Maurer (Toronto: Pontifical Institute of Mediaeval Studies, 1974). Of course, Eckhart wrote commentaries on Genesis, Exodus, Wisdom, Ecclesiastes, and the Gospel of John, as well as a brief commentary on the *Sentences* of Peter Lombard. For an informative synoptic account of Eckhart's Latin text, see Alessandra Beccarisi, "Eckhart's Latin Works," in Hackett, *Companion to Meister Eckhart*, 85–123.

5. Augustine is cited by Eckhart far more than any other authority, far more than Aquinas, and far more than Pseudo-Dionysius. On Eckhart's sources, see McGinn, *Mystical Thought of Meister Eckhart*, 162–82. McGinn also usefully reminds us that the level of citation should not be regarded as definitive in terms of making a judgment on which thinker had the greatest influence.

6. For an exhaustive account of the relation between Pseudo-Dionysius and Aquinas on the divine names, see Fran O'Rourke, *Pseudo-Dionysius and the Metaphysics of Aquinas* (1992; Notre Dame, IN: University of Notre Dame Press, 2005).

7. Famously, Pseudo-Dionysius talks in his *Mystical Theology* of the "superessential Godhead" (*hyperousias thearchia*) and identifies it with a unity that is impossible to name. The fact that he connects—but does not necessarily identify—the Godhead and the Triune God has proved a vexed issue. While the majority of interpreters have been satisfied that no real distinction is implied, a small minority have suggested that there is a real distinction. Thus, the pattern of interpretation is similar to that found in Eckhart studies and bears on it, since Eckhart's apophasis is grounded in the Dionysian tradition. John Jones is on the side of the majority. See especially his "Dionysian Mysticism: A Christian Conversion," chaps. 4 and 6.

8. For an account of how Eckhart breaks with Aquinas on the fundamental notion of the analogy of being, see Frank Tobin, *Meister Eckhart: Thought and Language,* Middle Ages (Philadelphia: University of Pennsylvania Press, 1986), esp. chaps. 2 and 3; Reiner Schürmann, *Meister Eckhart, Mystic and Philosopher: Translation with Commentary,* Studies in Phenomenology and Existential Philosophy (Bloomington: Indiana University Press, 1978).

9. See Sermon 9 in McGinn et al., *Meister Eckhart: Teacher and Preacher,* 255–61, esp. 257.

10. This is not quite the way Aquinas formulates it. He does not identify God with *esse* without qualification in the manner of either Eckhart or Scotus. Aquinas speaks rather of *esse seipsum* and avoids speaking as if being is univocally shared between God and created beings.

11. To the chagrin of Thomists such as Cornelio Fabro and Gustav Siewerth, Heidegger does not exempt Aquinas from the charge of ontotheology, that is, the charge that Being has been reified into the highest being. When Heidegger enlists Eckhart because of his "whylessness," he is thereby suggesting that this medieval Dominican did not fall foul of the ontotheological illusion. Of course, Heidegger makes a definitive break with medieval thought as early as his Habilitation on Scotus's doctrine of categories (1915). For a good account of this text which shows that Heidegger is dealing only in part with Scotus and in the main with Henry of Ghent, see S. J. McGrath, *The Early Heidegger and Medieval Philosophy: Phenomenology of the Godforsaken* (Washington, DC: Catholic University of America Press, 2006).

12. Tobin tries to reconcile different ascriptions of the creaturely realm in Eckhart's Latin works. If everything is *esse* and *esse* is divine, then everything is divine. This is one line of argument in Eckhart. But it is balanced by another line: here *esse* is associated with God (more in keeping with Aquinas); in this case, non-divine beings can be classed as nothing. See Tobin, *Meister Eckhart: Thought and Language,* 45–46.

13. For God considered as nothing, see Walshe, *Complete Mystical Works*

of *Meister Eckhart* S65 (Q6), S54 (Q23), S62 (Q82), S19 (Q71). For God as nameless, see S22 (Q53), S32a (Q20a), S67 (Q9), S49 (Q77); also S30 (Q45).

14. See Tobin, *Meister Eckhart: Thought and Language*, 39. Tobin is exemplary in chap. 2 on Eckhart's metaphysics and its critical relation to that of Aquinas, and almost as good in chap. 3 on Eckhart on predication.

15. For a translation of *Expositio libri exodi*, see McGinn et al., *Meister Eckhart: Teacher and Preacher*, 41–146.

16. Tobin, *Meister Eckhart: Thought and Language*, 146; also 131.

17. See the extraordinary Sermon 9 in McGinn et al., *Meister Eckhart: Teacher and Preacher*, 255–61.

18. Augustine's *Commentaries on the Psalms* are replete with phrases chastening our claims to have knowledge of God. Perhaps the most famous declaration is to be found in Sermon 117.3: *Si comprehendis non est Deus*. This phase echoes throughout Augustine's work. See Sermon 52.6.6; also *In Psalmos*, 85.12.

19. It would be a mistake to construe Augustine to be an entirely kataphatic thinker. Even if Augustine has respect for the human abilities of concept formation and language, their power is strictly limited. With respect to our language of God, we cannot proceed without the assistance of scripture and the theological tradition. And even then our finitude (not to mention sin) makes us fall short. To bring to mind two illustrations of this, see *De doctrina christiana* 1.6, and bk. 8 of *De trinitate*, arguably the text by Augustine most quoted by Eckhart. In the case of the latter, the confession of conceptual and linguistic inadequacy is beautifully placed after an exposition of scripture (bks. 2–4) and theological articulation (bks. 5–7), which provide the Christian community with the knowledge of who and what God is. Book 8 tells us that, at best, all knowledge of God is relatively adequate.

20. Books 9–11 of *De trinitate* are best understood to be speaking to the presence of God in the human soul, rather than being a replica of the divine Trinity. This is simply a highly influential caricature.

21. For German sermons that speak of ground, castle, or spark of the soul, see Walshe, *Complete Sermons of Meister Eckhart*, S2 (Q58), S7 (Q76), S8 (Q21), S11 (Q26), S18 (Q30), S21 (Q17), S31 (Q37), S32b (Q20b), S65 (Q6), S66 (Q10), S68 (Q11), S89 (Q47). For a synoptic discussion of the idea of ground and the images in which it is represented, see McGinn, *Mystical Thought of Meister Eckhart*, chap. 3, 35–52.

22. For German sermons in which there is discussion of the eternal birth of the Son in the soul, see Walshe, *Complete Sermons of Meister Eckhart*, S1 (Q57), S2 (Q58), S10 (Q25), S47 (Q46), L57 (Q12), S65 (Q6), S89 (Q47). For a balanced account of the eternal birth of the Son, see McGinn, *Mystical Thought of Meister Eckhart*, chap. 4, 53–70.

23. The Syrian monastic and liturgical context of Pseudo-Dionysius's texts has been a constant theme of the work of Alexander Golitzen. See especially

Mystagogy: A Monastic Reading of Dionysius Areopagita; 1 Cor 3:16, John 14:21–23, Cistercian Studies Series 250 (Collegeville, MN: Cistercian Publications, 2014).

24. Pseudo-Dionysius's commitment to hierarchy is indicated in the titles of such works as *Celestial Hierarchies* and *Ecclesiastical Hierarchies.* More generally, however, hierarchy is connected with initiation, which suggests a distinction between the elite and the common. Contemporary thinkers such as Jean-Luc Marion and Jacques Derrida take different sides of this argument. Marion defended hierarchy in his justly famous essay on Pseudo-Dionysius. See *The Idol and Distance: Five Studies,* trans. with an introduction by Thomas A. Carlson, Perspectives in Continental Philosophy 17 (New York: Fordham University Press, 2001; French original, 1977), 139–95. Derrida attacked Marion and negative theology in general (and Pseudo-Dionysius in particular) on the grounds of offense to the democratic principle that is subserved by deconstruction in "Sauf le nom (1987)." For an English translation, see *On the Name,* ed. Thomas Dutoit, trans. David Wood, John P. Leavey Jr., and Andrew McLoed, *Meridian: Crossing Aesthetics* (Stanford, CA: Stanford University Press, 1995), 33–85. For Marion's highly critical response to Derrida, see "In the Name: How to Avoid Speaking," with a response by Derrida, in *God, the Gift, and Postmodernism,* ed. John D. Caputo and Michael J. Scanlon, Indiana Studies in the Philosophy of Religion (Bloomington: Indiana University Press, 1999), 20–53.

25. See Tobin, *Meister Eckhart: Thought and Language,* 66.

26. A quick scan of Walshe's translations shows that the apophatic accent on namelessness and ineffability is strong in the following German sermons: S19 (Q71), S22 (Q53), S33 (Q20a), S57 (Q12); also S27 (Q9).

27. See Tobin's discussion of *ane* in *Meister Eckhart: Thought and Language,* 122–23. This word is equivalent to the modern German *ohne* (without)—a term used promiscuously by Jacob Boehme in his speculative form of mysticism to indicate the ultimate ground of reality prior to the personal God of Christian faith and prior also to the immanent Trinity.

28. Arguably, Johannes Scottus Eriugena is the first thinker to apply the term "Nothing" to God or the superessential divine.

29. Among other sermons that use Nothing as a name of God, see Walshe S54 (Q23), S62 (Q82), S65 (Q6).

30. In addition to McGinn, *Mystical Thought of Meister Eckhart,* chaps. 5 and 6, see McGinn, "The God beyond God: Theology and Mysticism in the Thought of Meister Eckhart," *Journal of Religion* 61 (1981): 1–19; "Meister Eckhart on God as Absolute Unity," in *Neoplatonism and Christian Thought,* ed. Dominic O'Meara (Albany: State University of New York Press, 1982), 128–39; and "A Prolegomenon to the Role of the Trinity in Meister Eckhart's Mysticism," in *Eckhart Review* (Spring 1997): 51–61. For Oliver Davies, see *Meister Eckhart: Mystical Theologian* (London: SPCK, 1991).

31. Eckhart is an object of critical analysis by Hans Urs von Balthasar in his articulation of a theological aesthetics. See *The Glory of the Lord: A Theological Aesthetics*, vol. 5, *The Realm of Metaphysics in the Modern Age*, trans. Oliver Davies, Andrew Louth, Brian McNeil, C.R.V., John Saward, and Rowan Williams; ed. Brian McNeil, C.R.V., and John Riches (San Francisco: Ignatius Press, 1991), 29–47. Balthasar seems to have read both the Latin and the German works. It is interesting that he commends Vladimir Lossky's *Théologie négative et connaissance de Dieu chez Maître Eckhart* (Paris: Vrin, 1960) as the definitive work on Eckhart (34). For an essay that analyzes in some detail Balthasar's complex reception of Eckhart, see Cyril O'Regan, "Balthasar and Eckhart: Theological Principles and Catholicity," *The Thomist* 60 (1996): 203–39.

32. The Heideggerian influence is present everywhere throughout Schürmann's *Meister Eckhart: Mystic and Philosopher*. This should not surprise us, given that the major influence on Schürmann's constructive thought is Heidegger. This is borne out by his *Heidegger on Being and Acting: From Principles to Anarchy*, Studies in Phenomenology and Existential Philosophy (Bloomington: Indiana University Press, 1987). While later in his career, John D. Caputo was more interested in the question of whether anticipations in Christian mystical thought of Heidegger and deconstruction might justify assigning mystical thought a measure of validity, earlier Caputo seemed to assume that the validity of Christian mystical thought pointed to recapitulations in modern philosophical thought. The exemplar of the latter is *The Mystical Element in Heidegger's Thought* (New York: Fordham University Press, 1986).

33. In addition to nn. 22 and 23 above, on the divine ground of the self and the trinitarian birth, respectively, see Walshe S60 (Q48), S66 (Q10).

34. Among the surprises of the German sermons are the following: (a) although it is hardly everywhere, the language of grace is operative; and (b) the emphasis on gift of existence mediated through the Spirit is frequent. For sermons that highlight grace, see Walshe S9 (Q86), S19 (Q71), S20 (Q44), S29 (Q39), S68 (Q11); for the Holy Spirit as the gift of existence, see S16 (Q29), S23 (Q47), S26 (Q57), S21 (Q377), S33 (Q35), S54 (Q23), S64 (Q11), S77 (Q63). It is not a little interesting that in a number of sermons gift in general and gift in and through the Spirit in particular are connected with the flow of goodness to give itself. See especially S26 (Q57), S54 (Q23). It is true that Eckhart sometimes confuses matters by suggesting that, provided detachment occurs, the divine birth has to occur. See S11 (Q26), S13b (Q5b), S60 (Q48). The language of necessity is likely a hyperbole intended to obviate the voluntarist picture of a capricious, unreliable God. The necessity here is aesthetic rather than logical or ontological. McGinn's chap. 5, "The Metaphysics of Flow," in *Mystical Thought of Meister Eckhart*, 71-113, is instructive in this regard.

35. For a presentation of the 1329 Condemnation and Eckhart's defense, see *Meister Eckhart: The Essential Sermons, Commentaries, Treatises, and Defense*,

trans. with an introduction by Edmund Colledge, O.S.A., and Bernard McGinn (New York: Paulist, 1981), 71–81.

36. See Louis Dupré, *The Common Life: The Origins of Trinitarian Mysticism and Its Development by Jan Ruusbroec* (New York: Crossroad, 1984).

37. For Jacob Boehme, see *Sämtliche Schriften*, ed. Will-Erich Peuckert and August Faust, 11 vols. (Stuttgart: Frommanns, 1956–61). I will pay particular attention to *De electione gratiae, oder Von der Gnaden-Wahl* (1623) (vol. 6) and *Mysterium magnum, oder Erklärung über das erst Buch Mosis* (1623) (vols. 7 and 8). Other texts that will be mentioned—although not discussed—include *Aurora, oder Morgenröthe im Anfange* (1612) (vol. 1); *De triplici vita hominis, oder Vom dreyfachen Lebens des Menchen* (1620) (vol. 3); and *Sex puncta theosophica, oder Von sechs theosophichen Puncten* (1620) (vol. 4).

38. Andrew Weeks underscores the alchemical and specifically Paracelsian background of Boehme's thought in his useful *Boehme: An Intellectual Biography of the Seventeenth-Century Philosopher and Mystic* (Albany: State University of New York Press, 1991).

39. See, e.g., Alexandre Koyré, *Mystiques, spirituels, alchemists du xvi siècle* (Paris: Vrin, 1961); also Steven E. Ozment, *Mysticism and Dissent: Religious Ideology and Social Protest in the Sixteenth Century* (New Haven: Yale University Press, 1973).

40. It is not surprising that Weeks is so good at tracing Boehme's alchemical background, including alchemy's adoption and adaptation in sixteenth-century Lutheran theology, given his mastery of the corpus of Paracelsus and deep knowledge of Valentin Weigel. See the following by Weeks: *Paracelsus: Speculative Theory and the Crisis of the Early Reformation*, SUNY Series in Western Esoteric Traditions (Albany: State University of New York Press, 1996); *Valentin Weigel (1533–1588): German Religious Dissenter, Speculative Theorist, and Advocate of Religious Tolerance* (Albany: State University of New York Press, 1999).

41. The parallelism between the cross/resurrection of Christ and the alchemical process of transmutation of base material into the philosopher's stone is fully in play in Paracelsus, Weigel, and Boehme. Certainly, the parallelism predates these figures. For a good account of just how early and how widespread the parallelism was, see Lawrence M. Principe, *The Secrets of Alchemy*, Synthesis (Chicago: University of Chicago Press, 2013).

42. One can read this projection into eternity to evince Gnosticism or apocalypticism, the latter insofar as the one who is slain is slain from the foundation of the world, the former insofar as the suffering of the historical Christ is a metaphor of the suffering of fallen Sophia or Acmaoth.

43. Weeks covers the biographical end of Boehme's contact with the Kabbalah through Abraham von Franckenberg. The most detailed treatment of the relation is provided by Robert Schulitz. See his "Einheit und Differenz: Die kabbalische Metamorphose bei Jacob Böhme" (Ph.D dissertation, University of Michigan, 1990).

44. For a synoptic account of the relation between Boehme's speculative mysticism and the Kabbalah, see Cyril O'Regan, *Gnostic Apocalypse: Jacob Boehme's Haunted Narrative* (Albany: State University of New York Press, 2002), chap. 9, 193–209.

45. Steven Ozment is especially strong on the trajectory of the *Theologia Deutsch*. See his *Mysticism and Dissent*, 18-25; also his *Homo Spiritualis: A Comparative Study of the Anthropology of Johannes Tauler, Jean Gerson and Martin Luther (1513–1516) in the Context of Their Theological Thought* (New Haven: Yale University Press, 1967), 86ff.

46. The Augustinian cast of the polemic against self-will as a choice for self rather than a choice for God is transparent.

47. The eleven volumes of Boehme's collected works sum to approximately six thousand pages.

48. *Sex puncta theosophica* arguably provides the best synopsis of Boehme's speculations about the movement from the divine Nothing to the Trinity and to the personal God of Christian faith. Other texts such as *Aurora* and *De triplici vita hominis* are mainly focused on the regeneration of the self in the context of a world marked by evil.

49. The best discussion of a division (*Schiedlichkeit*) between Unground and Trinity and Unground and wisdom is to be found in shorter texts of Boehme such as *Sex puncta theosophica*. This split is hardly a split at all, and real separation that Boehme hypothesizes occurs only with the appearance of eternal nature, which is both the contrary and basis of the personal God who is free and good, and yet to emerge. See Alexandre Koyré, *La philosophie de Jacob Boehme* (Paris: J. Vrin, 1929), 344-48; also my *Gnostic Apocalypse*, 32-37.

50. Eckhart in fact uses *Abgrund* rather than *Ungrund*. Here I view these terms to be equivalent.

51. I am not giving a causal account here. It may well be likely that the attribution of "Nothing" actually owes something to Kabbalistic ruminations on the *En Sof*.

52. Divine knowing or self-knowing that has engendered the subject–object split bears comparison with Neoplatonic reflections on the knowledge in the ordinance of the One. John Rist is especially illuminating on the latter. See his *Plotinus: The Road to Reality* (Cambridge: Cambridge University Press, 1967), 38–53.

53. Boehme's discussion of the three principles, that is, the principle of divine nature, the principle of divine spirit, and the temporal principle, is established as early as *Aurora* and is a constant in his writing thereafter.

54. For Boehme, there is a rough correlation between the principle of nature and Luther's God of wrath, on the one hand, and the principle of spirit and Luther's God of mercy, on the other. But, as a number of scholars have pointed out, the parallels are fairly approximate.

55. The influence of Boehme on Schelling is well attested. See especially

Robert Brown, *The Later Schelling: The Influence of Boehme on the Works of 1809–1815* (Lewisburg, PA: Bucknell University Press, 1977).

56. See Koyré's famous saying about contradiction being the condition not only of divine manifestation but also of self-manifestation (*La philosophie de Jacob Boehme*, 324).

57. Some texts of Boehme are almost exclusively spiritualistic, for example, *De triplici vita hominis*. Other texts such as *Aurora* and *Mysterium magnum* have significant portions devoted to what we might call a philosophical or theological anthropology.

58. Here I am speaking of words such as "signature," *mysterium magnum*, the use of salt, mercury, and sulphur as the three principles, and Paracelsian neologisms such as *illiaster* (from *hyle* [matter] and *aster* [star]).

59. Eckhart's suspension of the authority of divine command and relativization of the virtues was an object of fascination for John Jones. He was drawn to all those passages in Eckhart where he spoke of our relationship to God in the mode of "friend," and which spoke to "whylessness" beyond exchange and emphasized that virtue was not so much the goal as an effect of this whylessness.

60. More than Boehme's other texts *Aurora* provides an account of motivating experiences for the kind of speculative mysticism that Boehme goes on to articulate. Boehme provided a vision that is a sort of transport in which he sees into the divine meaning of things, and the origin and destiny of all reality.

61. Along with Koyré, the scholar who most emphasizes the problem of evil is Hans Grunsky; see his *Jacob Böhme*, Frommanns Klassiker der Philosophie 34 (Stuttgart: Frommann, 1956).

62. It is not an exaggeration to say that Boehme's account of the Luciferian fall is a prototype for Milton's account of Lucifer's fall and the production of chaos in book 2 of *Paradise Lost*.

63. Interestingly, McGinn divides the Rhineland assimilation of the work of Meister Eckhart over two books, dealing with Suso and Tauler in one volume and Ruusbroec in the other. See *The Harvest of Mysticism in Medieval Germany*, vol. 4 of *The Presence of God: The History of Western Christian Mysticism* (New York: Crossroad, 2005), 83–194 (Eckhart), 195–239 (Henry Suso), 240–96 (Johannes Tauler). See also McGinn, *The Varieties of Vernacular Mysticism 1350–1550*, vol. 5 of *The Presence of God: The History of Western Christian Mysticism* (New York: Crossroad, 2012), with Ruusbroec treated on 5–61. Throughout McGinn notes points of similarity and dissimilarity between Ruusbroec and Eckhart, but shows himself anxious to put Ruusbroec in his Low-Country context and establish the works of the Beguines as having real force on Ruusbroec's thought.

64. Dupré, *Common Life*; Rik Van Nieuwenhove, "Meister Eckhart and Jan van Ruusbroec: A Comparison," *Medieval Philosophy and Theology* 7 (1998):

157–94. Comparisons between Eckhart and Ruusbroec are threaded through Van Nieuwenhove's admirable *Jan van Ruusbroec: Mystical Theologian of the Trinity* (Notre Dame, IN: University of Notre Dame Press, 2003), esp. 81–84.

65. See *John Ruusbroec: The Spiritual Espousals and Other Works*, Classics of Western Spirituality, trans. with an introduction by J. A. Wiseman, O.S.B., preface by Louis Dupré (Mahwah, NJ: Paulist, 1985). See *Spiritual Espousals* (*SE*), 41–152; *Mirror of Eternal Blessedness* (*MEB*), 185–247; *The Sparkling Stone* (*SS*), 153–83.

66. The main vehicle for kataphatic description of the divine is Ruusbroec's strong emphasis on Christ as exemplar. For a clear account of his thought, see Van Nieuwenhove, "In the Image of God: The Trinitarian Anthropology of St Bonaventure, St Thomas Aquinas, and the Blessed Jan van Ruusbroec," *Irish Theological Quarterly* 66 (2001): 109–23.

67. See *SE*, 152; *SS*, 172. For discussion of apophasis in Ruusbroec, see Van Nieuwenhove, *Jan van Ruusbroec*, 81–85.

68. I am indebted to Van Nieuwenhove for drawing my attention to this (*Jan van Ruusbroec*, 54–55).

69. On "modelessness," see Van Nieuwenhove's discussion in *Jan van Ruusbroec*, 85–88.

70. I have provided a more literal translation here than that supplied by Van Nieuwenhove.

71. The rest/movement dichotomy is in line with Eckhart: Boehme has this as a binary also. Distinctions are not binary; real distinctions are binaries.

72. For "eternal birth," see *SP*, 146. Divinization does not absolve createdness; see esp. *MEB* 213, 237–39, 241–42, 246.

73. Van Nieuwenhove, *Jan van Ruusbroec*, chap. 3, 77–99.

74. Van Nieuwenhove is especially strong on this point (*Jan van Ruusbroec*, chap. 6, 77–99).

75. This trope of the self-diffusion of the ultimate, which is central to Christian Neoplatonism, finds expression in the thought of Plotinus and its first appearance in Plato's *Timaeus*. In the Christian Neoplatonism of Pseudo-Dionysius, it is meant to undergird metaphysically the view that self-gift defines the divine and that this gifting is neither contingent nor necessary. Perhaps the place in Ruusbroec's oeuvre where this point is most underscored is *A Little Book of Clarification*. See *John Ruusbroec*, 249ff., esp. 266. For divine *agapē*, see also *MEB*, 237.

76. For good synoptic accounts of Ruusbroec's engagement with the so-called heresy of the Free Spirit, see Wiseman's Introduction to *John Ruusbroec*, 3–7. The resistance to what Ruusbroec regards as an unbalanced form of spiritualism is perhaps clearest in *A Little Book of Clarification*.

77. Arguably, this is a central way in which Ruusbroec differs from the position articulated by Marguerite Porete in her classic *The Mirror of Simple Souls*.

78. Dupré thinks that the "common life" is nothing less than the hermeneutical key to Ruusbroec's entire work. Van Nieuwenhove does not go quite as far yet, nonetheless, highlights it (*Jan van Ruusbroec*, chap. 6, 157–91.

79. As a mystical theologian, Ruusbroec certainly deploys hyperbole, so it should not surprise that at moments in his work there are suggestions of union with God that relativize normal workings of and the normal place of virtue in the Christian economy. See especially *SE*, 139–43. In general, however, he makes clear that the practices of the Christian virtues of humility, compassion, mercy, purity, and so on, are essential to the definition of Christianity and constitutive of the common life. Not surprisingly, given its attempt to meet the challenge of the heresy of the Free Spirit head-on, the text where Ruusbroec is most insistent on the point is *A Little Book of Clarification*. Overall, however, as underscored by both Dupré and Van Nieuwenhove, throughout Ruusbroec's long writing career Christian life is defined by the virtues and the practices of prayer and liturgical observance.

80. The relativization of the virtues follows from Eckhart's rigorous denial of merit in the strict sense such that an exchange relationship is set up with God. Even in the bolder phrasing common to the German sermons, however, Eckhart does not suggest that the freedom from attachment is freedom for good or evil, as suggested by Schelling and in the twentieth century by Georges Bataille. Eckhart is convinced that only good follows from the surrender of attachment and the extinguishing of self-will. See Walshe, S9 (Q86), S11 (Q26), S15 (Q29), S17 (Q28), S18 (Q30), S23 (Q47). The existential correlative of this is that we experience ourselves as "friends" of God rather than subjects to be commanded.

81. Ruusbroec provides a copious treatment of all the Christian virtues, but the virtue that is the highest for him and the one that is regulative for all is Christian love. In this respect, he is closer to Bonaventure than to either Eckhart, who points to a union that goes beyond love, or Marguerite Porete, who points to a union that is deeper than love. The relation between Marguerite and the heresy of the Free Spirit remains a tangled one. McGinn touches on the relationship between Eckhart and Marguerite in *The Flowering of Mysticism: Men and Women in the New Mysticism, 1200–1350*, vol. 3 of *The Presence of God: A History of Western Christian Mysticism* (New York: Crossroad, 1998), 244–65, but he does not thematize it. For a thematic treatment, see Lydia Wegener, "Eckhart and the World of Women's Spirituality in the Context of the 'Free Spirit' and Marguerite Porete," in Hackett, *Companion to Meister Eckhart*, 415–43.

82. There are good reasons to think that, as elaborated in *Mysterium magnum* and *De electione gratiae*, the immanent Trinity is basically Sabellian in that Boehme affirms a unity of process and denies the identity of three persons. He is prepared to think of Father, Son, and Spirit as nodes or modes in the incipient process of divine self-development.

83. Hans Blumenberg, *Work on Myth*, trans. Robert M. Wallace (Boston: MIT Press, 1985), 259–60.

84. See my essay "Eckhart Reception in the 19th Century," in Hackett, *Companion to Meister Eckhart*, 629–67.

85. See Hans Martensen, *Between Hegel and Kierkegaard: Hans L. Martensen's Philosophy of Religion*, trans. Curtis L. Thompson and David J. Kangas, Texts and Translations 17 (Atlanta: Scholars Press, 1997). Martensen was a major conduit for German mystical theology in the nineteenth century, and especially of Eckhart and Boehme. While he may have been assimilating both from the beginning, in terms of publication, his work on Eckhart reception is much earlier than his work on Boehme reception. In his early text *Autonomy of Self-Consciousness in Modern Dogmatic Theology* (1839) Eckhart is his hero, but he feels positively about Suso, Tauler, and the *Theologica Germanica* (192–96). The one medieval excluded is Ruusbroec. Martensen has his reasons. There is, Martensen avers, no speculative tendency in Ruusbroec; his thought is too closely linked to doctrinal correctness and to the institutional (Catholic) church (156, 175, 196, 202–3).

86. There is a veritable industry here. Obviously, whatever the inherent scholarly limitations of the work, much is owed D. T. Suzuki for opening up discussion concerning the relation between the thought of Eckhart and Zen Buddhism in his *Mysticism: Christian and Buddhist; The Eastern and the Western Way* (London: Macmillan, 1957). There has also been considerable reflection on the relation between the thought of Meister Eckhart and the nondualist (*advaita*) philosophy of Adi Shankara (eighth century C.E.). Nor has the connection between Eckhart's mysticism and that of medieval Islam been neglected, as in the studies of his relation to Rumi and to Ibn 'Arabi. Much of the literature on the Eckhart–Rumi relation is popular. For a serious work on Eckhart and Ibn 'Arabi, see Robert J. Dobie, *Logos and Revelation: Ibn 'Arabi, Meister Eckhart, and Mystical Hermeneutics* (Washington, DC: Catholic University of America Press, 2009).

87. See the following works by Matthew Fox: *Meister Eckhart's Creation Spirituality in New Translation* (San Francisco: Doubleday, 1980); *Meditations with Meister Eckhart* (Rochester, VT: Bear, 1983); *Original Blessing: A Primer in Creation Spirituality* (Rochester, VT: Bear, 1983); and *Meister Eckhart: A Mystic Warrior of Our Time* (San Francisco: New World Library, 2014). While the comparative side of Fox's reading of Eckhart is evident from the beginning, in the work of 2014 it is even more to the fore. Although Fox ranges widely with regard to comparison, the relation between Eckhart and Rumi enjoys a certain kind of privilege.

88. See Nicholas Berdyaev, "Unground and Freedom," which functions as an introduction to *Six Theosophic Points and Other Writings*, trans. J. R. Earle (New York: Knopf, 1920; repr., Ann Arbor: University of Michigan, 1958), v–xxxvii. The influence of Boehme can be especially felt in the following works by Berdyaev: *Freedom and the Spirit*, trans. A. F. Clark (London: Geoffrey Bles,

1935); *Spirit and Reality*, trans. George Reavey (London: Geoffrey Bles, 1939); *The Beginning and the End*, trans. R. M. French (London: Geoffrey Bles, 1952).

89. The influence of Boehme on Bulgakov is to a significant extent mediated in and through the writings of Vladimir Soloviev and is further tempered through Bulgakov's commitment to the theological tradition. Boehme's thought is manifested in a general way in and through his commitment to a speculative form of theology and his sophiology. The influence of Boehme on Paul Tillich is also somewhat indirect. Boehme is mediated through Tillich's early appropriation of Schelling in his doctoral studies in Germany. See Tillich, *Mysticism and Guilt-Consciousness in Schelling's Philosophical Development*, trans. Victor Nuova (Lewisburg, PA: Bucknell University Press, 1974; German original, 1912). See also Daniel J. Peterson, "Jacob Boehme and Paul Tillich: A Reassessment of the Mystical Philosopher and Systematic Theologian," *Religious Studies* 42 (2006): 225–34.

4
Showings to Share: The Mystical Theology of Julian of Norwich

Marilyn McCord Adams

Called to Be Seers

In some mid-to-late twentieth-century circles, mystics were still getting a bad press. Pre–Vatican II Protestant "pop" culture type-cast monks in monasteries as irresponsible adults who withdrew from society to indulge their own private spiritual agenda, to lead a contemplative life that set them apart. Indeed (as the monks themselves thought), they were ranked above *hoi polloi*, who had no choice but to marry and reproduce and play their higher-up or lower-down roles in society. Such suspicions were succeeded by accusations from political and liberation theologians who pitted the individual against the social and insisted that the higher righteousness (genuine spirituality) would be expressed in political action to uproot systemic social evils. Once again, mystics were disparaged as irresponsible navel-gazing individualists.

Such critiques, of course, evidenced both appalling ignorance and polemical misunderstanding of the great contemplatives. After all, Augustine was bishop of Hippo, actively involved in institutional affairs and incidentally writing volumes that set the theological agenda for at least fifteen hundred years in the Western church. Bonaventure was called out of his university career to set the Franciscan order on a stable institutional footing after serious controversies had torn the movement following the death of Francis. Bonaventure's great contemplative treatises

were written for university-formed friars many of whom were also itin-
erant preachers. Teresa of Avila was motivated by her mystical flights to
reform the Carmelite order and—like St. Paul—to organize new communities of the strict observance and to see to their welfare.

In this paper, however, I want to focus on Julian of Norwich, an
anchoress, who took a vow to stay enclosed in her hermitage attached
to the church of St. Julian of Norwich for the rest of her life. By her
own lights, she was not an institutional "mover and shaker." She had no
institutional office among the clergy of the church nor teaching position
in a monastic school or university. Neither was she (like Catherine of
Siena) well placed to influence higher-ups in civil and ecclesiastical government.[1] Instead, she presents herself in her writings as a woman with
a vocation as a contemplative seer, called not only to see and attend but
to reflect upon and receive insights into the meaning of what she sees—a
role she represents not as something she was called to take up merely for
her own benefit, but one she was to fulfill on behalf of all Christians, of
all who are to be saved. Julian does not emphasize the image of the body
of Christ as one body differentiated into many members with complementary functions (cf. 1 Corinthians 12). Nevertheless, she does insist
that the showings are not some private privileged access, but showings to
be shared for the upbuilding of all members of the body of Christ in their
cradle-to-grave pilgrimage here on earth.

*Julian's threefold vocation is to see, to reflect and receive insight, and
to share.* Not every antemortem Christian who might read her book was
or is in a position to do this at the time of their reading it. I want to begin
by teasing out from what she writes and what she tells us what sorts of
skills and disciplines, what sort of spiritual posture suits one for this
role. What Julian sees is *God's purposes in creation, how the cosmos, our
present human predicament, and future destiny look from God's point of
view.* God shows it and she receives it, because all Christians to be saved
need to be strengthened by it, the better to persevere through this passing
lifetime. I turn briefly to sketch her estimate of the human predicament,
her distinctive vision of divine–human relations, and the theological
ground of her confidence that her shared showings should encourage us.
What Julian is shown is that *all Christians to be saved are destined to
be seers who eternally appreciate and delight in who God is, how God
loves, and what God does.* Julian's book not only records what she saw

and what she eventually understood the visions to mean; it is also full of advice—in contemporary terminology, we might speak of spiritual direction—to Christians trying to grow up in the knowledge and love of God enough to become contemplative seers. Like all authentic spiritual counsel, it is wisdom won through the counselor's own struggles to become a better lover of God.

Uncommonly Suited

From Julian's scant autobiographical remarks, readers can hardly avoid the conclusion that she was uncommonly suited for the role of seer.

Demanding Prerequisite

Julian herself insists that *the showings are not a reward for superior virtue*, or a sign that she is free from sin. For one thing, she does not think that competitions or comparisons to see who is the most virtuous are spiritually edifying. "To consider the sins of other people will produce a thick film over the eyes of our soul, and prevent us for the time being from seeing the fair beauty of the Lord" (76.197–98). On the contrary, as a seer receptive to the showings, Julian is acutely conscious of herself as a sinner. The more aware of God's love she is, the more she is able to face the truth of how vile sin is and how pathetic the human condition. Christ solemnly declares that she will remain a sinner to the end of her earthly life (37.117; 38–40.118–23; 63.175–64; 78.201).

What makes the role of contemplative seer so demanding is high standards, not of moral virtue but of focused longing. What sets Julian up to be an antemortem contemplative seer is her intense longing for union with Christ. Julian gives herself away right at the beginning (2:63–64), when she reports her bold youthful prayer for three things. First, Julian asked that if it be God's will, she be brought to understand Christ's passion. She desired to be there with Christ's friends and lovers at the foot of the cross and to suffer with him. She did not so much want a vision of Christ's passion, much less some form of conceptual analysis, but to feel his pains in her own body. Second, she prayed that if it be God's will, she might—while still a young woman—suffer physically a near fatal illness.

She wanted to receive the last rites, to pass through the hour-of-death demonic temptations and to be cleansed, to live more worthily of God and to die an even better death (2.64). Third, Julian prayed unconditionally to receive the three wounds: contrition, compassion, and a sincere longing for God (2.64).

Julian also reports, almost incidentally, that, by the time the prayer was answered (when she was thirty and a half), she had already detached herself from earthly things. So far as she could then see, the only point in prolonging this life would be to learn "to love God more and better, and so ultimately come to know and love him more in the bliss of heaven" (3.64). Likewise, in the midst of her visions and in the twenty-year aftermath during which she reflected on them before writing the long text of her book, Julian reports that her longing for Christ was insatiable: the more she had him, the more she wanted him (8.74; 10.77; 43.129; 51.149).

Multimedia Presentations

Julian's showings engage the whole person. Many follow the patterns typical of biblical prophecy (e.g., Jer. 1:11–14; Amos 7:7–9; 8:1–2): there is *a sensory presentation*—whether to her bodily eyes or to her sensory imagination, whether presented as something outside as if real, or in her mind's eye, or in a dream. This is accompanied by *intellectual visions* and *propositional understanding*, on the one hand, and *affections* (feelings, emotions, and moods) on the other. Thus, in the first revelation, the crucifix at which she is staring "comes alive" so that she sees Christ being crowned with thorns, sees "the red blood trickling down from under it, hot, fresh, and plentiful." This vision came with the strong conviction that God was showing it to her. At the same time, she is filled with joy, has "a mental vision of the Godhead," and understands the unity of the Trinity with Jesus and that "the Trinity is our Maker and keeper, our eternal lover, joy and bliss—all through Jesus Christ" (4.66-67).

Other showings recall the paradigm of biblical apocalyptic seers, in which the seer receives a sensory presentation, which prompts the seer's question "What is it?" and evokes the revealer's explanation of what it means. Thus, Julian sees a hazelnut-like thing in the palm of her hand. She asks what it is and receives the reply: "It is all that is made." Without forming words, she marvels, "Why doesn't it disintegrate?" The answer is formed in her mind: "Because God loves it." Meditation discloses three further propositional truths: that God made it, that God loves it, that God sustains it; that what God is, is inaccessible to us in this life; and that recognizing "the littleness of creation" is necessary to loving God appropriately in this life (5.68).

Heightened Sensory Capacity

Julian's reports of such showings evidence her remarkable capacities for noticing, remembering, and imagining sensory detail. Thus, in the first showing (of Christ's crowning with thorns) she "saw the red blood trickling down from under the garland, hot, fresh, and plentiful" (4.66). All the while she was receiving propositional truths, she continued to watch as

> great drops of blood rolled down from the garland like beads, seemingly from the veins; they came down a brownish red colour—for the blood was thick—and as they spread out they became bright red, and when they reached his eyebrows they vanished. . . . They were as fresh and living as though they were real; their abundance like drops of water from the eaves after a heavy shower, falling so thickly that no one can possibly count them; their roundness as they spread out on his forehead were like the scales of a herring. (7.71–72)

Likewise, in the second showing, she observed "frequent changes of colour. On one occasion I saw that half his face, from side to centre, was covered with dry blood, and that afterwards the other half similarly was covered, the first half clearing as the second came" (10.76). Again, in the fourth, she sees how his skin was broken by the flogging so that "there were deep weals in the tender flesh," whose bleeding was "so copious that had it been real the whole bed and more would have been soaked with blood" (12.82). And in the eighth, she watches his body dry up in death:

> I saw his dear face, dry, bloodless, and pallid with death. It became more pale, deathly and lifeless. Then dead, it turned a blue colour,

gradually changing to a brownly blue, as the flesh continued to die. . . . His nostrils too shrivelled and dried before my eyes, and his dear body became black and brown as it dried up in death; it was no longer its own fair living colour. (16.87–88)

Her vivid description continues:

Because of the pull of the nails and the weight of that blessed body it was a long time suffering. For I could see that the great, hard, hurtful nails in those dear and tender hands and feet caused the wounds to gape wide and the body to sag forward under its own weight, because of the time it hung there. His head was scarred and torn, and the crown was sticking to it, congealed with blood; his dear hair and his withered flesh were entangled with the thorns, and they with it. . . . Furthermore, I could see that the dear skin and tender flesh, the hair and the blood were hanging loose from the bone, gouged by the thorns in many places. It seemed about to drop off, heavy and loose, still holding its natural moisture, sagging like a cloth. (17.89)

When her daring prayer is answered and the Fiend comes in a dream to test her in what appeared to be the hour of her death, she sees him face to face:

It was like a young man's face, and long and extraordinarily lean. . . . The colour was the red of a tilestone newly fired, and there were black spots like freckles, dirtier than the tilestone. His hair was rust red, clipped in front, with side-locks hanging over his cheeks. He grinned at me with sly grimace, thereby revealing white teeth, which made it, I thought, all the more horrible. There was no proper shape to this body or hands, but with his paws he held me by the throat and would have strangled me if he could. (66.182)

Nor was the impression only visual. She reports that he came "with great heat and filthy smell" (66.182).

Later on, when she had been meditating on the parable of the Lord and the Servant (see below under "The Fall") for twenty years but still

had difficulty understanding it, she is instructed to discover its meaning in the sensory details, even the ones she finds "vague and unimpor-
tant": "how and where the lord sat; the colour and cut of his clothes; his
appearance, and his innate nobility and goodness; and how and where
the servant stood, what his clothes were like, and their colour and style;
his outward bearing and his inner goodness and loyalty" (51.144). Contemporary studies show what Julian implicitly knew: that sensory detail
strengthens our conviction that what we see is real. Heightened capacity
for sensory awareness is also correlated with ready belief in the reality of
God who reveals it.[2]

Unusual Empathetic Capacity

Moreover, only a person of unusual empathetic capacity could have experienced what Julian reports. Her early bold prayer expresses a desire not
so much to *see* Christ's passion but to sense it with her *bodily feelings*,
to experience literal com-passion, "to suffer with him" (2.63). With the
showings, her request was granted. She reports: "All the while he was suffering, I personally felt no pain but for him." In her estimation, the pain
was worse than that of her own dying (17.90), perhaps for two reasons.
First, because Christ's own pain was so great: the union of his human
nature to his Godhead strengthened him to suffer more than Adam's race
had throughout its history (20.94). Second, Julian reckons, because "of
all the pains that lead to salvation this is the greatest, to see your Love suffer" (17.90). During the passion, Christ's "friends suffered pain because
they loved him" (18.91). Although the pain was so great that it made her
wonder why she had asked for it in the first place, she comes to recognize that that was her lower nature protesting (19.93). The experience of
enduring the pain actually enabled her truly to feel "that I loved Christ so
much more than myself" (17.90). Love is the root of compassion. Julian's
great love for Christ opened her up to experience his sufferings in her
body. Those who love less will be less moved.

Trust and Reciprocity

If some of Julian's showings form-critically echo the revelation–question–answer of biblical apocalyptic (e.g., the hazelnut; see above under
"Heightened Sensory Capacity"), others break free of this form in favor
of reciprocal exchange. Thus, in the ninth revelation she sees Christ at

the point of dying suddenly become happy and cheerful. Julian *feels* cheerful, too. This is accompanied by a mental locution expressing Christ's question to her: "What is the point of your pain and anguish now?" Julian understands that Christ suffers because of his good will to bring us to higher bliss; that through our present pains and suffering we are now dying with Christ on the cross; and that as we deliberately endure that cross to the end we will suddenly be brought to unending joy (21.95–96). A further mental locution expresses Christ's question: "Are you satisfied with my suffering?" Her ready assent brings Christ's response: "Then I am satisfied, too" (22.96).

Still other stretches of her book seem to follow patterns of monastic meditation epitomized in St. Anselm's *Proslogion*. Faith seeks understanding. Anselm takes the initiative in praying for divine disclosure. He wrestles and waits until his prayer is rewarded with an "Aha!" disclosure, which he receives and ponders, questions and disputes, only to receive another "Aha!" which is also pondered, questioned, and disputed. Having received "the illumination" to understand that God is a being greater than which cannot be conceived and so not only extant (chap. 2) but necessarily extant (chap. 3), Anselm wants to know more: "What are you?" (chap. 5); "How can you be omnipotent if you cannot do all things?" (chap. 7); "How can you be merciful if you are impassible?" (chap. 8); "How can you be merciful if you are also just?" (chaps. 9–11).[3]

So, too, Julian is no merely passive receiver but does not hesitate to raise questions about what is shown. In the thirteenth revelation, she remembers her earlier longing for Christ and understands that nothing hinders us but sin. She asks, "Why sin?" and receives the answer: "Sin is necessary, but everything will be all right" (27.103). Further meditation leads her to press the question: "Why sin, when it results in such great harm to creatures?" (27.103; 29.106). She receives the answer that Adam's sin was the most harm that ever was or shall be done; that the atonement for Adam's sin is much more pleasing to God than Adam's sin was harmful; and that we should take our knowledge that God has made good on the worst harm as assurance that God will make good on all the rest (29.106). Later, it is what Holy Church teaches that prompts Julian's question: How is it that everything will be all right if some people will be damned in hell? Pursuing the question, she is told that she cannot understand now, that it is God's own secret what God will do on the last day to make everything all right (31–34.107–13). Again, Julian badgers God to clarify an apparent misfit between the showings and church teaching. Holy Church teaches that God reacts to sin with divine wrath, which must punish us if it does not forgive us (45.131–32). But no matter how hard she looked, Julian saw no wrath in God and—insofar as forgiveness involves setting wrath aside—she saw no forgiveness either. Instead, she saw that—so far from blaming or condemning us—God plans to compensate us for our sins with heavenly rewards (38.118–19; 45.131; 46.132–33; 48.136–37; 49.137–38). God's answer to this was the parable of the Lord and the Servant, of which more below (see under "The Fall"). Lastly, Julian confesses how she inquired out of curiosity whether someone she knew would persevere to the end. Receiving no reply, she learned to ask better (because more general) questions about human beings (35.113).

Such interrogative meditations presuppose longing that specially expresses itself in a striving to understand. St. Anselm knew that they also require skills, which he tried—in his classroom and in his exercise-book writings—to impart to his pupils. Likewise, seekers must begin with trust. Anselm is explicit that his monk pupils begin with *faith* in God as the source of the being and well-being of all else, as the Creator and Redeemer of Adam's race.[4] Such inquiry also demands a posture of humility that recognizes not only that human beings are "almost nothing"[5] but also are so sin-damaged that seeking would be fruitless without divine help.[6]

In the same vein, Julian's book stresses the importance of appreciating the "size gap" between God and creatures: "We have got to realize the littleness of creation and to see it for the nothing that it is before we can love and possess God who is increated" (5.68). She also emphasizes trust that God is *for* us and wants to help us. Mother Jesus is our nanny (58–60.164–71). By the time of her showings, Julian has settled into a posture of humility and trust that makes her teachable. Julian questions with the confidence of the uninhibited child who does not hesitate to expose her puzzlement to the parent whom she trusts to judge what explanations will be suitable and when it will be better to postpone fuller understanding (36.116–17). Julian's questions themselves are not childish, however. They arise out of her adult experience and show her to be articulate and tough-minded.

Overall, then, Julian was uncommonly suited to receive the showings. Nevertheless, she insists, they were not for her alone but for "all my fellow Christians." Their purpose was to comfort and instruct cradle-to-grave God-lovers, to encourage and assist everyone to be saved on their antemortem pilgrimage through this world of sin and suffering (8.74). There is a backstory as to why such showings are needed, one that reflects Julian's remarkable understandings of creation and the fall.

The Human Predicament

God's Good Purpose

Why did God create us in a world such as this? Julian sums up the message of her showings: Love was God's meaning (86.211–12). God loves creation: otherwise it would not have come into existence or continue in being (5.68). God loves humankind, with a love that had no beginning, with a love that will never end (5.67–68). Because love seeks union with its object, God unites Godself to human nature. Because—according to Julian's distinctive understanding—our soul is a composite of substance and sensuality (of a "higher" or "essential" nature and a "lower" nature), God unites to human nature in two stages. God creates all human souls at once and immediately joins our substance to the Godhead (to the whole Trinity) (55.159; 56.166). (Julian does not explain what sort of metaphysical union she has in mind, but evidently it is something between the mere dependence that all creatures—not only rational but also non-rational and inanimate—have on God as Creator and Sustainer and the hypostatic union that joins human and divine nature in one person in Christ.) The effect of this union is to make the soul holy (55.160). Julian is shown how the soul's substance or higher nature is kept safe and sound in God (45.131; 51.144; 53.156; 55.160), so that it has never consented to sin and never will (37.118). God unites our lower nature to God the Son in incarnation (55.160; 58.166), evidently into hypostatic union. Thus, God is and always has been in favor of both parts of our nature and is the cause that holds our substance and sensuality together (56.161). God intends that our higher nature should govern the lower. When that integration is achieved, all those who are to be saved will enter into joyful life together with God in a heaven of knowing and being known, of mutual delight and appreciation (27.103). Put otherwise, every human to be saved is predestined to become a seer and lover of God! But this requires the proper subordination of the lower nature to the higher. Christ conforms his sensuality to his higher human nature and thereby pioneers the integration that seers require (56.161).

The Fall

For those who are to be saved, Julian's God purposes a happy ending. But there is a plot complication that delays gratification for everyone. Perhaps the most memorable of Julian's showings is the parable of the Lord and the Servant with its striking picture of the Fall:

> I saw physically before me two people, a lord and a servant. And God showed me its spiritual meaning. The lord is sitting down quietly, relaxed and peaceful: the servant is standing by his lord, humble and ready to do his bidding. And then I saw the lord look at his servant with rare love and tenderness, and quietly send him to a certain place to fulfil his purpose. Not only does the servant go, but he starts off at once, running with all speed, in his love to do what the master wanted. And without warning he falls headlong into a deep ditch, and injures himself very badly. And though he groans and moans and cries and struggles he is quite unable to get up or help himself in any way. To crown all, he could get no relief of any sort: he could not even turn his head to look at the lord who loved him, and who was so close to him. The sight of him would have been a real comfort, but he was temporarily so weak and bemused that he gave vent to his feelings, as he suffered his pains. (51.141)

Julian explains that the servant's errand was to fetch "an earthly treasure which the lord loved"—"a repast, lovely and pleasing to the lord," "a meal" whose worth to the lord "depended on the servant's careful preparation of it, and his setting it before him personally." Again, she compares the servant's task to that of a gardener who has to do "the hardest and most exhausting work possible":

digging and banking, toiling and sweating, turning and trench-
ing the ground, watering the plants the while. And keeping at this
work he would make sweet streams to flow, fine abundant fruits
to grow; he would bring them to his lord, and serve them to his
taste. And he would not return till he had prepared the meal just
as he knew his master would like it. Then he would take it, and the
appropriate refreshment, bearing them with due ceremony to his
lord. (51.146–47)

The lord's reaction to the servant's fall was twofold: compassion and
pity, on the one hand; joy and anticipation in planning the honor he
would give the servant, on the other (51.144–46).

Meditating on its meanings, Julian comes to understand that the lord
is God, while the servant gets a double reading, the first of which is Adam
or Everyman, each and every member of the human race, and the second
of which is Christ. The "hardest and most exhausting work possible"
is the integration of our higher with our lower natures by bringing the
latter under the governance of the former. This task is intrinsically chal-
lenging, but it is made more difficult by the fact that our psychological
powers have been so damaged by the Fall that they are insufficient to "get
our acts together" and bring our lower and higher natures into proper
alignment.

This lack of coordination explains the inevitability of sin: the verdict
that no matter how hard we try, we will sin right up to our dying day
(37.117; 38–40.118–23; 63–64.175–79; 78.201). Julian does not mince
words: sin is really "vile" and "filthy," "black" and "shameful" (10.78),
horrible and horrifying (63.175; 64.178; 76.197; 78.201–2)—so much so
that we could not bear to confront it all at once. Sooner or later we will
have to face the truth about ourselves, but divine pedagogy is courteous
in disclosing it to us gradually (78.201–2). Sin is "unnatural" because
misalignment and malfunction "contradict our nature" (63.175). Julian
exclaims: sin is the sharpest scourge, the worst hell that a soul to be saved
can suffer (63.175; 72.190). In other words, it is hell to *be* a sinner, to be
such a caricature of what God created us to be.

Misalignment between sensuality and substance also gives rise to a dis-
abling "perception disorder." God indwells, the Trinity enfolds, unchanging and unchangeable divine love surrounds us. But we are "blind" and

"ignorant." We do not see God. We do not recognize the personal and loving presence that swaddles us (34.113; 47.134–35; 66.181; 85.210). We are not thoroughly convinced that God is *for* us. This perception disorder is a major source of antemortem misery:

> we are so spiritually blind and weighed down by our mortal flesh and murky sin that we cannot clearly see our Lord's blessed face. No, and because of this murkiness we have difficulty in believing and trusting his great love and our complete safety. And therefore I saw that we never cease from sighs and tears.

By contrast, even if we were "to be in the utmost pain," "if then we could see his blessed face, none of this pain would distress us" (72.190–91). What if—through the grace of God and "the hardest possible work"— someone were recovered enough from such blindness that she was able to receive and reflect upon revelations of divine love? What if she were to share what she learned with struggling and discouraged God-lovers alternatively tempted by laziness and despair? Surely, this would be an interim comfort and consolation!

Hopeful Disclosures

What would really help us to make our way through this passing lifetime is confidence that God is for us, that God is willing and able to make good on our present misery and the caricatures of God's image that we have become. Julian's showings are given to meet this crying need. Julian's twenty years of meditation on them put her in a position to articulate and to share essential good-news themes.

1. First and foremost, *Love is God's meaning. God's everlasting love for the human race is wholly unaffected by sin* (79.202–3). God sees the Fall and sees us in our fallen condition, but God is not angry with us, does not blame us (27.104; 28.105; 49.137–38, 140; 52.154; 53.155), and so has no need to forgive us (45.131; 52.153–54; 53.155). Indeed, given the "littleness of creation," God does not really expect more of us. Julian is told: "sin is necessary" (27.103). Evidently, the lord is not surprised when his servant, running off to do the errand in clumsy eagerness, takes a fall.

2. Second and importantly, *the Fiend is decisively defeated by Christ's passion*. Therefore, no matter how terrifying, no matter how much the fiends harass those who are to be saved, even though we will sin to our dying day, *the fiends will not finally overcome us*. God will keep us securely, and we will persevere to the end (13.83–84; 68.185).

3. Third and reassuringly, *God will do a great deed on the last day that will make everything all right*. What this cosmic deed will be is beyond our present comprehension (36.115–17). But Julian is given a picture of how God will make everything all right for individual sinners who are to be saved. When we get to heaven, God preempts apologies or expressions of humility by greeting us with gratitude: "Thank you for all your suffering, the suffering of your youth" (14.85). That is, "thank you for persisting in 'the hardest possible work'—the work of struggling through the trials and distortions of a cradle-to-grave human life." Such divine honors will be public and permanent. They will cancel our shame, fully compensate us for the hell of being lifelong sinners, and fill us with everlasting joy (14.85–86; 38.118–19). Our sins will not be eternally despised or forgotten, but will be worn by saved sinners as honorable battle scars (38.119; 39.121).

4. Fourth and in the meantime, *Mother Jesus is always working to help us learn to subordinate our sensuality to our higher nature, to rear us up into those virtues that will enable us to enjoy him forever* (58.166–67). Mother Jesus guides us by his laws (55.158), and sometimes punishes to correct faults (61.171–72). Like any mother, Jesus sometimes allows his children to learn the hard way but never allows the situation to become dangerous or eternal-life-threatening for them (61.172). When we fall, it is the gracious touch of Mother Jesus that enables us to get up again (52.153). Whenever we are frightened, whether by suffering or our own disobedience and failures, Mother Jesus wants us to run to him at once and cling to him forever (61.172).

"One-ing" as Ground and Key

The way Julian sees it, what drives God's whole creative project is a divine desire for "one-ing."

Metaphysical One-ings

First, there is (the above-mentioned but less than precisely defined) *metaphysical one-ing*. She speaks of God as the "foundation of our nature" (56.162) and "the ground of our life and existence" (78.201), as if the Godhead is the matrix in which all creatures are embedded and on which they are all dependent. Again, Julian is shown how God unites our higher nature or substance to Godself at creation. "All souls to be saved in heaven are forever joined and united in this union and made holy in this holiness" (53.157). Later on, God unites our lower nature or sensuality to God the Son in the incarnation. Alternatively, Julian can speak almost pantheistically, declaring that God "*is* everything that we know to be good and helpful" (5.67–68; 9.75). She reports that her twelfth revelation "shows Our Lord *to be the being of all that is*" (1.62). Typically, she retreats from this to the language of indwelling: "God indwells our soul" and "our soul dwells in God" (54.157). The human soul is a "glorious city," "a resting place" (81.206) in which Christ makes himself completely at home (67.183). According to Julian's sixteenth revelation, "the Blessed Trinity, our Creator in Christ Jesus our Saviour" lives there, in the soul, eternally (1.63). Willy-nilly, God and the soul are intimately present to one another. Willy-nilly, the soul is caught up into functional collaboration with the indwelling Godhead. God is always working in us, and God is working in our working.

Statutory Identification

Second, and of equal importance, is Julian's notion of *statutory identification*. As already noted (see above under "The Fall"), in the parable of the Lord and the Servant, the servant gets a double reading: on the one hand, he is Adam, Everyman, each and every member of the human race; on the other hand, he is Christ. Representing Adam's race as one man gives us to understand that "in the sight of God, everyman is one man and one man is everyman" (51.144), in the sense that God "loves all who are to be saved as if they were one soul" (37.118). Representing Adam and Christ by the same figure signifies that "God makes no distinction in the love he has for the blessed soul of Christ and that which he has for the lowliest soul to be saved" (54.157). "Jesus is everyone that will be saved, and everyone that will be saved is Jesus" (51.149). According to Julian's distinctive understanding, our higher human natures are just as holy as Christ's is. But our whole souls—the composite of substance and sensuality—are a mess. Statutory identification of our whole souls with Christ's whole soul begets a quasi-legal imputation of lovability and worth that excuses us from blame. "While we are yet sinners," the Father counts us as "dear lovely children," because "the Father cannot and will not blame us more than his own dear Son Jesus Christ" (51.148).

Moreover, Julian appears to regard this imputed lovability and worth as underwritten by Christ's "hardest possible work":

> When Adam fell, God's Son fell. Because of the true unity which had been decreed in heaven, God's Son could not be dissociated from Adam. . . . Adam fell from life to death, first into the depths of this wretched world, and then into hell. God's Son fell, with Adam, but into the depth of the Virgin's womb—herself the fairest daughter of Adam—with the intent of excusing Adam from blame both in heaven and on earth. And with a mighty arm he brought him out of hell. (51.147–48)

Julian does not elaborate on which (if any) of the traditional atonement theories she is endorsing. With Holy Church she can say that the passion of Christ buys us out of hell, or that hell is harrowed of souls that are his—which hints at a ransom theory (where Christ's suffering and death pays the devil a ransom for sinners) (12.83; 22.97–98; 23.99). Again with Holy Church, she insists that the Fiend is overcome by Christ's passion—which could suggest a *Christus Victor* theme (where the cross is a contest—just before Julian's era, a jousting match—between Christ and the devil) (13.83–84). Her comment that "our good Lord Jesus has taken upon himself all our blame" (51.148) sounds like an anticipation of Luther's Glorious Exchange (where faith is a *reciprocal* trade of our guilt for Christ's righteousness), except that Julian does not say that in taking our blame Christ himself becomes blameworthy (even statutorily) (51.148).

Transitive Solidarity

Third and closely related is the one-ing of *solidarity*. Christ falls into "this wretched world" to suffer in solidarity with Adam, with Everyman, with each and every individual human being. Falling into the womb, Christ "accepted great hurt, the hurt that was our flesh, in which from the first he suffered mortal pain" (51.149). God "the Father deliberately allowed his own Son to suffer in his human nature Everyman's pain, without sparing him" (51.150). Strengthened by his divine nature, Jesus suffers in his human nature more than the human race could suffer from the beginning to the end of time (20.94). "Fairest Lord Jesus" did not look so fair on the hard wood of the cross. Julian learns that Jesus allows his body to be twisted and tortured to keep up the family resemblance with fallen humanity that now caricatures God's image (10.77-78). Jesus not only suffers *for* us to defeat the Fiend. Julian declares that—although risen and impassible (!)—Jesus suffers *with* us so long as any of us are still muddling through this passing lifetime (20.94). Love drives extravagant solidarity. Jesus assures Julian that he would have done and suffered more for us and with us, if it were possible (22.97–98). Jesus willingly does and suffers whatever is necessary, because he is determined to have us as his joy and his crown (51.151).

Like other lovers of Christ, Julian returned the favor to the best of her abilities. She prayed for and experienced Christ's pain in her own body (3.65–66; 17.90), pain that seemed to her to surpass the pangs of death. Despite the intensity of the pain, the showings brought Julian to choose Jesus for her heaven, to the point where she preferred to continue to suffer with him until judgment day than to enter heavenly bliss without him (19.91–93). Not only does Julian show solidarity with Christ in suffering, but when the apparent hour of her death arrives, she imitates Christ in scorning the Fiend through "real hard work" (13.84; 69.186).

Along the way, it dawns on Julian that God's statutory identifications— of each and every human being with Adam, and of Adam with Christ— mean that the one-ing of solidarity ought to be transitive. Given Christ's solidarity with Adam, a God-lover's solidarity with Christ ought to pass over into solidarity with all those who are to be saved. At the beginning of her book, Julian represents herself as detached from the world. She reattaches to her fellow Christians through her love for Christ who suffers for them and with them (28.104–5; 37.118; 57.164; 78.202; 79.202–3). This is how she comes to understand that the showings are for all those to be saved. It is also what confronts her with Christ's daunting invitation:

to share his preference to suffer through until judgment day rather than enter heavenly bliss without them.

Helps for Future Seers

All human beings to be saved are predestined to be seers. But we will not be able to enter into this calling unless and until our perception disorder is overcome. Julian is confident that, at death, "eternally 'hid in God,' we shall see him truly and feel him fully, hear him spiritually, smell delightfully, and taste him sweetly! We shall see God face to face, simply and fully. The creature made by God, shall see and eternally gaze upon him, his maker" (43.130). *Then* our blindness will be cured, our spiritual senses fully revived. In the meantime, Christians to be saved face a lifetime of "the hardest possible work" to bring substance and sensuality into proper alignment, so that the lower nature is conformed to the higher. *Pace* Ignatius Loyola, Julian nowhere advises us here and now to undertake specifically cognitive exercises the better to mimic her heightened capacities for sensory detail. In the life to come, we will *see*. There will be no call to imagine. The key to our rehabilitation is not so much what we see or feel antemortem, but that we learn to trust God to be *for* us no matter what. To this end, Julian urges spiritual exercises that engage the whole person. Her many and nuanced recommendations may be summed up in three.

1. Sin and Self-Knowledge

First, future seers should keep at the spadework of self-knowledge. Eventually, we will have to face the whole truth about our own sin-wrought disfigurement. Because this would be too ghastly for us to face all at once (46.132; 78.201–2; 82.207), divine pedagogy stages a series of partial disclosures through a process that strings us out in the polar tension between what Holy Church teaches and what Julian saw about God's attitude toward sinners. Shown just the right amount, the disintegrated soul reacts the way Holy Church says it should: it fears divine wrath and reprobation. When the soul is convinced that it is fit for hell, the Holy Spirit nudges it with the grace of contrition, which prompts it to beg for mercy and forgiveness and to flee to Jesus, only to experience a friendly welcome (39.120; 40.120–21). The teaching of Holy Church accurately grasps the dynamic that fallen human nature "believes" in. Even though it is not really true that God is angry or reproving, fear that God is plays an important role in our spiritual growth and recovery. Cycling and recycling—through the humiliation of self-knowledge, fear of divine wrath and damnation, the wound of contrition and the panic of begging for mercy, only to be astonished by God's unchanging and unchangeable love—dig down to bedrock, enabling us to *experience* both the depth of our weakness and wretchedness and the wideness of God's mercy. Julian even suspects that this is one reason why sin was necessary: if we did not keep falling flat on our faces and making filthy messes of ourselves, we would not be able to learn what God's love means (58.167; 59.167; 61.172). Each revelation of who we are strikes terror; each friendly welcome stirs trust. Both work to restructure the self to make it whole. Julian assures us that mercy and grace assist at every step (56.161–62). Julian warns: because we have to keep at it until we die, our cradle-to-grave lives will be one continual penance (81.206).

2. Prayer as Collaboration

Julian is firm: God wants us to "work away" at our praying. The reason is simple: prayer helps us to align the appetites of our lower nature with those of our higher nature, whose will is always conformed to God. To be sure, prayer is a deliberate act of the soul, but it is covertly collaborative. Julian learned that God is the foundation of our praying. God moves us to pray for what God wants to give us. When we do pray, we will what God wills for us. Put otherwise, prayer "ones" our desires with God's. Because God is always working secretly toward our personal reconfiguration, we should keep at it whether we feel like it or not, even in seasons of dryness. In prayer, our blindness may even be temporarily lifted so that we perceive God's presence. Over time, persistence in prayer makes our soul more sensitive to the omnipresent and ever-loving Godhead (41.123–25; 43.128–30).

3. Patient Solidarity

Julian is realistic. She sees this world as a prison and this passing lifetime as a penance filled with suffering and shame. But she is shown that the sufferings of this present life are nothing compared with the glory to be revealed (Rom. 8:18). On the last day, God will do something that will make everything all right, and God-lovers will enter into eternal bliss. Julian warns: making such "heavy weather" of our present difficulties is spiritually counterproductive because it flirts with accusation and mistrust of God's goodness. Instead, we should use the one-ing of solidarity to reframe our antemortem ills. God the Son took our flesh and suffered his passion as an act of solidarity with Adam's race. Julian herself prayed to feel Christ's pains in her own body as an act of solidarity with Christ. So, too, future seers can practice by deliberately choosing to be patient, by accepting their present suffering as an act of solidarity with Christ and with Everyman (21.95–96; 64.177; 73.192). Over and over again, we can prefer to suffer our whole cradle-to-grave lifetime rather than come to paradise without them!

The spiritual exercises that Julian commends are ones she learned by doing. Julian learned "the hard way" from experience that engaged her whole person. In Julian's showings, Christ is presented as the paradigm alignment of substance and sensuality. Mary is also offered to Julian as a role model of response to divine love (25.101–2). Julian's book implicitly presents Julian as an example, a teacher closer to us who, throughout her cradle-to-grave life, was tempted in many things as we are and sinned to her dying day, a guide who is able to sympathize with our weakness and show us how to cooperate with Mother Jesus and to grow up as seers already in this passing life (cf. Heb. 4:15).

Notes

1. Julian of Norwich, *Revelations of Divine Love*, trans. Clifton Wolters (Harmondsworth: Penguin Books, 1966), 2.63; 9.75–76 (= chapter 2, page 63; chapter 9, pages 75–76). Parenthetical references in the text are to *Revelations of Divine Love* following this pattern.

2. For a case study in how this works, see T. M. Luhrmann, *When God Talks Back: Understanding the American Evangelical Relationship with God* (New York: Vintage, 2012), esp. chaps. 6–7, pp. 157–226.

3. Anselm, *Proslogion* in Schmidt, *Opera Omnia*, 1:93–122.

4. Anselm, *Monologion*, in Schmidt, *Opera Omnia*, 1:5, 13 (prologus and chap. 1).

5. Anselm, *Monologion*, in Schmidt, *Opera Omnia*; 1:51 (chap. 31).

6. Anselm, *Proslogion* in Schmidt, *Opera Omnia*, 1:97–100, 111–13 (chaps. 1, 14, 16).

Works Cited

Anselm of Canterbury. *Opera Omnia*, vol. 1. Edited by F. S. Schmidt. Stuttgart-Bad Cannstatt: Friedrich Frommann, 1968.

Julian of Norwich. *Revelations of Divine Love*. Translated by Clifton Wolters. Harmondsworth: Penguin Books, 1966.

Luhrmann, T. M. *When God Talks Back: Understanding the American Evangelical Relationship with God*. New York: Vintage, 2012.

5
The Ignatian Mystic

Phyllis Zagano

Does Ignatian spirituality admit mysticism? Many discussions about mysticism and the apostolic life separate the two, as if mysticism is solely the passive and privatized experience of God, while the apostolic life involves only activity in the world, even as it is Christ-centered. So the two broad categories of contemplative and active, easily represented by the Mary and Martha of scripture, seem at odds both in life and in prayer.

Such a view disconnects the paths in the ways of holiness, restricts mystic experience, and supports a false dichotomy between two types of prayer, broadly categorized as passive-contemplative and active-imaginative prayer. The wall built between these two broad categories divides but does not separate the activities of prayer. Neither is the divide helpful in creating the interior recognition that a mature prayer life involves many activities, some more recognizably receptive or contemplative and some more recognizably active, each type within the general categories of adoration, petition, contrition, and thanksgiving. Within these, even as one or another might be deemed contemplative or active, are understandings of the *apophatic* (negative) and *kataphatic* (positive) ways of understanding God, with the *apophatic* view that God is ultimately unknowable, while the *kataphatic* view focuses on how and on the fact that God can be known. These two views are not as contradictory as they might seem. As in all things, balance is necessary to support the spiritual life.

Can the follower of Ignatian spirituality be called a mystic? In this paper, I examine particular concepts of mysticism and the spiritual life in light of Ignatian practice. The discussion shows how Ignatius's recommendations for specific prayer exercises and his various rules present a broad base upon which the individual can rest a mystic involvement that leads to an active and engaged apostolic life. Specifically, I present a description of the *Spiritual Exercises* as they unfold within the retreat setting and as they then extend to daily life, and demonstrate how the balance between and among various modes of prayer supports the development of both a mature interior life of prayer and a mature spirituality of action. In sum, I argue that the Ignatian mystic lives a mysticism of service, in which the experience of God propels mission, service, and prayer.

Ignatius and the Spiritual Exercises

Some find that the spirituality of Ignatius of Loyola, the Basque founder of the Society of Jesus, the Jesuits, cannot fit into any category of mysticism or mystic experience.[1] Such considerations depend on an enclosed view of contemplative prayer and a definition of mysticism that relegates it only to its interior manifestations and denies the value of positive emotive reactions to prayerful experience. Yet it is in Ignatian spirituality that the concepts of contemplative mysticism and active responses inside and outside of prayer are joined: the interior "mystical" life of prayer feeds and directs the exterior "apostolic life" of action in the world, which in turn redirects the individual to prayer. Hence the term "contemplative in action" for the individual living what is known as Ignatian spirituality and what is more truly understood as Ignatian mysticism.

So much has been written about Íñigo López de Loyola (1491–1556) since his founding the Jesuits in 1540,[2] that even the briefest history of his life seems redundant. Even so, reminders of some milestones can help refresh the picture of him. Thirteenth child and youngest son of minor Spanish nobility, Ignatius was seriously wounded at the Battle of Pamplona in 1521. His recovery in his family castle found him with little to read or think about, and he considered the vanities of his life and their implications during his recovery. Especially taken by a *Life of Christ* and by a book of lives of the saints, which reinforced his relatively neglected religious upbringing and practice, Ignatius found that his daydreams of battle glory quickly evaporated, while those of doing something else stayed on. Soon he wondered: What if he were to do what St. Francis did, or St. Dominic? Once healed of his wounds, yet still with a persistent limp, he experienced visions—of Mary the Mother of Jesus, and of the Trinity—that set him further on a path of self-discovery, first to Manresa, where he prayed for hours on end, then to the Holy Land, then to studies in Alcalá and Paris, where he gathered companions and formed the Society of Jesus. His additional visions—of creation, the Eucharist, and the humanity of Jesus—propelled both his interior life and his active ministries. Before his death in 1556, both his *Spiritual Exercises* and the Jesuit Constitutions had received papal approval.

The *Exercises* are most often described as a book of instructions for the retreat director who, over a period of thirty days more or less, guides the individual retreatant through four "weeks" of exercises. The four parts of the *Exercises* may be broadly termed as intended, first, to bring the retreatant to an understanding of self as created and redeemed; second, to move the retreatant to choose a positive means of following Christ; third, to realize the cost of such following; and, fourth, to recognize that calling's ultimate joy.

The purpose Ignatius gives for the *Spiritual Exercises* is "the conquest of self and the regulation of one's life in such a way that no decision is made under the influence of any inordinate attachment" (*Sp. Ex.* 21).[3] The role of decision making in Ignatian spirituality is crucial in understanding the way the Ignatian mystic sees the world and all in it.

The First Principle and Foundation, given to the exercitant in the preparation days before beginning the First Week of the Exercises, presents the underlying theme for the meditations, considerations, and rules that follow and can be seen as a précis of the expected movements of the four weeks. The First Principle and Foundation comprises a series of statements of fact the retreatant is invited to consider that begin: "Man is created to praise, reverence, and serve God our Lord, and by this means to save his soul." The simplicity of the statement belies its depth, for, as a means of learning decision making, the experience of the *Exercises* always refers back to this essential point of reflection deeply and personally for the exercitant: Why do I exist? The further statements in the Principle and Foundation reinforce the fact of God's personal, intimate creation of and relationship with the individual and with all creation, stating that (1) all creation is aimed at assisting the individual in his or her personal end; (2) the individual's use of creation is to be solely for the furtherance of that personal end, and anything that is a "hindrance" must be eliminated; (3) such an attitude requires complete indifference to all created things insofar as the individual is able, and, specifically, "we should not prefer health to sickness, riches to poverty, honor to dishonor, a long life to a short life . . . [and] all other things"; (4) and, finally, "Our one desire and choice should be what is more conducive to the end for which we are created" (*Sp. Ex.* 23).

In following the distinct movements of the heart, such a process, directed both at learning ways of praying and of decision making, can enable the exercitant to carry forth from the experience of the thirty-day retreat tools to live an authentic mysticism of action in the world. In fact, each of the goals—if they can be termed such—of the *Exercises* forms the lynchpin of a developed spirituality and provides means to help the retreatant continue sure-footed on a path he or she chooses freely with continually developing insight and self-understanding gained through regular prayer and introspection.

It is here that conversations about the *kataphatic* (positive) and *apophatic* (negative) modes of prayer come into play as criticisms of Ignatian methodologies. A misconception that Ignatian prayer is restricted to meditative application of intellect, reason, and will to particular Gospel passages leads some to dismiss Ignatian spirituality as a whole, sometimes presenting an argument that John of the Cross picks up where Ignatius leaves off, and that Ignatius's *Exercises* and rules and practices should be abandoned by the mature person of prayer. So follows the contention that the true mystic learns more from John than from Ignatius, and even that Ignatian prayer—as it is poorly characterized—is only for beginners.

Consolation and Desolation

The criticism that Ignatian prayer must be eventually "outgrown" comes from the misunderstanding of Ignatius's descriptions of and understandings of the value of the individual's learning to distinguish interior consolation and desolation in prayer. Crucial to the *Exercises*, and to

Ignatian spirituality, is the interior recognition of what might broadly be called positive (consoling) and negative (desolating) emotions or movements of the heart by the retreatant, or exercitant.

The initial methods of prayer in the *Exercises* include deeply imaginative work. Through a structured series of meditations with what is called "composition of place," Ignatius suggests that the individual notice everything in the scene of a specific Gospel passage: all the sights, sounds, smells, even tastes and physical feelings attendant to placing oneself in the picture. The individual is directed to pay attention to feelings: to joy, sorrow, happiness, fear, excitement, anxiety, calmness, upset, and the entire panoply of human emotion. So the individual may imagine a personal role in the birth of Jesus, as participant or onlooker, and consider as well the feelings such imaginings evoke.

Using the many Gospel passages from which the director is free to choose as the retreat continues, the exercitant refines understandings of the concepts of consolation and desolation within prayer, broadly understood as positive or negative emotions but eventually refined to be understood as indications of what is from God and what is not from God. That there are three possibilities for intuition is key to Ignatian discernment: suggestions are either from the self, from the Creator and Lord, or from what Ignatius calls the "Enemy of Human Nature," the devil. While many suggestions can at first be sensed as positive, an increasingly refined sense of emotional responses eventually allows the mature person of prayer to understand better whether an individual concept, idea, or suggestion for action fills the desires of God, or of evil, or of the narcissistic self from which all persons must escape.[4]

The discernment of spirits can at first be a confusing concept, because both good and evil spirits, the desires of God and the desires of the Enemy of Human Nature, can have similar, if not the same, effects. That is, an interior prayer, or a discerned concept for action, can bring joy, happiness, excitement, and calmness, yet still not be the effect of God's desire for the soul, but rather a trap of evil or of the narcissistic self.

Ignatius explains the confusion, depending on the state of the individual soul, as follows. Persons accustomed to moving from one bad action to another will not have any sensitivity to an objectively negative action; in fact, "the enemy is ordinarily accustomed to propose apparent pleasures," and "fills their imagination with sensual delights and gratifications, the more readily to keep them in their vices." Here, Ignatius teaches, the good spirit provides the remorse of conscience to meet the challenges of the evil one (*Sp. Ex.* 314).

Alternatively, the person striving to eliminate negative actions in life faces an evil spirit that will "harass with anxiety" and raise "obstacles backed by fallacious reasonings" to prevent the soul from choosing God's path. In this case, the good spirit brings positive emotions, consolations, even inspirations and tears to support genuinely forward momentum (*Sp. Ex.* 315). So Ignatius defines the effects of consolation and desolation, and he writes even more specifically about these in the following paragraphs of the *Spiritual Exercises*. Spiritual consolation, Ignatius says, brings a feeling of love for God, so much so that the individual loves all creation in God to the point of tears emanating from that love. The tears may be sorrow for action or for the sufferings of Christ or for any other positive reason. Ignatius defines consolation as "every increase of faith, hope and love, and all interior joy that invites and attracts to what is heavenly and to the salvation of one's soul by filling it with peace and quiet in its Creator and Lord" (*Sp. Ex.* 316).

Spiritual desolation, on the other hand, is the opposite. Desolation, for Ignatius, is marked by "darkness of soul, turmoil of spirit, inclination to what is low and earthly, restlessness rising from many disturbances and temptations which lead to want of faith, want of hope, want of love" (*Sp. Ex.* 317). The distancing from God causes the negative character of thoughts marking spiritual desolation.

Eventually, the individual recognizes an internal "feeling" attached to each of these states or ways of response.

The key, as Ignatius explains in these, the Rules for Discernment appropriate to the First Week of the Spiritual Exercises, is in managing the interior life and one's choices so that no decision is taken within times of desolation, specifically because it is in times of desolation that the evil one can more easily guide the soul. Patience here becomes the guiding virtue, where the individual trusts that the desolating feelings will pass and whatever consideration brought up by or clouded by them can be completed in times of peace and calm.

Here also, Ignatius carefully explains that there are three ways in which the individual can fall into desolation: (1) due to inattention to the regular practice of prayer; (2) due to God's loving invitation to trials;

and (3) due to God's desire to present a deeper self-knowledge, specifically that it is impossible for the individual alone to attain any spiritual consolation. Crucial is the understanding that all is gift, and pride and vainglory can move the individual to believe that consolation is both due to his own action and within his own power.

So arises again the problem of prayer. The misconception regarding Ignatian prayer is that it depends solely on consolations, and on possibly self-generated good feelings that confirm fanciful ideas of the mystical life. Such evidences the very narcissistic traps Ignatius strove to avoid and too broadly characterizes *kataphatic* (positive) prayer as a way to understand God through what God is, perhaps implying that God is first of all known by positive feelings in prayer. When *kataphatic* prayer is mischaracterized in this fashion, it is understandable that some contemplative followers of the ways of John of the Cross would deny the value and even efficacy of Ignatian prayer. Properly understood, however, Ignatius and John are not totally opposed one to another. As Paul Bernadicou, building on Lucien Roy, wrote some years ago, the distinctions between the outlooks of Ignatius and John are not that great when considered in the context of their complete writings. Roy's five distinctions are educative: (1) for Ignatius God is in his gifts, while for John God is other than gifts; (2) Ignatius values consolations, while John does not and warns they must be rejected; (3) Ignatius encourages individuals to look for consolations, while John considers such pursuits foolish; (4) Ignatius finds that patterns of consolations support proper decision making, while John finds them a means to lead one astray; and (5) Ignatius says certain kinds of higher consolations support the notion that they are God's enlightenment, while John opposes determinations made with feelings or interior illuminations. Roy points out, however, that Ignatius and John agree that consolations are *only* means to the goal, which is God and an understanding of God's desires for the individual. Even so, it is clear that the positive appreciation of consolation can also be a step backwards along the spiritual path, where the consolation, not God's desire for the soul, becomes the object sought after and the trap for the person seriously engaged in prayer.[5]

Where intimacy with God is understood as the goal, however, the approaches of Ignatius and John are not contradictory but rather build one upon the other even to the point of complementarity. John's warnings are against spiritual narcissism, whereas Ignatius's teachings are against personal narcissism. Each warning encourages the individual to break from self. The enclosed, comfortable, and essentially undisturbed "contemplative" prayer against which John warns is the comforting self-reflection of narcissistic desires; the exciting yet unreflective and self-directed "action" that Ignatius warns of can come from the same narcissistic roots. Where the one creates false interior solace and reinforces spiritual narcissism, the other engenders similar good feelings but, lacking genuine discernment of God's desires for the individual or the world, focuses on the individual rather than on God. Each can be replete with consolations, but false ones.

Ignatian Discernment

A key to the active imaginative prayer in the *Exercises* is the Colloquy, the deeply personal imaginative conversation with Jesus introduced in the First Week. The first of these presents Jesus on the cross, and the retreatant is invited to imagine speaking to the bloodied, disfigured, tortured man-God and to imagine his sweat and smell. The initial questions tend to stay with the exercitant as the days unfold: "What have I done for Christ? What am I doing for Christ? What ought I do for Christ?" (*Sp. Ex.* 53). In ensuing exercises, the individual is invited to converse with Jesus, and with Mary his mother, and with God, essentially using the instructions regarding the Colloquy from this first exercise: "Speaking exactly as one friend speaks to another, or as a servant speaks to a master, now asking him for a favor, now blaming himself for some misdeed, now making known his affairs to him, and seeking advice in them" (*Sp. Ex.* 54).

The Colloquy serves as a review and reinforcement of each prayer period, as the exercitant essentially takes the insights gained and brings them to conversation first with Jesus, then with Mary, and finally with God. Each conversation sheds light on the points developed and prepares the retreatant to better follow Ignatian practices after the close of the retreat.

The insights gained through the understandings of feelings of consolation and desolation, including insights gained through colloquies, carry over to everyday determinations through the discernment of spirits. Within the complex of Ignatian practice is the daily or twice-daily Examen of Conscience, or Examen of Consciousness,[6] whereby the individual quickly and with gratitude reviews the day's activities. Here, there is a clear distinction in the *Exercises* between the searching for sin in the day's activities and the review of God's care for the individual and the individual's grateful response (or nonresponse).

The Examen typically follows these steps: (1) first placing oneself in God's presence and care; (2) next briefly and gratefully reviewing the gifts of the day (or part of the day); (3) then asking for guidance of the Spirit in understanding personal responses and emotions; (4) then reviewing the entire day (or part of the day), focusing on one or a few specific instances; and, finally, (5) asking for guidance in a deeply personal conversation with the Lord. Some teachers reverse the second and fourth steps somewhat, and in fact they are interchangeable depending on the ways the person has developed his or her relationship with a personal Jesus over the years. The point is to place one's strengths and God's gifts before the Lord in gratitude and to examine personal response in God's light and in view of individual and personal purpose, one's end.

The Ignatian Examen is in no way a passive exercise, even as it may include a deeply contemplative understanding of self and of God's desires. The Examen does not eliminate the reality of the Jesus of the Gospels with whom the individual has presumably developed an intense and intimate relationship through dedication to active imaginative prayer as it has suited the occasion. In fact, it is the crucified Jesus who in history and in the life of the world is constantly before the Ignatian mystic.

How does this relate to mysticism? The hypothesis of this article is that Ignatian mysticism is a mysticism of action, born of deep personal experience of God as Creator and Lord, through the development and maintenance of an intimate relationship with Jesus Christ. Therefore, an understanding of the movements of the heart within prayer—an understanding of consolation and desolation—leads to an understanding of the movements of the heart in life, in the activities of life as they are examined once or twice daily in the Examen.

These understandings and practices, which lead to a personal "election" or decision regarding the individual's life within the enclosed *Exercises*, are then carried forward to daily discernment of activities in service of the church and of the world. Here, as Michael Buckley writes, the individual's interior understandings and external choices lead to the deeply personal realization of both the personal and the ecclesial "struggle for human salvation" and to both personal and ecclesial understandings of each individual's "radical nature as the beloved of Christ."[7] Every personal choice balances private discernment—of the needs and struggles of the whole church (the people of God) in concert with the authority of the church—with the individual's strengths and abilities. Such, as Brian O'Leary points out, is the tension Ignatius accepted and determined to live with.[8] Such is the tension the Ignatian mystic embraces.

Daily discernment follows the patterns established in the *Exercises* flowing from the Meditation on Two Standards, that of Satan and that of Christ (*Sp. Ex.* 136–147), whereby within the retreat context the exercitant places himself or herself within imaginative scenes, the one before the standard, or flag, of Satan, the other before the standard of Christ. The military phraseology, perhaps better suited to Ignatius's baroque era, serves to distinguish the matter of life choice in general, and, as the meditation is reflected upon and recalled in times of discernment, it helps distinguish the smaller choices of daily life. The meditation, coming as it does during the Second Week, establishes the strong dichotomy of choice that marks Ignatian mysticism: one is either choosing the positive, life-giving, and fulfilling way of following Christ, or one is not. As such, this meditation presages the pinnacle of the *Exercises* and the crux of each individual's personal discernment: the desire to be with Jesus in all, even insults and derision, or not.

To solidify the understanding of the choice to follow the standard of Christ, and to delineate its invitation and its consequences, Ignatius presents the considerations on Three Classes of Men (*Sp. Ex.* 149–157), which lead into additional meditations on Gospel scenes of the life of Jesus. Another, more general reflection in the Second Week is that on the Three Kinds of Humility. Each comes before and essentially leads toward the Making a Choice of a Way of Life, which in and of itself is eventually mirrored within daily personal discernment.

The Three Classes of Men is a consideration of the ways in which individuals deal with daily decisions and provides a methodology for deepening the determination to follow the standard of Christ. The three classes comprise the first, whose members would like to be free of restraining attachments but put off definitive action to an undefined future; the second, whose members would like to free themselves of these attachments but in such a way as to retain control over them; and the third, whose members are graced with true indifference and who contentedly keep or relinquish these attachments depending on God's personal desire for them within their own lives.

The considerations of the Three Kinds of Humility serve to deepen the understanding of the choice to stand with Christ in all decision making, and describe the three kinds as, first, the individual who determines not to commit any sort of serious, or mortal, sin; second, the individual who accepts and lives a perfect indifference (as in the Three Classes of Men) and will under no circumstances commit any sort of less serious, or venial, sin; and third, the individual who, with perfect humility, identifies totally with Christ in all choices, even to the point of being poor, insulted, and "accounted as worthless and a fool for Christ, rather than to be esteemed as wise and prudent in this world" (*Sp. Ex.* 167). The third kind of humility circles back to the third class of persons, which comprises individuals for whom the sole choice is the greater glory of God in Christ Jesus and delimits the consequences of such a choice.

Clearly, in the context of the long retreat, as well as in the context of the shorter, yet traditional eight-day retreat, the director, following the lead of the Spirit at work in the retreatant, will suggest more or less concentration on these considerations in the Second Week. The Meditation on Two Standards and the materials in the Three Classes of Men and Three Kinds of Humility are important and applicable, if not exactly during the retreat, certainly later, as the exercitant carries the fruits of the retreat into daily life.

These two considerations—and within the long retreat they are truly more considerations than meditations—come before the Introduction to Making a Choice in Life (*Sp. Ex.* 169), but within the context of the Second Week's exercises on Jesus's public life. With more or less emphasis in the context of the retreat, the considerations and ways of making choices form the heart of Ignatian spirituality as a mysticism of action. They serve as a continual backdrop to the reflective questions on choices in life, either as the choice of a permanent state in life or as an independent daily choice within that larger context, and often help in recognizing the temptations against proper choosing given in the further Rules for the Discernment of Spirits, which are more commonly presented in the Second Week of the Exercises (*Sp. Ex.* 328–336). These rules state that only God can bring true consolation, and especially without any previous cause, and that "both the good angel and the evil spirit can give consolation to a soul, but for a quite different purpose" (*Sp. Ex.* 331). Here Ignatius teaches that the onset, experience, and aftermath of consolation must be carefully observed, and especially the trajectory of thoughts leading up to an apparently "good" decision or choice. Ignatius is quite specific, warning that once the "enemy of our human nature" has been detected, the entire course of thoughts must be reviewed. Quite simply, persons often make bad decisions in haste, because, in colloquial terms, it seemed like a good idea at the time.

The repetitive, even overlapping, nature of the *Exercises* and their constant reinforcement of themes—always aimed at recognition and affirmation of the end for which the person is created—again come into play as the foundation for decision making. The end for which the person is created: "For the praise of God our Lord and for the salvation of [one's] soul" (*Sp. Ex.* 169) determines the means to be used, no matter whether the choice is a permanent vocational choice or, later, one or more discrete choices within the context of that greater choice. The key to choosing, building on the rules for discernment within prayer and on the daily repetition of the Examen, is in recognizing how and when a correct choice can be made.

Ignatius initially lists three times of choosing: first, when the will is so attracted to the choice that it accepts it without hesitation; second, when the evaluation of consolations and desolations and "discernment of diverse spirits" sheds light on the matter; and, third, in what Ignatius calls a "time of tranquillity," when the soul is peaceful. Within this third "time," Ignatius points to two ways of making a correct choice: in the long retreat on the manner of a way of life if such is appropriate and possible, but also within daily life on various matters that arise (*Sp. Ex.* 175–178).

The six points regarding the first way of choosing are (1) to think of the matter; (2) to keep one's end in mind; (3) to ask the Lord to show what would better serve his glory; (4) to balance the advantages and benefits, the disadvantages and dangers of the choice at hand; (5) to consider what seems most reasonable; and (6) to offer the choice in prayer, asking that God accept it as meeting his service and desires (*Sp. Ex.* 179–183).

There are four rules regarding choosing in this third "time": (1) that the greater or lesser attachment to the object of consideration is only for the love of God; (2) that the determination matches the advice the individual would give a total stranger on the matter; (3) that the choice would be the same at the moment of death; and (4) that the choice is what one would like to have made when presented at the last judgment. Finally, the choice is offered to the Lord, as in the First Way of choosing, "that the Divine Majesty may deign to accept and confirm it if it is for His greater service and praise" (*Sp. Ex.* 184–188, 183).

As with all things, the confirmation depends on offering the choice to God in a time of personal peace—Ignatius warns against making a decision in a time of desolation—and the various tools for discernment learned throughout the retreat can be brought to bear both inside the retreat and in daily life. It is worth repeating here that the standard all determinations are measured against is God's personal desire for the individual to freely and fully live his or her end or reason for being.

Applications of the Exercises

The movement of the *Spiritual Exercises* brings the retreatant next to the passion and death of Jesus, and it is here that the matter and manner of choice play out both in the presentation of the various scenes of accusation, judgment, torture, denial, and eventual death and burial of Jesus Christ. The exercitant's own life story plays behind (and sometimes within) the meditations on the appointed Gospel passages such that each point in each meditation becomes a point of personal discernment: Will his or her choice match the choice of Jesus? If so, will his or her choice result in the cruelty Jesus experiences, interiorly or exteriorly? Can the exercitant choose, repeatedly, to suffer (really or metaphorically) the fate of Jesus?

On approaching the meditations on the passion, the retreatant is directed to ask for "sorrow, compassion, and shame because the Lord is going to his suffering for [his or her] sins" (*Sp. Ex.* 193). Such can evince a powerful emotional reaction, as Jesus's story unfolds in the mind's eye and the retreatant is directed to "grieve, be sad, and weep" (*Sp. Ex.* 195) in the consideration of Christ's suffering—and his desire to suffer—such that it reflects back on the call of Christ the King (as opposed to the call of the Enemy of Human Nature) and Jesus's invitation of *laborare mecum*—to labor with him—in all. The overriding directive of the Third Week is to join Christ in sorrow, anguish, tears and deep grief because of what Christ suffers—in the present tense—for the individual personally (*Sp. Ex.* 203). Ignatius was suspicious of his own experience of tears when they accompanied deep consolation, and he wrote that the "gift of tears" ought not be asked for. However, he also wrote (to Francis Borgia) of three kinds of tears: those arising from thoughts of personal sin or that of others; those arising from contemplating the life of Christ; and those arising from the love of the divine persons.[9] So the directive to ask for tears in the Third Week when asking to join Christ in his own sorrow comfortably fits into the Ignatian patterns of prayer.

Following several days of working through the events of the passion, many directors then invite the exercitant to spend an entire day of repetition of the passion. The exercise combines with consideration of the fact of Jesus's death, as well as with the deep sorrow and weariness of Mary and of the disciples (*Sp. Ex.* 208, Seventh Day). At this point, the depth of confusion at the results of the actions of forces opposing Jesus and his message becomes evident and, although the exercitant is well aware of the coming resurrection, he or she has no guarantee of it in this particular retreat. The psychology of this part of the *Exercises* is clear: one moves from confusion to insight, and the insight here gained is a deepening of the challenges of the chaos of sin and evil to staying the course as a follower of Jesus.

Outside the retreat setting, the profound memory of the passion and of the emotional response it evokes when fully entered into is carried over to the daily life of the Ignatian mystic, who increasingly and repeatedly sees the anger of the Enemy of Human Nature as it is played out in so many ways in private and public spheres. The issues of the day, the damages done to innocent humanity, to the environment, and to personal freedoms are mirrored by personal injustices, insults, and abuses where they are suffered for cause.

Here the practice of discernment is key: individuals may suffer injustices, insults, and abuses for many reasons, all ultimately the result of evil. But the task of the person discerning with Ignatian methods is to separate those manifestations of negativity caused by positive actions—literally of following Jesus—and those caused randomly. Either can present a false notion within the individual that he or she is the direct target of evil. Whereas such might be true, such might equally be false, and, if false, it will invite the individual into a prideful stance that eventually, if not immediately, becomes harmful and quite negative.

Therefore, the Fourth Week of the *Spiritual Exercises* is necessarily short, and the grace the exercitant asks for is to "rejoice intensely because of the great joy and the Glory of Christ the Lord" (*Sp. Ex.* 221). The better formulation might be "rejoice profoundly." The retreatant is initially invited to consider a scene not recorded in Gospel accounts: that Jesus appears first to his mother, Mary. In whatever way the exercitant imagines this scene—whether within the house of Mary, or in her garden, or in some other place—the point of the meditation is to demonstrate in the mind's eye that the resurrection brings Jesus fully human and fully divine now displaying his glory and divinity first to his mother, she whom all natural understanding would say he loved most. Jesus's role here, again first to his mother, is as consoler. The exercitant is asked to notice how he consoles his mother, who has, after all, lost her son.

This first apparition of Jesus as consoler can help assuage the grief the exercitant feels and felt most deeply while meditating on Christ's passion; in daily life the recollection of Jesus as consoler can serve to assuage grief during the individual's life as a passionate follower of Jesus. Following the close of the retreat, recollection of such consolation, either intellectually or viscerally or both, can bring deep relief during times of trial related to the mission, the activity of the Ignatian mystic.

Various Gospel narratives of the resurrection used in the Fourth Week can deepen the graced understandings of the final accounts of Jesus in scripture. In the closing days of the retreat, the retreatant is invited "to strive to feel joy and happiness at the great joy and happiness of Christ" (*Sp. Ex.* 229) on awakening. That practice, carried into daily life, will bring with it a personal determination to face the day's challenges with a deep and confirmed understanding of the resurrection as a historical fact and as a present reality and deep gratitude for the gifts of life.

The final part of the *Spiritual Exercises* consists of the Contemplation to Attain the Love of God, which has as its basis the point that the lover always seeks to share gifts with the beloved. The retreatant is directed to ask for "an intimate knowledge of the many blessings received" (*Sp. Ex.* 223)—in creation and redemption, and personal gifts and graces, all of which the individual is moved to return gratefully to God. Here Ignatius's prayer known as the *Suscipe* sums up the energies the retreatant will take to the world:

> Take, Lord, and receive all my liberty, my memory, my understanding, and my entire will, all that I have and possess. Thou hast given all to me. To Thee, O Lord, I return it. All is Thine, dispose of it wholly according to thy will. Give me thy love and Thy grace, for this is sufficient for me.

Ignatian Mysticism in the World

While the schema of the retreat is enclosed, it gradually and increasingly becomes obvious that its exercises, reflections, tools, and experiences are meant to be carried to the world as the exercitant reenters daily life. One of the earliest considerations given as the prelude to the long retreat, the First Principle and Foundation, carries throughout as a background theme and now becomes a measure of daily activity. Its points, having been repeated over the course of thirty (or, less intensely, eight) days, echo the structure of the meditations as a whole and of the Examen in particular. That the individual is created to praise and serve God; that all created things can assist in that goal and are discarded if they do not; that indifference allows free action and choice; and that the only choice should be what is in concert with the individual's Christ-centered end is the measure of the mysticism of action now enlivened and deepened by the experience of the *Exercises*.

The individual who has experienced the *Spiritual Exercises* in any of their many modes, either as a thirty-day or an eight-day enclosed retreat, or through what is called the Nineteenth Annotation over as many as thirty-two weeks, can find his or her outlook so shaped that that configuration to Christ is his or her only option. What does this imply, both for interior prayer and external action?[10] That choosing freely to live as a disciple of Christ is both possible and probable given the graces of the *Exercises*.

Returning to the implicit criticisms of John of the Cross regarding Ignatian prayer, it is easy to see where Ignatian practice can be misconstrued insofar as it is so obviously directed at discernment and decision making. John clearly states that interior consolation is not something to be sought. Yet Ignatius's warnings mirror those of John in that Ignatius directly states that interior consolation might not always signal a proper course of action. So their basic advice is nearly equal, except that John is speaking of an interior life of prayer, where Ignatius is speaking not only of that life but also of the life of action.

Ignatius does, in fact, deal with what John would call true mystical experience, specifically in the case of deep consolation without prior cause mentioned earlier, the unsought and unexpected deep and undeniable recognition of a truth or of the presence of God. Ignatius clearly warns that thoughts in such a time of deep consolation without prior cause must be carefully distinguished from those that follow. This is not exactly the same as John's suggestion that all desire, even the desire for the knowledge of God, be given up in prayer. Ignatius's warning, however, supports such an attitude if the considerations of the ways consolations can come to the individual—from the self, from God, and from evil—are kept in mind. For Ignatius, consolations without prior cause are determined by the will of God, and, while it is characteristic of God to bring true happiness and spiritual joy to the individual, it is equally real that the evil one will "propose fallacious reasonings, subtleties, and continual deceptions" against God's desire for the individual in their aftermath (*Sp. Ex.* 329–330, 336).

More finely, as Ignatius explains in the further Rules for Discernment that he places as appropriate for the Second Week of the *Spiritual Exercises*, both good and evil can cause consolation, each for its own opposite purposes. In fact, he writes it is "the mark of the evil spirit to assume the appearance of an angel of light," only to lead the individual deeper and deeper into what eventually becomes a bad (and by that time inevitable) smaller or even larger choice. So, where appropriate, the individual within retreat is instructed to review carefully the entire course of thought, noting at what point the turn to the subject and away from Christ took place when the end of the trajectory of thought clearly weakens resolve or peace. The rule here given supports the reason for the Examen as a daily or twice-daily practice to be carried beyond the retreat, since bad choices have a way of multiplying their interior reasons until their ultimate negative nature cannot be easily felt or understood (*Sp. Ex.* 332–334). The Ignatian mysticism of action always requires freedom, and sometimes that freedom is constrained by false reasons.

As Ignatius points out in these further rules, the action of what he called the "good angel" is delicate, absorbed easily by the soul like a drop of water on a sponge in the individual striving to live positively, whereas the action of the evil spirit is quite the opposite, resounding like a splash of water upon a rock. The action of these spirits is quite the reverse, where the individual, already caught in a web of negativity, is in the process of going from bad to worse. Here the action of the evil spirit is quiet, while the action of the good angel is noisy and counterintuitive. In daily life, the two can be termed ways of "nagging." In the calm soul striving to live in God's care, the evil spirit will present thoughts that "nag" and disrupt peace; in the damaged soul living negatively, it is the good angel that is disruptive (*Sp. Ex.* 335).

Again, in carrying the *Spiritual Exercises* to a life of active involvement and engagement with the world, Ignatius's advice does not counter the warnings of John of the Cross. In considering consolation without previous cause, Ignatius teaches that the moment of consolation must be carefully distinguished from the time following, because the enthusiasm of immediate response may not be from God, but rather from the self or even from the good or evil spirit. In any event, the responses must be carefully discerned separate from the incidences of consolation (*Sp. Ex.* 366).

Conclusions

Though I have not here examined the contemplative prayer of the Ignatian mystic, it is fair to recognize that, within a lifetime of prayer, many, if not most, individuals are invited into a prayer more easily understood as a prayer of quiet, or even of union, that may or may not bring with it the consolations Ignatius describes and of which John warns. Of course, those who pray truly contemplatively are always at risk for deep desert experiences. While the *Spiritual Exercises* themselves do not deal with the specifics of Dark Night as explicated by John of the Cross, they do teach means of dealing with it as it arises. In fact, Ignatius's teachings, especially regarding decision making in times of desolation, well serve the individual whose prayer and life have moved into the type of darkness and desolation John describes.

Even so, in essential methodology and ways of understanding God, Ignatius and John process the interior life in distinct ways. While the *Spiritual Exercises* move through the purgative and illuminative stages and aim at unitive experiences (all clearly defined in John), the relatively short and enclosed experience of the *Spiritual Exercises*, particularly in the long retreat, are best undertaken when the individual is living in relative quiescence. Thereby, any addressing of Dark Night experiences would be done retrospectively, as the *Spiritual Exercises* take place outside the normal stream of life.

John of the Cross describes and seeks to comfort and guide those who experience the Dark Night, but Ignatius's methodology can and does apply to the extended experiences of the Dark Night as they arise in life and, less directly, within retreat.[11] The Dark Night (first, of the soul), initially marked by an inability to practice discursive meditation combined with a lack of emotional satisfaction from the spiritual journey even as a deep commitment to Christ is maintained, is a confusing and distressing time into which any person dedicated to a life of prayer can be plunged.[12] The deepening of this Dark Night to what is known as the Dark Night of the Spirit, described in John of the Cross's *The Dark Night,* Book II, includes, most obviously, as Kieran Kavanaugh and Otilio Rodriguez point out, "Darkness and affliction . . . that stem from the divine–human conflict (Chaps. 5–6); the remembrance of past prosperity with a hopeless feeling about the present situation (Chap. 7); and the powerlessness of the soul's faculties, unprepared to receive the divine object."[13]

The Ignatian mystic can well enter these stages in the spiritual journey and continue to live a life of prayer without refreshment or even conscious engagement with God. But the Ignatian mystic invited to this portion of the interior life and unable to engage in active-imaginative prayer has tools to engage and be engaged with God's light in darkness. The Ignatian mystic will move quietly and confidently to a passive-contemplative prayer, unafraid of the "dark," knowing full well that the darkness can be the result of too much interior light. So long as a positive apostolic life is maintained, the Ignatian mystic can be assured that God is present even in apparent absence, even without the consoling feelings and understandings of earlier prayer. In fact, Ignatius teaches that times of consolation must be recalled when times of desolation arrive. While times of desolation in prayer cannot be equated with the Dark Night—the entire construct of the Dark Night includes desolation but goes far beyond it in terms of God's absence—Ignatius's instructions are helpful, particularly his warnings about decision making in times of desolation.

The prayer of the contemplative mystic, characterized by John of the Cross, and the prayer of the mystic of service, characterized by Ignatius of Loyola, in the end can be seen as mirroring each other in outlook and effect. There are times within the Ignatian retreat when the individual may be invited to contemplative prayer, even the "dark" prayer of unknowing that strips away all activity and knowledge and shines such a bright light that the individual is interiorly blinded. What the individual "knows" at this time is that there is nothing that can be known about God. Such would be true *apophatic* prayer. But the Ignatian mystic of service continues to live in the world and continues to evaluate choices, to make decisions, to seek a life in consonance with God's personal creation of him or her. Such a life brings God deeply into prayer, and the apparent knowledge of what God is in the *kataphatic* modes of prayer propels free action.

The wall between the two broad categories of prayer is helpful in categorization but not helpful in living the spiritual life. The mystic of whatever description—contemplative or active— needs to use whatever he or she can to maintain commitment to overall choice and the daily supportive choices that grow from the knowledge of who God is and how God comes deeply and personally into daily life. There is in the mature life of prayer both the *kataphatic,* or positive, and the *apophatic*, or negative, ways of understanding God. It is the balance that supports the mystic's spiritual life, in the case of the Ignatian mystic, a mature spirituality of service marked by the freedom of indifference and the joy of the resurrection.

Notes

1. The theme is well examined by Harvey D. Egan, who contends that "Ignatius was an incomparable mystic whose mystical and apostolic gifts are

really two sides of the same coin," and that Ignatius's mysticism caused his apostolic intensity (*Ignatius Loyola the Mystic*, Way of the Christian Mystics 5 [Wilmington, DE: Michael Glazier, 1987], 19). As Evelyn Underhill points out, "The concrete nature of Ignatius' work, and especially its later developments, has blinded historians to the fact that he was a true mystic" (*Mysticism: The Nature and Development of Spiritual Consciousness* [1900; repr., Oxford: Oneworld, 1993], 468). This paper follows that theme, arguing that following Ignatius's methodology and fully accepting his premises cannot help but encourage the mystic life of action in any prayerful person.

2. The first seven gathered in 1534. "The Formula of the Institute of the Society of Jesus" was approved by Pope Paul III in 1540, and again by Pope Julius III in 1550.

3. Louis J. Puhl, *The Spiritual Exercises of St. Ignatius* (Chicago: Loyola University Press, 1951), 11.

4. Evidence of Ignatius's own escape from narcissism, which becomes increasingly obvious as a theme in the *Spiritual Exercises*, is evaluated in David A. Salomon, "Forging a New Identity: Narcissism and Imagination in the Mysticism of Ignatius Loyola," *Christianity and Literature* 47, no. 2 (Winter 1998): 195–212. William W. Meissner, a Jesuit and psychiatrist, develops Ignatius's narcissistic issues and their resolutions in greater detail in *Ignatius of Loyola: The Psychology of a Saint* (New Haven: Yale University Press, 1994). Meissner plainly states, "All of Ignatius' spiritual experiences, including his mystical states, may or may not have been induced by divine influence. Ignatius devised his rules in order to make this determination" (p. 149).

5. Paul J. Bernadicou, "What Role Does Consolation Play in the Spiritual Life?" *Science et esprit* 49, no. 2 (1997): 187–92; Lucien Roy, "Faut-il chercher la consolation dans la vie spirituelle?" *Sciences ecclésiastiques* 9 (1956): 109–70.

6. The Examen is not a review of the day's mistakes, as in an examination of conscience prior to confession, but a graced grateful look at where and how God's gifts were accepted. The term "Consciousness Examen" came into popular use in the mid-1970s. See George A. Aschenbrenner, "Consciousness Examen," *Review for Religious* 31 (1972): 14-21; reprinted in *Notes on the Spiritual Exercises of St. Ignatius of Loyola*, ed. David L. Fleming (St. Louis, MO: Review for Religious, 1983), 175–85.

7. Michael J. Buckley, "Ecclesial Mysticism in the *Spiritual Exercises* of Ignatius," *Theological Studies* 56 (1995): 441–63.

8. Brian O'Leary, "The Mysticism of Ignatius of Loyola," *Review of Ignatian Spirituality*, no. 116, 38, no. 3 (2007): 77–97.

9. Meissner, *Ignatius of Loyola*, 294.

10. See, e.g., Joseph A. Tetlow, *Choosing Christ in the World: A Handbook for Directing the Spiritual Exercises of St. Ignatius Loyola according to Annotations Eighteen and Nineteen* (St. Louis, MO: Institute of Jesuit Sources, 1999).

11. Darkness arises in at least two specific places in the long retreat: in the First Week and in the Third Week. The genuine experiences of darkness are retroactive, however, insofar as they relate to the retreatant's history, even as they are quite real within the retreat. William Connolly advises the director not to interfere at these points in the retreat ("Experience of Darkness in Directed Retreats," *Review for Religious* 33 [1974]: 609–15; reprinted in Fleming, *Notes on the Spiritual Exercises*, 108–14).

12. John does not use the exact terms "dark night of the soul" or "dark night of the spirit," but these have become common parlance. See Kevin Culligan, "Dark Night and Depression," in *Carmelite Prayer: A Tradition for the 21st Century*, ed. Keith J. Egan (New York: Paulist Press, 2004), 119–38.

13. From "The Dark Night," in *The Collected Works of St. John of the Cross*, trans. Kieran Kavanaugh, O.C.D., and Otilio Rodriguez, O.C.D. (Washington, DC: ICS Publications, 1991), 379–80.

6
Teresa of Avila on the Song of Songs

Lawrence S. Cunningham

*Only the touch of the Spirit can inspire a song like this
and only personal experience can unfold its meaning.*
—Saint Bernard of Clairvaux

It was a momentous occasion when the late Pope Paul VI named Saint Catherine of Siena and Saint Teresa of Avila as "Doctors of the Church." In addition to the honorific, Pope John Paul II named St. Thérèse of Lisieux a doctor of the church. Apart from the honorific of "Doctor" was the implicit recognition that these figures had a coherent set of teachings. That recognition further demanded that inquiry into the nature of that teaching (*doctrina*) was not only useful but pertinent. With such a declaration it became obvious that theologians would no longer be allowed to relegate these writers to the sidelines as mere "spiritual writers." They were to be read with more scholarly attention. Such an inquiry meant further that the corpus of writing was necessarily open to investigation. It was also recognized that such an investigation meant recourse to all of the evidence which, in the case of women doctors, meant that it was not expected that there be found systematic treatises but threads of learning woven into diverse genres of writing. In the case of Saint Teresa of Avila, however, we do have some major books on which a full investigation can be based whereas in the latter case of Saint Thérèse of Lisieux, we have one volume compiled from some late autobiographical reflections and some scattered letters and belletristic fragments of poetry and plays. Even apart from the honorific title of "Doctor," Teresa of Avila is generally recognized as a major spiritual writer who lived and wrote

131

at an especially fecund time of Catholic spiritual writing. In the case of Thérèse of Lisieux, however, there was extended discussion in Rome as to whether she had a coherent body of teaching (i.e. a *doctrina*) that would merit her being named a doctor of the church.

Anyone teaching the history of the Christian spiritual tradition in general and the mystical tradition in particular must take into account the writings of Saint Teresa of Avila, even though in a survey course certain choices of what to read must be made. Typically, when I have constructed such courses in the past, my own choice was to put *The Interior Castle*, Teresa's most mature work, on my syllabus. If time afforded, we might also read her autobiography and her earlier treatise *The Way of Perfection*, since that text allows us to see the development of Teresa's mind when she wrote *The Interior Castle*. It is probably most typical of survey courses to omit *The Book of Foundations*, leaving that to the specialists on Carmelite history, and to ignore completely her minor works and her letters. Recently, however, I have been looking at those minor works to study them in relation to the larger writings of the saint. This essay takes up for examination a very short text of seven brief chapters whose original title was *Conceptions of the Love of God upon Certain Words of the "Song of Solomon."*[1] I am fully aware that this is a minor work, and I recognize that even as sympathetic a Teresian scholar as the late E. Allison Peers has judged it as "the weakest of Saint Teresa's works, both in subject-matter and in expression."[2] Though I do not question the judgment of Peers, I find that this is a work not to be neglected.

Pace the judgment of Peers, Teresa's text is of some interest, if only to pay tribute to the saint's willingness to use fragments from the Song as a launching point to instruct her fellow sisters at a time in sixteenth-century Spain when vernacular commentaries on scripture were highly suspect and when commentaries on Sacred Scripture by women were unheard of. After all, it was expected that reflections on scripture were to be done only by those theologically trained (*los letrados*, the "Lettered Ones"). While this text is not exactly a commentary (she uses only two verses as a starting point for her "meditations" [her word] and later refers to only a few more verses of the book), even to choose such a vehicle was daring. As is well known, her confessor urged her to burn the manuscript as something unseemly for a nun to write, and it was only after her death that it saw its way into print. It is also an interesting text in that it fleshes out some insights that Teresa had already discussed in two larger earlier works, namely, her autobiography and *The Way of Perfection*. Further, the text sheds light on *The Interior Castle*. Finally, this minor treatise had at least one careful reader in Saint Thérèse of Lisieux, who not only admired the work but hoped in the future to write her own reflections on the Canticle.[3]

There are no clear markers in the text that allow us to date the work with absolute precision, but some allusions indicate that it was composed in Avila sometime between 1566 and 1572, with the real possibility that Teresa rewrote sections of it during that period. Her Carmelite sisters were her intended audience, and the text even reads as if it were the recording of live conferences. It was most likely written, however, to be circulated to the various communities of the Reform. The chapter divisions and headings are the work not of Teresa herself but of the editor Jerome Gratian (1545–1617), the Carmelite confessor of the saint, when he posthumously published the manuscript in her collected works in 1611. While Teresa herself referred to the text as "meditations" one can also think of the work as a set of instructions directed to her Carmelite sisters on contemplative prayer. The chapters, in short, were like conferences for her sisters, meant probably to be read to them as part of their formation.

The Text and Contents

In her prologue to this work Teresa noted how she loved the words from the Song of Songs even though she barely understood them in Latin (Teresa most likely heard the words of the Song most frequently in their application to Mary in the *Little Office of the Blessed Virgin Mary*), but in the last few years she says that she gained a better comprehension of them so that by explaining them she might bring consolation to her sisters of the Reform. She quite explicitly discusses these words to illuminate the path to prayer. In other words, this text is a form of spiritual guidance for the sisters of her community and not anything designated for general consumption. They were meant to be "in house."

In her opening chapter she admits how difficult it is to unpack the words of scripture for those who lack the learned languages; even when the words are explained or paraphrased in the vernacular difficulties remain. Still, Teresa had a profound respect for the biblical text and understood its riches: "For one word of His will contain within itself a thousand mysteries" (*MSS* 1.2). Thus, she interrogates the phrase "Let him kiss me with the kiss of the mouth" (Song 1:1), which opens the biblical text, concluding that the kiss signifies peace and friendship. In the second chapter she discusses nine erroneous or false kinds of peace, concluding with a paean of praise for the religious life and a stipulation that the peace which is true is that peace desired by the bride in the Canticle.

It is tempting to see those opening chapters as a kind of résumé of the penitential life, in which the aspirant can sort out and avoid those delusory forms of peace that may be a snare for the novice in the spiritual life. It is probably the case that Teresa is too impressionistic a writer to have framed her meditations according to a rigid plan of the penitential, illuminative, and unitive stages, but it is also the case that Teresa does want to insist on fundamental monastic ascesis as a first stage in the life of perfection before that true peace which she describes in the next chapter may be attained. That peace, Teresa says in the opening of chapter 3, is rooted in faith and love where "the soul does not want to benefit by what the intellect teaches it, for this union between the bride and bridegroom has taught it other things the intellect cannot attain to and the soul tramples the intellect underfoot" (*MSS* 3.3). Indeed, the third chapter could be described as an extended meditation on the union of a person's will with the will of God. Teresa insists that doing God's will constructs a wall of resistance to the evils of the world as well as providing the power to do God's service. In this meditation, she holds up the example of Jesus in the garden of Gethsemane, where Jesus submits to the will of God; it is that fusion of wills, human and divine, that permits a person to speak the language of love found in the Song of Songs.

The description of true peace is, of course, the serene tranquility in which the three Augustinian powers of intellect, will, and memory are quieted. That rest was the goal of the spiritual life, as Teresa learned from her readings from the *recogido* teachers (beginning with Francisco de Osuna's *Third Spiritual Alphabet*, which she had read as a young nun, as she tells us in her autobiography), as well as from the good advice she received from her various mentors. That true peace brings her to the prayer of quiet, only then to advance, as she will trace out later, to the prayer of union in its several discriminations. Teresa will refine her understanding of the prayer of quiet in chapter 5 of the *Meditations* in her comment on Song 2:3 when she glosses the phrase "I will delight to sit in his shade." That "shade of divinity" provides what one scholar has called the "Dionysian clincher," making the recipient impervious to all forms of discursive thinking—an authentic form of unknowing.[4]

If the prayer of quiet brings tranquility to the three powers of intellect, will, and memory, thus taming our restless heart and mind, there is yet a further depth of prayer to be attained. In chapter 4, commenting on the text "Your breasts are better than wine and give forth the most sweet fragrance" (Song 1:2–3), Teresa argues that, beyond interior and exterior peace, there is yet a deeper union in God. Inspired by the biblical text, she likens this relationship to that of an infant lovingly nourished at the breast of her mother. She notes that a suckling infant "doesn't understand how it grows nor does it know how it gets its milk, for without its sucking or doing anything often the milk is put into its mouth" (*MSS* 4.4).

Chapters 5–7 can be understood as an extended meditation on the significance of the prayer of union. Teresa describes the gift of the Holy Spirit given in the prayer of union to enkindle the flame of love (chap. 5); the suspension of the faculties through inebriation with that love (chap. 6); and, finally, not only how the prayer of union fortifies those who experience it and suffer for God and neighbor, but also how the grace of union is a gift for the church such that any sister who is granted the prayer of union should not think it to be only for her own self (chap. 7). Interestingly enough, Teresa uses the example of the Samaritan woman in John 4 to make her point. That woman who met Jesus at the well left him there to go into the village to announce his presence to others. One almost senses a Teresian moment here; from the living waters she has the strength to go forth to share her knowledge with those who lacked her knowledge.

How do the teachings on prayer found in this brief work comport with Teresa's more extended comments on the path of prayer found in the more expansive treatments in her larger works? A number of observations are in order.

First, in many other places Teresa is interested in beginning at the beginning, in the sense that she attempts to help the aspirant sister move from the recitation of formulaic prayers and structured meditations to a deeper experience of God. In fact, one could say that moving beyond formal meditation is a critical issue for both Teresa and John of the Cross. The issue can be simply stated: if discursive meditation involves both intellect and acts of the will, does prayer become "better" by thinking more deeply and in a more focused manner? Teresa thinks not. The whole point of Teresian (and, of course, Sanjuanista) spirituality is to go beyond discursive vocal prayers and meditation into the various stages of the prayer of quiet. This is not to say that she eschewed meditation but, rather, that she used it as a launching pad into a deeper union with God.[5]

In her other works, Teresa maps out more fully the "stages" of prayer, but the map is not always described in the same way. In *The Book of Her Life*, using the extended metaphor of water from a well, an aqueduct, a river, and falling rain, Teresa outlines a progressive set of steps moving from reflection to the prayer of quiet, to the "sleep of the faculties," and to what she calls variously union, ecstasy, and raptures. By contrast, in *The Way of Perfection* (much like the schema in her meditations on the Song of Songs) she distinguishes active recollection and the prayer of quiet. Finally, in *The Interior Castle* her map is much more elaborate, since, beginning in the Fourth Mansion of the castle, she describes passive recollection and then the prayer of quiet, while in the final mansions or dwelling places she discriminates the prayer of union, ecstasy, and, finally, spiritual marriage. It is interesting that in that final mansion Teresa alludes only twice to the Song of Songs (*Mansions* VII 3.13 and 4:11), although it is so central to *Brautmystik* ("bridal mysticism").

There is nothing out of order in recalling Teresa's various maps of the spiritual journey, since her goals are not systematic but experiential in intent. That intent is to describe for her sisters how prayer is union with God and how God is revealed in prayer. Her various classifications may well have been drawn from the images she puts to use in fashioning her treatises, so that the various stages of prayer in her autobiography depend on the fecundity of the image of water (in a well, via waterwheels and aqueducts, streams, rivers, and, finally, rain), while her descriptions in the *The Interior Castle* are driven by the architecture of the castle itself. Teresa's map of the prayer life is one in which she says, in effect, that it is "like this" or "like that."

Teresa was less than precise in the way she discussed the stages of prayer in her various works. There is a somewhat amusing aside in *The Interior Castle* that illustrates the point. In a discussion of a kind of rapture she calls "flight of the spirit," Teresa says, "It seems the trough of water we mentioned (I believe it was in the fourth dwelling place, for I don't recall exactly) filled so easily and gently, I mean without any movement."[6] Her translator, in a note, thinks she had in mind not *The Interior Castle* but her water metaphor in *The Way of Perfection*.[7] There is no reference to the water metaphor in the fourth dwelling place, but she does refer to a book she had written fourteen years earlier, which is, of course, *The Way of Perfection*. The point to be made in the last analysis is that her metaphors, *exempla,* and tropes are less important than her clear trajectory in mapping the spiritual journey itself. Teresa herself makes this clear in the epilogue of *The Interior Castle* when she notes that, while she discussed seven mansions in her book, "in each of these there are many others, below and above and to the sides, with lovely gardens and fountains and labyrinths" (*Epilogue* 3).[8]

Some Conclusions

It would be special pleading to argue that Teresa's meditations on the Song of Songs is central to her spiritual doctrine, but it would be false to argue that her text is unworthy of examination. Teresa was the heir of a long spiritual trajectory mediated to her from her Carmelite tradition and amplified by her close acquaintance with learned spiritual guides who brought their insights from Ignatian, Dominican, Franciscan, and Augustinian sources. Her acquaintance with bridal mysticism is patent, as her exposition of the Seventh Mansion of *The Interior Castle* makes clear. That particular reading of the Song of Songs has an ancient spiritual ancestry going back as far as Origen of Alexandria's prologue to his commentary on the biblical book. Like Saint John of the Cross in his prologue to the *Spiritual Canticle*, Teresa understands that the poetic language of the *Song of Songs* has a deep meaning that is so profound that the Holy Spirit reverts to the vocabulary of poetry and poetic expression to make the point.

Teresa's *Meditations on the Song of Songs* must be read, then, not only in terms of its own value as part of her corpus, but as part of that long tradition of spiritual and mystical comment on the Song of Songs itself. It is, in short, part of a longer vision (a *doctrina?*) of what constitutes the mystical path as Teresa both experienced it and mediated it to her Carmelite communities. Her encounters with various verses in the Song of Songs resonated with her experience in such a way that they became a platform by which she could encourage her fellow Carmelites to see if they could discern similar experiences, as she said near the end of her text: "When I began, my intention was simply to explain how you can find comfort when you hear some words from the *Song of Songs* and how, even though they are obscure to your understanding, you can reflect upon the profound mysteries contained in them" (*MSS* 7.9).

Epilogue

These brief reflections were written in 2015 as part of my own study of Teresa of Avila during the year in which we celebrate the five hundedth anniversary of her birth. It was a good time to go back over texts I have taught over the decades and to acquaint myself with those writings of the great saint to which I had paid insufficient attention. It was a happy coincidence that the general editor of this volume asked me to contribute something to honor the memory of the late John Jones, who died all too young. John never edited any of my books, even though Crossroad had published three of my books before John became an editor. I did, however, have many conversations with him and happily consulted with him on various manuscripts that were under review for publication. We would meet usually during the hectic to and fro of the annual meetings of the American Academy of Religion. John had a grace rarely given to the young: wisdom. It was a wisdom that shone forth in his person, not one that was exhibited for admiration. He had a deep and abiding concern for the mystical tradition, both by education and by instinct. His communications with me when he was gravely ill were never alarmist, and my promise of prayers was gracefully received. We were not close, but I considered him a friend. John was a student of Dionysius the Areopagite, contributing some important essays on that enigmatic genius. In his memory and because of our friendship I close with some words from *The Divine Names*: "The sacred theologians [i.e. the psalmists] sing a hymn of praise to the Good for giving friendship and peace to all beings which is why all good things show friendship, inherent harmony, and their descent from the one Life."

Notes

1. That title was given to the work by Jerome Gratian when he compiled Teresa's collected works in 1611. The definitive English translation uses the title *Meditations on the Song of Songs*; see *The Collected Works of St. Teresa of Avila*, trans. Kieran Kavanaugh, O.C.D., and Otilio Rodriguez, O.C.D., 3 vols. (Washington, DC: ICS Publications, 1982), 2:207–60. I will cite that text in the essay as *MSS* in parentheses. In this essay I have enjoyed the benefit of the work of Kevin Culligan, O.C.D., who shared pages from his forthcoming study guide to this text of Teresa's *Meditations*.

2. E. Allison Peers, *Mother of Carmel: A Portrait of St. Teresa of Jesus* (New York: Morehouse-Gorham, 1946), 117.

3. See Thomas R. Nevin, *The Last Years of Saint Thérèse: Doubt and Darkness, 1895–1897* (New York: Oxford University Press, 2013), 3, 171. Evidently, her prioress quashed the idea of her writing such a commentary. As was the case with Teresa's superiors, it was unthinkable for a nun to write a commentary on Sacred Scripture since she had no formal training.

4. Luis M. Giron-Negron, "Dionysian Thought in Sixteenth Century Spanish Mystical Theology," *Modern Theology* 24 (2008): 699.

5. On these refinements, see "How to Pray: From the Life and Teachings of Saint Teresa," in *Carmel and Contemplation: Transforming Human Consciousness,* ed. Kevin Culligan and Regis Jordan, Carmelite Studies 8 (Washington, DC: ICS Publications, 2000), 115–35.

6. *The Interior Castle* VI.5, in Kavanaugh, *Collected Works of St. Teresa of Avila,* 2:387.

7. Ibid., 481.

8. Ibid., 452.

7

Is Darkness a Psychological or a Theological Category in the Thought of John of the Cross?

Edward Howells

For John of the Cross, is darkness a feeling, or is it a theology of the transcendence of feeling, in relation to a transcendent, "dark" God? It appears to be both. In the *Ascent of Mount Carmel*, John introduces the "dark night" primarily as a psychological experience on the spiritual journey. He calls it a "path of dark contemplation and aridity, in which he [the individual] feels lost."[1] At the same time, he says that he is not going to use "experience or science" to explain it, because these can deceive us, but rather "sacred scripture" through which the Holy Spirit speaks.[2] He proceeds to treat the dark night as a theological reality, given by God for the soul's good to help it progress to the goal of union with God.[3] We need the teaching of scripture and the Holy Spirit to understand the nature of the dark night, or it would remain obscure.[4] The dark night is both an experience, told in psychological terms, and something that cannot be adequately explained without turning to its theological rationale, as given directly by God, exceeding the psychological.

An enduring difficulty in interpreting John of the Cross's notion of the "dark night" is how to understand these psychological and theological aspects and their relation to one another. Should one or the other be given priority, and in what precise combination? To put it another way, what is the status of the *experience* of the dark night in theological terms? Historically, interpretations have tended to swing between poles, at one time emphasizing the psychological and at another, the theological. In the early decades of the twentieth century, for instance, prominent neoscholastic writers on John, such as Réginald Garrigou-Lagrange (1923) and Jacques Maritain (1932), sought to make John into a systematic theologian of the mystical life, compatible with Thomas Aquinas.[5] This was a highly theological reading, regarding psychology as an important element in mystical theology but always subordinating it to scholastic theological categories. Where perceived disagreements were found between the psychology and scholastic theology, the theology was given priority.[6] But after the Second World War, a new generation of scholars, no longer sympathetic to neoscholasticism, sought to emphasize the psychological detail, experiential language, and human process in John's thought, against what they saw as oversystematization and a dogmatic straitjacket. Max Huot de Longchamp (1981), for instance, points to the elements of "dynamism" and "process" in mystical transformation as central to John's teaching, contrasting this approach with that of "the systematisers" such as Garrigou-Lagrange, while allying himself with writers such as Henri Sanson (1953).[7] The same reaction can be seen in studies that emphasize John's literary production, such as Colin Thompson's *The Poet and the Mystic* (1977), which treats the literary form of poetry and commentary as key.[8] In recent decades, a further swing can be identified, now against psychology. It is not the psychology of the previous interpreters of John of the Cross that is in view, however, but the broader rise of nontheological approaches to the mystical exemplified by William James's *Varieties of Religious Experience* (1902). As mystical states have been increasingly treated in solely psychological terms, theologians such as Denys Turner (1995) have called for a return to a theological interpretation of John's mysticism as opposed to one based on psychological states or experiences.[9] Without wanting to go further into this history, I mention it here to indicate that the relationship between the psychological and theological aspects of John's thought is an enduring question and far from settled today. In the end, the question is not choosing *between* psychological and theological accounts, as strict alternatives, but how best to hold the two together coherently, while observing their distinction.

John of the Cross's notions of "darkness" and "dark nights" provide a valuable focus for this analysis, for several reasons. First, darkness is a controlling metaphor in two of his major works, the *Ascent of Mount Carmel* and *Dark Night*. Second, to start from John's own use of metaphor and language in his written texts recognizes that this is the best basis for analysis, rather than introducing abstractions or paraphrases of his teaching that already favor a certain kind of interpretation. Third, the metaphor of darkness is a vital meeting point for theology and psychology. I will argue for a position that is closest to the group of scholars that I have identified as the post–Second World War reaction to neoscholastism. Both psychological and theological elements are given adequate attention in this approach, and there is a strong attempt to hold them together satisfactorily. In contrast, both the neoscholastic approach and the more recent reaction to William James give theology a priority that leaves too little room for psychology.

A particular risk in any interpretation of John of the Cross is to regard a single moment in his various itineraries of mystical transformation as definitive of his whole teaching, at the expense of the rest. For instance, the following passage from the *Dark Night* offers just such a vantage point on the relationship between theology and psychology in darkness:

> Why, if it is a divine light (for it illumines and purges a person of his ignorances), does the soul call it a dark night? In answer to this, there are two reasons why this divine wisdom is not only night and darkness for the soul, but also affliction and torment. First, because of the height of the divine wisdom which exceeds the capacity of the soul. Second, because of the soul's baseness and impurity; and on this account it is painful, afflictive, and also dark for the soul.[10]

Darkness here is understood as caused principally by the excess of divine light. It is a kind of darkness that only theology can explain, because it is felt to be in excess of human capacity and unknowable without theological illumination. Both the soul's "capacity" and its "baseness and impurity" are in opposition to the light, which means that it is felt as darkness. From this passage alone, it might be concluded that John's psychology is finally trumped by a theology of the divine darkness, which wholly exceeds and opposes it. Closer inspection, however, shows that the passage comes late in the *Ascent–Night*, with three books of the *Ascent* and the first book of the *Night* already in the background. In those books,

John says very little about the ability of the soul to perceive God's nature as an excess of light: the experience is overwhelmingly negative, of deep psychological darkness with no way out. John should not then be thought of as seeking to leave that kind of darkness behind at this point. Rather, he is adding a new theological possibility: that the soul, having reached this stage of transformation, can begin to see within the psychological darkness a simultaneous presence of divine light. The introduction of theological darkness does not supersede the psychological darkness but expands it into something that is simultaneously both dark and light. The new theological key, in which dark and light belong together rather than opposing each other, enlarges and complexifies rather than removes the psychological darkness that dominates the process of transformation up to this point.

We know little about how John reacted to his incarceration in Toledo for nine months at the hands of hostile Carmelite friars. There is only a passing reference to it in one of his letters.[11] But it is reasonable to suppose that it gave him a deep insight into the psychological detail of the spiritual journey, especially in the close psychological conditions of his experience of imprisonment. In the *Ascent of Mount Carmel*, the first of his major works, written not long after his escape from prison, he chooses a theology that engages with humanity at the point of its greatest suffering, which he locates in Jesus' cry of dereliction, "My God, my God, why have you forsaken me?"[12] Starting from here, human psychology is marked by the darkness of suffering, while also being gripped, at the same time, by the divine movement toward resurrection. John first links psychology and theology at the point in Christ's life where he was "annihilated in his soul, without any consolation or relief."[13] John is less interested in the external physical manifestations of Jesus' suffering than in how he suffered inwardly as one rejected and abandoned by the Father, even while remaining divine. This furnishes his starting point for speaking of the divine presence in terms of a psychology of darkness and loss.

What Is the Dark Night?

In the *Ascent of Mount Carmel* and *Dark Night*, which together form one sequence, the dark night is overtly a series of steps or "nights" of purgation, moving from the appetites which are purified by active detachment in relation to the objects of the senses to the purgation of more inward attachments of the spirit, including the mental "images" and "forms" of the higher faculties of intellect, memory, and will. Purgation can be attained both actively and passively, that is, both by one's own effort, as an ascetical program, and by the "inflow" of grace, through the gift of the theological virtues of faith, hope, and love, so that the soul adheres more closely to God and becomes correspondingly more detached from created possessions. The pairs of sensory/spiritual and active/passive make a fourfold division that structures the books of the *Ascent* and the *Night*.[14] But John also introduces a threefold scheme early on, corresponding to the traditional stages of purgation, illumination, and union.[15] Here, darkness is usefully accorded three distinct yet complementary senses. First, darkness is to follow Christ into the "complete nudity, emptiness and poverty" of his death on the cross, which is a state of being "brought to nothing."[16] This is a point of entry into Christ and also when "the spiritual union between his [the individual's] soul and God will be effected."[17] Darkness is felt negatively, as suffering like that of Christ, but it is given a positive role as a Christlike self-gift to which God responds by uniting the soul with God, in the manner of the Son's relation to the Father. It is dark in the sense that Jesus suffers in order to make this gift, a point to which I shall return.

Second, darkness expresses the epistemological challenge of moving from a mediated approach to God, through created means that point to God remotely, such as spiritual exercises, mental images of God and so on, to an immediate relationship, where God's uncreated light is in direct contact with the human soul. John regards this transformation as one for which the soul is ill prepared, because of both its small "capacity" and its "baseness and impurity," so that it is experienced as darkness.[18] Before it can apprehend the excessive divine light that engulfs it, there is a difficult process of growth by which the soul is "fortified" so that it "becomes capable" of receiving and recognizing the divine light.[19] No natural means exist in human knowing for experiencing God's immediate presence, so one must be formed in the soul by grace, and this takes time. God feels increasingly absent as the soul realizes that what it is longing for cannot be known naturally, which leads to the defining experience of the dark nights, where the soul feels as if "two contraries" are at war within it, one longing for God's immediate presence, and the other seeking him through inadequate human means.[20] The division is strongly felt in the higher faculties of intellect, memory, and will. Darkness is especially related to the intellect, as natural knowing requires mental images and forms of creaturely objects, which are absent in the immediate relation to God, rendering the intellect "dark." John calls this the "means or road of faith," correlating faith with the intellect.[21] A similar "voiding" or emptying occurs in the memory and will, correlated with hope and love respectively, which experience "oblivion" and a loss of delight.[22] Most of the *Ascent* is taken up with this opposition between the natural operations of intellect, memory, and will and the deeper yearning for God's presence, while the infusion of God's presence by the theological virtues of faith, hope, and love in the three faculties cannot yet be positively felt.

Third, darkness comes to express a more paradoxical position as transformation progresses, where the initial shock of the soul's incapacity and impurity begins to turn into a positive sense of God's presence, as already seen in the first long quotation. At this late stage, darkness continues to signal the difference between the divine and the human in the soul's experience, but darkness is no longer the sign of the soul's opposition to God, which has now been purified. John understands this in terms of Dionysius's "ray of darkness," as a state that is both light and dark at once. The soul is moving from a simple darkness, caused by its incapacity and impurity, to an experience of being both humanly exceeded by the divine light and positively able to apprehend it, at once.[23] John calls this "dark contemplation."[24] By contemplation, he means knowledge of the immediate presence of God; while, by darkness, he signals that the means by which the light is known, which is no longer through creaturely forms but by direct contact with God's uncreated form, remains in tension with the soul's knowledge of creatures. As both light and dark, it is "like the very early dawn just before the break of day."[25]

In each of these three senses of darkness, darkness and light are closely juxtaposed. The soul's feeling of abandonment by God is capable, in John's view, of becoming a transformed capacity within the soul for feeling God's immediate presence. In book 1 of the *Ascent*, before the immediate presence of God is introduced, John points out that purgation is because of "a more intense enkindling of another, better love (love of one's heavenly Bridegroom)."[26] Purgation is never a merely natural process of self-discipline or preparation for grace but already a response to the divine light. From the start, therefore, the theology of God's immediate presence and the soul's psychology are linked. John treats psychological experiences of darkness as a proper way to express the life of grace, in a series of steps moving toward God's immediate presence.

As soon as John allies darkness with particular psychological feelings and states, however, difficulties arise. Whether the feelings are of pain or delight, it must be asked whether John is identifying a particular psychological process as normative for the journey of transformation. Are certain psychological states and experiences a condition for receiving the divine light? If so, John seems to be limiting the divine presence to one particular trajectory in human experience, which is reductive for theology. Hans Urs von Balthasar suggests that this is indeed a difficulty with John's thought. John reduces the way of Christ for the whole church to the way of inner darkness. He says, "The internal coherence of the entire corpus is so great that, despite all the open-ended freedom it imparts, it appears as *the* way to God. . . . The possible varieties of perfect faith and contemplation cannot be determined by one single experience, and within this variety the various forms of active Christian life must be allowed to make their contribution."[27]

Von Balthasar thinks that John excludes trajectories other than his way of dark contemplation, particularly the various forms of the active life. Yet it is not a decisive problem, he goes on to say, because it is possible to interpret John's psychology as linked to theology not primarily in the single experience of the dark night but in the "renunciation of divine experience by the Son in *forma Dei*," which, for the sake of redemption, is "the condition of the 'ordinary' man," shared by all humanity.[28] The dark night can then be seen as *just one example* of following in the way of Christ, rather than the only way, and, insofar as it conforms humanity to Christ's renunciation, as a way for all. Von Balthasar's argument is persuasive, because John situates his psychology of darkness in relation to the person of Christ initially, only extending it to the various experiences of the dark night felt by individuals on the basis of this universal claim. It is worth turning to John's starting point to observe how this connection between theology and psychology is first made.

The Connection of Psychology and Theology
in the Person of Christ

The initial connection between psychology and theology, for John, is at the moment of Jesus's cry of dereliction on the cross, where Jesus is both in an immediate union with the Father, corresponding to the divine light, and suffering the psychological darkness of a sense of abandonment and annihilation by God. It is important to recognize that psychological darkness *as pain* is not inherent in Jesus's condition. God's light, as infinite, is always in excess of humanity, but it is only felt by Jesus as pain, and thus as "opposed" or "contrary" to the soul, on account of others' imperfections, which he takes on himself. In our case, the imitation of Christ causes pain because of human incapacity and sin.[29] When the soul reaches union and has been purified and enlarged by grace, there is still darkness, but there is no pain.[30] Without pain, is there any role left for psychological darkness? Before asking that question, we should note that John has cleared aside two false directions. On the one hand, he sees darkness as more than a particular psychology of pain. It has the amplitude of the divine darkness as well. It includes pain but should not be reduced to it, which alleviates the risk of theological reductionism. On the other hand, he wants to pull back from the other extreme, which is simply to oppose the darkness of psychological pain with the light of God's immediate presence. He suggests that the two are really linked, though there is also a distinction between them.

If darkness as pain is distinct from theological darkness, where is the connection to be found? Turning back to the suffering of Christ, John says:

> At the moment of his death he was certainly annihilated in his soul, without any consolation or relief, since the Father left him that way in innermost aridity in the lower part. He was compelled to cry out, My God, my God, why have you forsaken me? (Mt. 27:46). This was the most extreme abandonment, sensitively, that he had suffered in his life. And by it he accomplished the most marvellous work of his whole life, . . . the reconciliation and union of the human race with God through grace.[31]

Jesus's psychological suffering, in which he is "annihilated," "in innermost aridity" and in "extreme abandonment," is felt "at the same moment" as "the reconciliation and union of the human race with God." In Jesus's case, there was a *causal* link between the suffering that he was made to bear and the reconciliation of the human race: "by it he accomplished" reconciliation. But it is notable that, though he could have, John does not suggest a redemptive notion of suffering in relation to us here, in which suffering is chosen as valuable in itself for moving toward union with Christ. Rather, it is the temporal simultaneity that he emphasizes: "*at the moment* of his death he was certainly annihilated in his soul."[32]

John sees no necessary connection between Christ's psychological pain and God's immediate presence. Rather, by drawing attention to the simultaneity of "at the moment," he seeks only to make the negative case: to deny that God *cannot* be present in pain. John says that those who, like Job's comforters, conclude that God has forsaken the person who suffers pain are to be resisted in the strongest terms.[33] Nevertheless, the historical revelation of Jesus indicates that God *chooses* to be fully present at the same moment as human pain. John would say, as Aquinas does, that it is "fitting" for Jesus to suffer, but that it is not possible to give "necessary" reasons why he does.[34] Revelation alone tells us that there is a real connection in Christ's person between the psychological darkness of pain and the theological darkness of God's immediate presence. Similarly, for us, the darkness of felt abandonment by God presents a special invitation to union with Christ, offering a point of access to the divine presence, but it is one without natural cause or rationale: it is beyond natural explanation.

Darkness as "Impasse"

John's reluctance to see a causal link between darkness as pain and darkness as divine light can be interpreted in a stronger sense. Returning to the second, epistemological meaning of darkness, John describes a process in which the soul loses its familiar way of relating to creatures in the natural process of knowing. The soul's natural means of knowing is incapable of apprehending the uncreated divine light, with which it is coming into contact, other than as a "contrary." John's "two contraries" of the felt opposition between the natural human means of knowing and the divine light, expresses the absolute incommensurability of the divine light with human experience and reason.[35] Darkness as pain arises, then, not from anything the soul is receiving from God, but because *it cannot know what it is experiencing*: it suffers from the ungraspable character of what it is trying to know. The darkness is of the subjective disorientation of the whole experiencing apparatus, not of anything objective about God. It is "dark" in two senses: first, because of the loss of the "particular forms" of knowledge, which have no "proportion" to God, to make way for the "general, pure act" of the divine being; and, second, because the mind is emptied or "voided" at its roots, in the operations of the higher faculties of intellect, memory, and will, as it tries to work without the mental forms of creatures.[36] Even though psychological darkness and the divine light are said to be coming into contact here, John emphasizes precisely the disjunction and lack of a meeting point. The divine light cannot be felt. There is real pain, and pain felt because of God's presence, but it is merely a subjective reaction. The soul feels a "disinclination to fix the imagination or sense faculties upon other particular objects, exterior or interior," and a wish to refrain from spiritual "acts and exercises" in relation to God—not because it does not want God but because it perceives now that there is no means to God's immediate presence through creaturely objects and forms.[37]

Denys Turner focuses on this moment of disjunction between theology and psychology in John's thought in his *Darkness of God*, as part of his larger argument in the book, which seeks to wrest Christian mysticism from psychological and experiential reductionism. In discussing John, he says,

> What is John describing in all that detailed psychology of "mystical experience"? . . . The answer must be: he describes no experience *of* anything "mystical" at all, but only of what we might call the "experiential feedback of that which is truly "mystical."". . . Again and again John places the action of grace itself beyond our power of experience. Faith . . . is not an experience; it is an excess of light to the soul, productive in it of the darkness of unknowing, and its presence is known only through what it deprives us of.[38]

The soul experiences a psychological response to the excessive character of God's being, rather than having a direct experience *of* God's being. The darkness is purely subjective, as "feedback," rather than of an object.

Against Turner, however, is the fact that this is only a moment in John's understanding of the process of mystical transformation. Darkness is not a single experience but an ongoing subjective response to God's immediate presence, with which the soul has further to go, beyond the stage of "contraries." There is a real antagonism between psychology and theology at this point, and it is a vital transition point on the journey, dominating the *Ascent–Night*, but beyond it, the soul's disorientation and confusion give way to a realization that the soul is being "fortified" so that it "becomes capable" of apprehending and knowing the divine presence.[39] A psychological connection *is* being forged in the human person, only it is at the level of grace, beyond anything that can be anticipated.

Constance Fitzgerald has usefully coined the phrase "impasse" to interpret John's view of darkness at this point.[40] "Impasse" implies the discontinuity of "contraries," where the soul realizes that humans and God have nothing in common by which God's immediate presence can be known on the human side. Yet, as a subjective response, impasse also sets the experience in continuity with what went before and what comes after. In an experience of "impasse" one feels entirely imprisoned and unable to move, but one still has a choice as to how to respond. One can remain stuck, or regard it as pointing to new possibilities for thought and action that were not there before. For John, this is precisely the role of darkness in the ongoing process of transformation. When impasse is pursued not as a defining experience but as a passage to something else, it can be used in a way that subverts itself: darkness deconstructs the process of reasoning that introduced it. At the height of impasse, the soul begins to detach from the experience, which allows it to seek something new by means of the break. The experience is of being "dissolved," of a "cruel spiritual death . . . like hanging in midair, unable to breathe," and of "torment" and "terror."[41] Yet, at the same time, the effect is positive: "The divine extreme strikes in order to renew the soul and divinize it."[42] Fitzgerald notes that, though impasse is a wholly negative experience in itself, in the wider context of a person's ongoing life, it can be used positively. As a way of introducing something new, it can even be developed into a skill over time. Through a seasoned response to impasse, experiences of impasse are welcomed and cultivated by a soul that knows how to direct them into generating new possibilities. The moment of discontinuity between psychology and theology is transformed by this move, from sheer opposition into a positive psychological means of understanding the divine presence. This is what John means when he says that the "voiding" or negation of the intellect, memory, and will is also their growth into a new capacity.

The Soul's Deep Capacity for God

John situates the point of discontinuity and breakdown between the soul and God at the heart of his understanding of the renewal of the soul's psychology by theology. Connections that cannot be made between psychology and theology in conceptual or static terms can be asserted of an individual's psychological *process* that has discontinuity at its heart. When John says that the soul "becomes capable" of receiving the immediate divine presence, he does not mean that an internal continuity of nature is established between the creature and God.[43] In the *Living Flame of Love*, John applies the phrase "the deep caverns of feeling" from the *Flame* poem to explore this transformation of the faculties of intellect, memory, and will. He suggests that the faculties are deeply connected to God precisely in the emptiness of their yearning for God, "since anything less than infinite fails to fill them."[44] In this voiding or emptying, he says, "The capacity of these caverns is deep, because the object of this capacity, namely God, is profound and infinite. Thus in a certain fashion their capacity is infinite, their thirst is infinite, their hunger is also deep and infinite, and their languishing and suffering are infinite death."[45] The key phrase, "in a certain fashion their capacity is infinite," signals John's caution in asserting that the soul's psychology has become continuous with the divine presence. The three faculties are not in themselves made infinite and simply divine. Rather, they have a "thirst" and "hunger" corresponding to God's infinite nature, which stretches them out infinitely *toward* God. They share in God's infinite nature, as John says elsewhere, "by participation"—by participating in an infinite nature that belongs to God rather than to them.[46] The process of reaching out in an infinite thirst and hunger toward God, however, is regarded by John as a new capacity for receiving God's presence positively, without merging the divine and human natures.

How can a capacity formed out of an essential lack, a lack of divinity, become something positively identified with divinity in the soul? Starting with a view of the natural soul as a hierarchy of powers, with the bodily senses at the bottom and the higher faculties of intellect, memory, and will at the top, John tries to spell out the kind of human structure that can sustain this paradoxical simultaneity of ontological difference and unity. Pursuing his discussion of the "deep caverns of feeling," he says that the soul attains a new "feeling of the soul." This is "the power and strength that the substance of the soul has for enjoying the objects of the spiritual faculties"—that is, for enjoying God's infinite nature directly.[47] The "substance of the soul" is John's term for the spiritual center point or apex of the soul, usually hidden, in which it relates to God directly. The additional "feeling of the soul" is a new power, which makes the substance of the soul able to feel God's immediate contact positively, where before God's presence was excessive and hidden. The three higher faculties, John says, then work in relation to the "feeling of the soul" much as the bodily senses relate to the "common sense" in bodily knowing, that is, as an archive and receptacle of forms, receiving the uncreated form of God passively, so that it can be known.[48] The mention of the bodily senses at this point does not signify a return to created or "particular" forms but, rather, indicates that, even without created forms, the higher faculties in their transformed capacity can differentiate what they receive in relation to God's immediate presence, to feel and know it. They can "feel and enjoy the grandeurs of God's wisdom and excellence" with their new "capacity for feeling, possessing and tasting them all."[49] John effectively introduces a strong duality into the soul with the emergence of the "deep caverns of feeling," where God's immediate presence is felt by a cognitive structure that works in parallel with the bodily senses, without overlapping with them at any point.[50] In their natural orientation, the higher faculties work in relation to the bodily senses by means of created mental forms, while in their new spiritual orientation, they work solely in relation to God and without created forms.

What does this mean? It is difficult to see how two distinct ways of knowing could work together while dealing with ontologically divided objects, one human and the other divine, within the same soul. John's answer rests on a dynamic notion of the soul's operation when it is in the state of quasi-infinite yearning for God's immediate presence. The soul that has grasped the fact that, in relation to God's immediate presence, it is *"impossible* for it to lift its eyes to the divine light," begins to see that this has some positive value in terms of its interior "depth," or, as he calls it here, its "abyss."[51] Union with God becomes possible when the soul recognizes that, as an abyss of infinite yearning for God, it is "like" God, who in Christ has shown an infinite yearning for the human soul. The impasse that makes it yearn infinitely for the other is precisely its capacity for God. It is God who first crosses the ontological divide between divine and human, in the incarnation, but, in doing so, an abyssal desire is instigated in the soul that seeks return to God. When the soul turns to God out of this abyssal desire, two abysses join in their mutual emptiness, longing for each other, "like to like."[52] Their emptiness is not identical. God's is an emptiness that crosses the ontological divide, while the soul's is merely receptive. But in its receptivity, the soul takes on the likeness of the divine abyss, so that it can be joined to divinity positively and possess the union within its own expanded nature. The depth of the faculties of intellect, memory, and will unites with God in a new kind of awareness that can apprehend and discern God's presence immediately.

John appeals to the marriage relationship of bridal mysticism to make sense of this joining of theology and psychology in the soul's transformed capacity. Since the soul's longing for God is a participation in God's own longing for the soul, "a reciprocal love is thus actually formed between the soul and God, like a marriage union and surrender, in which the goods of both . . . are possessed by both together."[53] The central moment is one of both unity and difference, as they long for each other out of what they do not have, namely, the other, as much as out of the love that they share. The marriage metaphor allows John to assert that there is a dynamic unity of diverse theological and psychological elements, and that this takes place "within" the soul. John explains this psychology further with reference to the acquired dynamics of the Trinity. The soul is being transformed "into" the Trinity.[54] Following Augustine, John regards the soul as made in the image of God, with a correlation between the soul's higher faculties of memory, intellect, and will, and the three persons of the Trinity, Father, Son, and Holy Spirit.[55] The capacity of the soul to reach out infinitely toward God "in a certain fashion" and to unite with God enables it to possess God as God possesses divine being in the relations of the Trinity. Just as the Holy Spirit is constituted by the relationship between the Father and the Son, so the soul unites with God by sharing in the love with which God loves God in the Trinity, that is, the Holy Spirit. When the soul loves God in mystical union, it "loves God, not through itself but . . . through the Holy Spirit, as the Father and the Son love each other."[56] This provides the soul with a unity differentiated not simply between the soul and God but from within the divine unity, so that God's ontological otherness is not compromised by the union. The soul can unite with divinity in fully human terms, in a union differentiated, first, in the Trinity and, second, in the ontological distinction of creation in the incarnation, holding these differences within the unity of Father and Son.

The key moment of transformation occurs when the soul recognizes its difference from God, most directly felt in the experience of impasse, and is able to identify this difference as *included* in its sharing of the unity of the Trinity. While impasse signals the incommensurability of the divine and human natures, further transformation indicates a unity compatible with the impasse, by means of the maximal combination of simultaneous unity and distinction of the Trinity. In the *Spiritual Canticle*, this is the moment when the Bridegroom, wounded by the soul's love, appears to the soul in the incarnation as a wounded stag, now for the first time "in sight on the hill." God becomes visible at this point because the soul realizes that its yearning for God is equally God's yearning, joined in their mutual "wound" of love. They join in their woundedness, in the respect that, as John says, "among lovers, the wound of one is a wound for both, and the two have but one feeling."[57] The soul sees that it is no longer alone in its yearning, but that God also yearns for it, and that out of its awareness of this love as shared it can feel the unity with God that is the Holy Spirit. God's presence is felt in the "breeze" of contemplation, which is the breath of the Holy Spirit, shared between the Father and the Son.[58] The soul differentiates both itself and God as partners within the single bond of the Holy Spirit.

Conclusions: Implications for the Relation
of Psychology and Theology

For John of the Cross, darkness is, first of all, the growing awareness of the one who longs for God's presence that human psychology is wholly unable to accommodate itself to the divine nature. The pain of this realization, however, which is itself psychological, increases to the point of "profound darkness" and "dark death," which turns the soul's experience of impasse around, pointing to the graced possibility for the inclusion of an otherness in the soul that is divine.[59] Using the dialectic of Dionysius, John suggests that any psychology of the divine presence, however negative, has a positive corollary, without which it could not be stated at all. There must be something in human nature that is aware of God's immediate presence, even if the experience is of the impossibility of experiencing God as God. Rather than simply finding a positive capacity in human nature to answer to this conundrum, John uses the Dionysian paradox of simultaneous darkness and light to accommodate the rift *between* theology and psychology within his transformed psychology. It is true both that God cannot be experienced humanly and that God is experienced in a fully human way. This is nonsense until John's particular working out of the metaphor of darkness is appreciated: darkness is not any single experience but the ongoing experience of one whose reality is infinitely deeper than one's experiences, being open, especially in the inability to understand oneself fully, to what is wholly other.

Darkness is a process. Impasse is a vital experience, but less significant in itself than as something that changes a person's perspective by demanding a response at a deeper level. The person must ask not simply, What am I experiencing? but, out of confusion, Who am I here? At that point, the merely psychological question becomes a theological one, because the current, natural "I" is not enough: nothing in the soul's experience offers itself as a means to grow beyond the impasse. Rather, the impasse can only be left to work on itself, to subvert itself. When the "I" surrenders to what is beyond it, in an unlimited personal longing for completion by the other, John suggests that something truly different enters human psychology. Surrender in total desire for and dependence on the other points not simply beyond the "I" but to something deep within the "I," namely, the divine source from which its humanity and all of creation flow. The soul comes to see that its deepest reality is an open-ended relationality, which finally demands God's immediate presence as its goal. This goal is reached when the soul takes on the expanded dimensions of the relationality of the Holy Spirit, as sheer gift, in its humanity.

John's view of the soul's transformed psychology is marked by a deep duality, as we have seen. He describes two parallel psychologies within a single soul, which work in ontologically different ways. But this duality is merely an exaggerated case of what is already natural to the soul. The darkness of impasse is a constant feature of ordinary human experience. Dynamically, the soul is constantly trying to reach out to and grasp what it is not, and this characterizes the human mind at its deepest. Theological transformation is an extension of this natural duality. There is great difficulty in reconciling the two poles of the soul's relationality when they are ontologically opposed, in relation to God, but the same basic desire of the mind to embrace what is other is at work.

Theological transformation introduces not something new into psychology but an enhanced ability to appropriate the mind's deeply relational and "other-centered" character. John takes the view that theology and psychology are united in this "center" of the soul, rather than remaining opposed or separated. By "center" he means two things. First, the center is the soul's awareness of its fundamentally relational character, which in union is an awareness of sharing in the divine relationality which holds together the divine and the human. While in its old, natural center it sought to know God as an object outside it, as another creature in the world, from which it was profoundly absent, now it "knows things better in God's being than in themselves."[60] It finds its knowledge of God within its awareness of its own relationality, as a participation in the relationality of Trinity. The soul is able to articulate this central relationality within it, where before it was inchoate and hidden. When drawing on this awareness while also seeking to know things in the world, the soul has a perspective in which "all things seem to move in unison," however diverse they are in creation. The soul can hold their diversity together in relation to their fontal origin in the Trinity, with which it is united.[61] Second, this deepened center is also a center of agency. John describes the relational dynamism of the center as conveyed to the whole soul by means of an "overflow": the "sweetness" of union at the center "overflows into the effective and actual practice of love, either interiorly with the will in the affective act, or exteriorly in works directed to the service of the Beloved."[62] In this sense, John adds, "the power to look at God is, for the soul, the power to do works in the grace of God."[63] The mutual gaze of contemplation at the center of the soul, giving a heightened awareness of the divine presence, is the same dynamic that energizes the body and action in the world, producing deliberate action flowing from God's immediate presence.

Psychology and theology are thoroughly united, but John relies on the metaphor of darkness to sustain this unity, as also containing a deep distinction. Darkness effectively guards against the tendencies of both theology and psychology to a kind of abstraction that obviates the personal, dynamic relationality that he has carefully built up. Darkness achieves this, first, by requiring a personal frame of reference. As we have seen, the experience of impasse demands a shift from the experience itself to a deeper consideration of personal and interpersonal depth in relation to God. Darkness brings a turn to the subject, and to a subject that is wholly other-directed, unable to be a subject without the other. Second, darkness sets this subjectivity in an ever-expanding framework, by emphasizing the otherness of the God whom the soul seeks. "Dark" relationality puts the desire for what is *infinitely* beyond the subject at its heart. Third, darkness expresses the unfolding character of the soul's union with God, in a temporal process. The soul is always moving into the unknown, in continuing surrender. Even in union, when this movement is seen to be reciprocated and upheld by the divine presence, which brings light, the soul's movement toward the other is one of risk and adventure, and dark in this sense. In each case, darkness keeps the dynamism in play.

Psychology and theology are kept in movement by darkness, so that while they are united, they do not merge or collapse into one another. They are united in a darkness that moves constantly from a psychology of sheer impasse to one whose capacity is expanded by theology to hold infinite otherness within itself, in a psychology wholly open to and dependent on the theological other for its own internal completion. This is possible only over the course of time, in a process of personal transformation, as a movement between elements of unity and distinction in relation to God that become increasingly juxtaposed, toward the goal of holding them at the same moment, as Christ does, in mystical union.

Notes

1. "Camino de oscura contemplación y sequedad en que a ella le parece que va perdida" (A Prol. 4, p. 71 [256]). Citations of John of the Cross use the following abbreviations: A = *Ascent of Mount Carmel* (*Subida del Monte Carmelo*); N = *Dark Night* (*Noche Oscura*); C = *Spiritual Canticle* (*Cántico Espiritual*, B redaction); F = *Living Flame of Love* (*Llama de Amor Viva*, B redaction). The English translation used is *The Collected Works of John of the Cross*, trans. with an introduction by Kieran Kavanaugh and Otilio Rodriguez (Washington DC: Institute of Carmelite Studies, 1979); the edition of the Spanish original is *Obras Completas de San Juan de la Cruz*, ed. Lucinio Ruano, 14th ed. (Madrid: Biblioteca de Autores Cristianos, 1994). Following the specific locator for the passage in the work, page numbers are given first to the English translation and second (in square brackets) to the Spanish edition.

2. "Ni de experiencia ni de ciencia . . . la divina Escritura" (A Prol. 2, p. 70 [255]).

3. A Prol. 1, 3-5, 8.

4. A Prol. 2.

5. Réginald Garrigou-Lagrange, *Christian Perfection and Contemplation according to St. Thomas Aquinas and St. John of the* Cross, trans. Sr. M. Timothea Doyle (London: Herder, 1937, 1958), originally published as *Perfection chrétienne et contemplation selon saint Thomas d'Aquin et saint Jean de la Croix* (1923); Jacques Maritain, *Distinguish to Unite: Or, The Degrees of Knowledge*, trans. Gerald B. Phelan from 4th French ed. (1959; repr., Notre Dame: University of Notre Dame Press, 1995), originally published as *Distinguer pour unir, ou les degrés du savoir* (1932).

6. For example, Maritain insists that John has a notion of "silent concepts" which "play the formal part" in mystical knowledge of God, to account for the discrepancy between Aquinas's view that God cannot be known in this life without created intermediaries and John's rejection of created intermediaries. He tries to correct John in favor of Aquinas (*Distinguish to Unite*, 281).

7. Max Huot de Longchamp, *Lectures de Jean de la Croix: Essai d'anthropologie mystique,* Théologie historique 62 (Paris: Beauchesne, 1981), esp. 83–146, 391–414. Huot de Longchamp says that "language is the key word" of his investigation (p. 390), referring this move (p. 35) particularly to Henri Sanson, *L'esprit humain selon Saint Jean de la Croix* (Paris: Presses universitaires de France, 1953).

8. Colin P. Thompson, *The Poet and the Mystic: A Study of the Cántico Espiritual of San Juan de la Cruz*, Oxford Modern Languages and Literatures Monographs (Oxford: Oxford University Press, 1977).

9. Denys Turner, *The Darkness of God: Negativity in Christian Mysticism* (Cambridge: Cambridge University Press, 1995), treated further below.

10. "¿Por qué, pues es lumbre divina—que, como decimos, ilumina y purga el alma de sus ignorancias—, la llama aquí el alma noche oscura? A lo cual se responde que por dos cosas es esta divina Sabudería, no sólo noche y tiniebla para el alma, mas también [le es] pena y tormento: la primera es por la alteza de la Sabiduría divina, que excede al talento del alma, y en esta manera le es tiniebla; la segunda, por la bajeza e impureza della, y desta manera le es penosa y aflictiva y también oscura" (N 2.5.2, p. 335 [527]).

11. Letter 1 (July 6, 1581). The reference to being swallowed by a whale, like Jonah, can also be linked to N 2.6.1, 3.

12. A 2.7.11, p. 124 (Matt. 27:46). See the full citation below.

13. Ibid. See the full citation below. Iain Matthew calls this the "hinge" chapter of the *Ascent–Night* ("The Knowledge and Consciousness of Christ in the Light of the Writings of St. John of the Cross" [D.Phil. dissertation, University of Oxford, 1991], 256).

14. A 1.1. Book 1 is the active purgation or night of the senses; books 2 and 3 the active night of the spirit; book 4 (which is called the *Dark Night* book 1) is the passive night of senses; book 5 (*Dark Night* book 2) the passive night of the spirit. In fact these elements are more mixed than the scheme suggests.

15. A 1.2.

16. A 1.13.3–4. "Toda desnudez y vacío y pobreza" (A 1.13.6, p. 103 [289]). "Viniere a quedar resuelto en nada" (A 2.7.11, p. 125 [311]).

17. "Quedará hecha la unión espiritual entre el alma y Dios" (A 2.7.11, p. 125 [311]).

18. N 2.5:2, as quoted in the long quotation above.

19. "Amparando la natural" (F 1.27, p. 590 [934]). "Pueda recibir la unión" (N 2.12.4, p. 356 [550]). One must look to the *Living Flame of Love* for the full expression of this expansion of the soul, though it begins in the *Ascent-Night* (also F 1.36; 3.18, 22).

20. "Dos contrarios" (A 1.6.1; also C 8.3; F 1.22).

21. "Medio o camino . . . lo cual es la fe" (A 1.2.1, p. 74 [260]).

22. A 2.6.1–4. E.g., "las cuales tres virtudes todas hacen . . . vacío en las potencias" (A 2.6.2, p. 119 [305]). "Un olvido grande" (A 2.14.10, p. 145 [332]).

23. "Rayo de tiniebla" (A 2.8.6, p. 128 [314]); also N 2.5.3; C 14 & 15.16–17; F 3.49.

24. "Oscura contemplación" (A Prol. 4, p. 71 [256]).

25. "La cual es ya inmediata a la luz del día" (A 1.2.5, p. 75 [261]).

26. "Otra inflammación mayor de otro amor mejor, que es el de su Esposo" (A 1.14.2, p. 105 [291]).

27. Hans Urs von Balthasar, *The Glory of the Lord: A Theological Aesthetics*, vol. 3, *Studies in Theological Style: Lay Styles* (Edinburgh: T&T Clark, 1986), 105-71, here 169.

28. Ibid., 169.

29. N 2.5.2. John's two reasons for darkness—first, human incapacity, and, second, sin—correspond to the scholastic distinction between elevating grace and healing grace, also used, for instance, by Thomas Aquinas, *Summa Theologiae*, IaIIae 109:2.

30. A point briefly touched on at the end of the *Ascent–Night* (N 2.23.12; 24.2–3) and developed further in C 14 & 15.21; 20 & 21.16; F 1.36; 3.7.

31. "Cierto está que al punto de la muerte quedó también anihilado en el alma sin consuelo y alivio alguno, dejándole el Padre así en íntima sequedad según la parte inferior, por lo cual fue necesitado a clamar diciendo: *Dios mío, Dios mío, ¿por qué me has desamparado?* (Mt. 27:46); lo cual fue el mayor desamparo sensitivamente que había tenido en su vida . . . que fue reconciliar y unir al género humano por gracia con Dios" (A 2.7.11, p. 124 [310–11]).

32. My emphasis.

33. A Prol., 4.

34. Thomas Aquinas, *Summa Theologiae*, IIIa 1.

35. A 1.6.1; also C 8.3; F 1.22.

36. (i) A 2.8.3, 5; 12.5–7; F 3.46–47. (ii) A 2.6; 7.4.

37. "Ve no le da ninguna gana de poner la imaginación ni el sentido en otras cosas particulares, exteriores ni interiores. . . . Sin actos y ejercicios" (A 2.13.3–4, pp. 140–41 [327]).

38. Denys Turner, *The Darkness of God: Negativity in Christian Mysticism* (Cambridge: Cambridge University Press, 1995), 245–46.

39. F 1.27; N 2.12.4 (see n. 19 above); F 1.36; 3.18, 22.

40. Constance Fitzgerald, OCD, "Impasse and Dark Night," in *Women's Spirituality: Resources for Christian Development*, ed. Joann Wolski Conn (New York: Paulist Press, 1996), 410–35.

41. "[De]suece la sustancia espiritual . . . de manera que si a uno suspendiesen o detuviesen el aire que no respirase" (N 2.6.1, 5, pp. 337, 339 [530, 531]). "El gran tormento . . . el gran pavor" (C 13.4, p. 459 [786]).

42. "El divino embiste a fin de renovarla para hacerla divina" (N 2.6.1, p. 337 [529]).

43. N 2.12.4 (see n. 19 above).

44. "Pues no se llenan con menos que infinito" (F 3.18, p. 617 [982]).

45. "Es, pues, profunda la capacidad de estas cavernas, porque lo que en ellas puede caber, que es Dios, es profundo e infinito; y así será en cierta manera su capacidad infinita, y así su sed es infinita, su hambre también es profunda e infinita, su deshacimiento y pena es muerte infinita" (F 3.22, p. 618 [984]).

46. "Por participación" (A 2.5.5, p. 117 [303]).

47. "Por el sentido de el alma entiende aquí la virtud y fuerza que tiene la sustancia de el alma para sentir y gozar los objectos de las potencias espirituales" (F 3.69, p. 637 [1016]).

48. "El sentido commun" (F 3.69, p. 637 [1017]).

49. "Siente y gusta el alma profundamente las grandezas de la sabiduría y excelencias de Dios. . . . La virtud y capacidad que tiene el alma para sentirlo, poseerlo y gustarlo todo" (F 3.69, p. 637 [1016–17]).

50. I have given an analysis of this point elsewhere; see Edward Howells, *John of the Cross and Teresa of Avila: Mystical Knowing and Selfhood* (New York: Crossroad, 2002), 29–31.

51. "Esle imposible alzar los ojos a la divina luz. . . . Un abismo" (F 3.71, p. 638 [1018]; my emphasis).

52. "Semejante a su semejante" (ibid.).

53. "Y así entre Dios y el alma está actualmente formado un amor recíproco en conformidad de la unión y entrega matrimonial, en que los bienes de entrambos . . . los poseen entrambos juntos" (F 3.79, p. 641 [1024]).

54. E.g., C 39.3.

55. C 1.6; F 1.15. The soul is already in the image of the Trinity from its creation, but in union this image is perfected and made evident, where before it was hidden.

56. "Ama el alma a Dios no por sí . . . porque ama por el Espíritu Santo, come el Padre y el Hijo se aman" (F 3.82, p. 642 [1026]); also C 13.11, as immediately below.

57. "Que el ciervo vulnerado: . . . En los enamorados la herida de uno es de entrambos, y un mismo sentimiento tienen los dos. . . . Por el otero asoma" (C 13.9–10, pp. 460–61 [788]).

58. "Al aire de tu vuelo y fresco toma: . . . El Espíritu Santo, que es amor, también se compara en la divina Escritura al *aire*, porque es aspirado de el Padre y del Hijo" (C 13.11, p. 461 [788]).

59. "Una profunda y honda muerte . . . en este sepulcro de oscura muerte" (N 2.6.1, p. 337 [530]).

60. "Las conoce mejor en su ser que en ellas mismas" (F 4.5, p. 645 [1030]).

61. "Todas las cosas criadas . . . hacen el mismo movimiento" (F 4.4, p. 644 [1029]).

62. "[La] dulzura . . . redunda en el ejercicio de amar efectiva y actualmente, [ahora interiormente] con la voluntad en acto de afición, ahora exteriormente haciendo obras pertenecientes al servicio de el Amado" (C 36.4, p. 547 [879–80]).

63. "Poder mirar el alma a Dios es hacer obras en gracia de Dios" (C 32.8, p. 536 [869]).

8
The Contemplative Turn
in Ficino and Traherne

Mark A. McIntosh

> You never Enjoy the World aright, till you see how a Sand Exhibi-
> teth the Wisdom and Power of God: And Prize in evry Thing the
> Service which they do you, by Manifesting His Glory and Goodness
> to your Soul, far more then the Visible Beauty on their Surface, or
> the Material Services, they can do your Body.[1]

Few passages from the Anglican priest and poet Thomas Traherne (1636–
1674) are better known and beloved than this evocation of the contemplation of God in nature. The delightful itinerary of human perception
that Traherne proposes—from the tiny grain of sand to the immense,
pervasive beauty of divine wisdom—lures the reader into a beguilingly
cheerful labyrinth of contemplation: even the tiniest things, if not eyed
in a merely reductive or utilitarian way, can become thoughts that draw
the mind up into joyful converse with that eternal goodness whence all
things flow.

In this brief essay, I want merely to explore a "usefulness" to contemplation, a use whose meaning and significance may well have been
lost to view in modernity. For, as Traherne's era passed through wars of
religion and civil wars, the rise of new philosophy and new science, the
very possibility and the real meaning of this contemplative moment were
being lost. By the rise of the Romantic era, it had come to seem like little
more than an occasion for artistic souls to express themselves exquisitely.
The beauty of the world was no longer a crucial ally in the return of the

creatures through the contemplation by human minds of God's goodness in creation, ascending in yearning by means of the creatures' beauty to its first and final cause. Natural beauty had come to seem more like an obfuscating husk that cloaked matters best subjected to the practical investigations of immanent natural causation by modern science—or else to be a mendacious bid to deceive and lead astray the naive. In that atmosphere, it became increasingly difficult to see what point there could be to a contemplative appreciation of nature—other than as an inspiration for heightened aesthetic subjectivity, so severe was the new division between the natural and the supernatural. As John Henry Newman was to remark in the early nineteenth century:

> The system of physical causes is so much more tangible and satisfying than that of final, that unless there be a pre-existent and independent interest in the inquirer's mind, leading him to dwell on the phenomena which betoken an Intelligent Creator, he will certainly follow out those which terminate in the hypothesis of a settled order of nature and self-sustained laws. It is indeed a great question whether Atheism is not as philosophically consistent with the phenomena of the physical world, taken by themselves, as the doctrine of a creative and governing Power.[2]

Newman's phrase "taken by themselves" is of course the fatal issue: for most of the history of Christian thought, the phenomena of the physical world could only be "taken by themselves" by means of willful ignorance or a suspect moral vision. As Thomas Aquinas had observed: "As a work of art manifests the art of the artisan, so the whole world is nothing else than a certain representation of the divine Wisdom conceived within the mind of the Father."[3] And for this very reason, a failure to perceive and to praise God's goodness in creation, to behold the world contemplatively, was seen as a derogation of human duty. Bonaventure had lamented this:

> As long as man stood up, he had the knowledge of created things and through their significance was carried up to God, to praise, worship, and love Him. This is what the creatures are for and how they are led back to God. But when man had fallen, since he had lost knowledge, there was no longer anyone to lead the creatures back to God.[4]

For the great Franciscan, the apprehension by humankind of the divine intelligibility, the creative artistry of Wisdom, crucially achieves both the full likening and return of the creatures to their primordial truth in God's knowing of them, and fulfillment of the mind's true calling to ascend to the eternal via the temporal. To fail in making this contemplative turn is thus not missing out on a pleasant opportunity for aesthetic pleasure, but a fatal outcome of the Fall's degenerative momentum.

Early modernity seems to be the moment when, in terribly generalized terms, we might say that Western culture loses touch with this contemplative calling of humanity—even as an aspect of its own vocation now disfigured by sin. In this essay I want to open some perspectives on the meaning and significance of contemplating God in creatures as those views were still available to the West in the late flowering of Christian Platonism that we find in Traherne, and in his important predecessor and interlocutor, Marsilio Ficino (1433–1499).[5] The exciting discovery in the later twentieth century of several unknown Traherne manuscripts means that his significance in early modern thought will only grow; and among the interesting features of Traherne is his notebook of Ficino quotations and annotations.[6]

So what is contemplation for? Why are human beings called to recognize the invisible wisdom and power of God in the visible things God has made (Rom. 1:20)? Certainly for Traherne, as for the rest of the Christian tradition, the contemplation of God in nature is in part a preparation for the unmediated contemplation of God in heaven, and it is also of course an appropriate act of reverence and praise for the Creator on the part of the creatures. But even beyond this, as I hope to show, certainly for Traherne and (perhaps) Ficino, there is a sense in which it is also a drawing of creation onward, almost eucharistically, into its full potential and meaning—as though the full truth of the creatures cannot be realized until the divine generosity and self-giving at their core become acknowledged and named, received and offered back in praise and thanksgiving to their Source. Perhaps we could think of the contemplative turn as a vital renewal and refreshing of the primordial divine speaking at the heart of each creature; for when a human or angelic mind is actualized by thinking the intelligible form (or idea) of a thing in contemplating God's beauty within it, we could say that at this moment the created thing is restored to oneness—in and through the contemplative movement of the mind—with the divine idea by which the creature is spoken continuously into existence in the eternal Word.

In a letter of 1494, for example, Ficino speaks of how, by God's mercy, the words of a prophet who speaks of earthly things sometimes become filled with the divine power of the primordial Speaker, so that a creaturely thing named in human words becomes resonant again with the divine speaking and wisdom that is its creative ground. The distinguished Ficino scholar Michael Allen comments that here Ficino is pointing to the "interweaving of the Logos in the unfolding of the things of nature, the *res creatae* that depend for their very existence on the divine utterance."[7] My suggestion is that the contemplative's beholding of God's intelligible beauty in creatures is analogous to the prophet's naming of God's power in creatures; in both cases, the human mind (precisely by its intelligent apprehension of a creature) fosters a replenishing within the world of that ravishingly intelligible divine speaking by which the creature is and toward which it will be consummated.

This contemplative turning or ascent of the mind—from the finite individual creature to the radiant fullness of the creature's eternal archetype in the mind of God—might even be seen as a kind of momentum within created time itself. Augustine, for example, perhaps with a kind of serious playfulness, imagines the gathering pendulum swing of time as coming into being precisely through the angelic contemplative turning from beholding the creatures in themselves to beholding them in their archetypal forms in God:

> The holy angels, whose equals we shall be after the resurrection, if to the end we hold to Christ our Way, always behold the face of God and rejoice in His Word, the only-begotten Son, equal to the Father; and in them first of all wisdom was created. They, therefore, without any doubt know all creation, of which they are the creatures first made, and they have this knowledge first in the Word of God Himself, in whom are the eternal reasons of all things made in time, existing in Him through whom all things have been created. And they have this knowledge in creation itself, as they look down upon it and refer it to the praise of Him in whose immutable truth they behold, as in the source of all creation, the reasons by which creatures have been made. There the knowledge they have is like

day, and so that blessed company, perfectly united by participation in the same Truth, is the day first created; here among creatures their knowledge is like evening. But immediately morning comes (and this happens on all six days), because the knowledge angels have does not remain fixed in a creature without their immediately referring it to the praise and love of Him in whom they know not the fact, but the reason, for its creation.[8]

It is as if the angels' referring their knowledge of the creatures to the praise and love of God is a kind of deep ordering rhythm building up the noetic patterns and structures of the world, structures that govern our perception of all things in their transience and their ultimacy, and so our perception of time itself. And Ficino clearly enjoys this possibility. Whenever we turn, he says (echoing Augustine), from thinking about reality by means of created things to the principles and causes of those things, then we have turned from knowledge that "is called by the theologians 'evening' knowledge" to what "is called 'morning' knowledge."[9] We can see how this pendular contemplative momentum is, for Ficino, at work throughout all the levels of reality—the expressive outflow of radiant divine beauty attracting the ardent contemplative upward yearning of the creatures back toward their source. He says:

Beauty is a certain act or ray from it [the Good] penetrating through all things: first into the Angelic Mind, second into the Soul of the whole, and the other souls, third into Nature, fourth into the Matter of bodies. It adorns the Mind with the order of Ideas. It fills the Soul with the series of the Reasons. It supports Nature with the Seeds. It ornaments Matter with the Forms. But just as a single ray of the sun lights up four bodies, fire, air, water, and earth, so a single ray of God illuminates the Mind, the Soul, Nature, and Matter. And just as anyone who sees the light in those four elements is looking at a ray of the sun itself and, through that ray is turned to looking at the supreme light of the sun, so anyone who looks at and loves the beauty in those four, Mind, Soul, Nature, and Body, is looking at and loving the splendor of God in them, and through this splendor, God Himself.[10]

Importantly, for Ficino, as for Traherne (and most of the Christian tradition prior to modernity), it is the radiance of the intelligible form that beckons the contemplative mind, and therefore it is the particular calling of human beings to awaken to the true meaning, the divine splendor, of that which is arousing them. Contemplation is the means by which the hidden divine beauty within creation can be recognized and acclaimed; it is the means by which creation continues its unfolding pilgrimage from "evening" knowledge to "morning" knowledge, from the night of this world to the light of everlasting day.

But why would such a contemplative ascent, an imitation of the angelic "turning" from the mundane existence of the creatures to their eternal ideas in God, carry such significance? We see Traherne clearly holding this same view:

> The Services of Things and their Excellencies are Spiritual: being Objects not of the Ey, but of the Mind: And you more Spiritual by how much more you Esteem them. Pigs eat Acorns, but neither consider the Sun that gav them Life, nor the Influences of the Heavens by which they were Nourished, nor the very Root of the Tree from whence they came. This being the Work of Angels Who in a Wide and Clear Light see even the Sea that gave them Moysture. And feed upon that Acorn Spritualy, while they Know the Ends for which it was Created and feast upon all these, as upon a World of Joys within it: while to Ignorant Swine that eat the Shell, it is an Empty Husk of no Taste nor Delightfull Savor. (I.27)

Traherne carefully guides the mind along the contemplative itinerary, teaching his readers to journey with the angels up through the causes to the ends of the tiny acorn and so at last into the divine bounty and beauty that is the real core of the creaturely acorn. In this way one comes to feast "upon a World of Joys" hidden within the acorn, and thus Traherne would have us make present within the world, through this contemplative replenishing and refreshing, an influx of the primordial generosity of God. I'm suggesting, then, that this contemplative turn might be seen as a kind of advancing of the creature toward its consummate existence, its archetypal being in its creative or exemplar idea in the eternal Word.

Adam in paradise, says Traherne, was happy though without the things we esteem ("gorgeous apparel, palaces, gold and silver, coaches," etc.), for he was "entertained only with celestial joys, the sun and moon and stars, beasts and fowls and fishes, trees and fruits, and flowers, with the other naked and simple delights of nature" (III.67). This paradisiacal vision could still sense the hidden presence of the Giver in each gift, and Traherne's chief concern is to renew this contemplative delighting in the divine presence in all things, and so realize the truth of all things in God. The point, he writes, is not what objects are before us, but "with what eyes we beheld them, with what affections we esteemed them":

> All men see the same objects, but do not equally understand them. Intelligence is the tongue that discerns and tastes them, Knowledge is the Light of Heaven, Love is the Wisdom and Glory of God, Life extended to all objects is the sense that enjoys them. . . . All objects are in God Eternal: which we by perfecting our faculties are made to enjoy. (III.68)

Tasting the divine goodness in all things with the tongue of the mind, says Traherne, is the way to make real in them now something of the full savor of their archetypal reality in the mind of God.

In Thomas Aquinas's relatively early formulation (in *The Disputed Questions on Truth*) regarding this "life" of the creatures in the Word, he had strongly pointed to this eternal agency:

> The intellection of the Word is his act of existence, and so is the likeness of the things he possesses. Therefore, a likeness of a creature existing in the Word is also his life. Similarly, this likeness of the creature is, in a way, the creature itself—that is, in the same way that the soul is said to be, in some fashion, all things. Consequently, because the likeness of a creature existing within the Word in some way produces the creature and moves it as it exists in its own nature, the creature, in a sense, moves itself, and brings itself into being; that is, in view of the fact that it is brought into being, and is moved by its likeness existing in the Word. Thus, the likeness of a creature in the Word is, in a certain sense, the very life of the creature itself.[11]

As the "very life of the creature itself," the divine idea of the creature existing eternally in the Word bears within itself the authoring power, the agential beauty that is the real meaning of the creature's mundane existence. And in a world where the truth and significance of creatures are so often distorted and indeed mortally wounded by sin, the contemplative "re-cognition" of this truth becomes of life-changing significance. So perhaps we could understand the real meaning of the contemplative turn in this way: as the work of the contemplative mind, holding up into prayerful offering the mystical truth of the creature, reuniting it with its overflowing creative agency within the Word.

In this way, the work of the contemplative mind holds creatures up into consummate reality, rekindling within them their fullness and final end— perhaps even in analogy to the eucharistic offering, in which the gifts and creatures of bread and wine, held up into the offering of the Word made flesh, are replenished beyond all creaturely limits and thus become more really themselves, more really food and drink, precisely in being offered up into the authoring Word of their existence. It is thought provoking to see C. S. Lewis, an eminent scholar of Renaissance literature after all, noticing in Traherne something very like this capacity of contemplative mind and its priestlike responsibility within the created order. He states:

> Remember too what Traherne says, that our appreciation of the world—and this becomes fully conscious only as we express it in art—is a real link in the universal chain. Beauty descends from God into nature: but there it would perish and does except when a Man appreciates it with worship and thus as it were sends it back to God: so that through his consciousness what descended ascends again and the perfect circle is made.[12]

There is perhaps some kinship between the contemplative turn and the aesthetic imagination, for in each case the creaturely mind is at work bringing into intelligible light the hidden fullness and divine significance of things. Commenting on this artistic analogy to the contemplative in Ficino, Louis Dupré observes:

> The beauty of the cosmos and the human ability to improve it through art found their definitive meaning in Ficino's Neoplatonic

philosophy of universal love. Beauty, being the radiance of the divine form, incites a cosmic love that unites all creatures in their return to the divine One. This harmony of all forms inspires the human mind to a contemplation of God's beauty.[13]

Certainly, the divine beauty in all things incites contemplative yearning, as Dupré argues; I only want to suggest that, even beyond this, the contemplative turn sends creatures back to their creative and life-giving truth in God—and that, perhaps, making such an offering is the very heart of human being. Traherne surely intends to make exactly this eucharistically oriented point:

> The Idea of Heaven and Earth in the Soul of Man, is more Precious with GOD then the Things them selvs, and more Excellent in nature. . . . The World within you is an offering returned. Which is infinitly more Acceptable to GOD Almighty, since it came from him that it might return unto Him. Wherein the Mysterie is Great. For GOD hath made you able to Creat Worlds in your mind, which are more Precious unto Him then those which He Created: And to Give and offer up the World unto Him, which is very Delightfull in flowing from Him, but much more in Returning to Him. Besides all which in its own Nature also a Thought of the World, or the World in a Thought is more Excellent then the World, because it is Spiritual and Nearer unto GOD. (II.90)

In this important passage, Traherne not only deploys the classical notion (also seen in the passage from Thomas above) that the mind or soul is in a sense all things by virtue of its ability to conceive them intelligibly, but he also suggests that it is indeed the human calling given by God—to receive God's good gifts for the very purpose of sharing them back again in great thanksgiving, receiving and returning all things in the image of that eternal trinitarian receiving and returning, which is the infinite act of existence itself and the inexhaustible life of God. Moreover, as Traherne adds, God seems to delight in this mutual involvement of creatures in their own return, " for GOD hath made you able to Creat Worlds in your mind, which are more Precious unto Him then those which He Created." Again, I want to suggest that this spiritual insight of Traherne's might, perhaps, share a certain kinship with Aquinas's teaching regarding the exemplary agency of creatures in the Word: what Aquinas considers from the eternal standpoint in God, Traherne considers from the creature's standpoint in time, as it comes to a delighted recognition of its own and all other creatures' cherishable and intelligible truth in God.

For Ficino, this contemplative practice is undoubtedly a preparation for eternity, for, he proposes, when our mind enjoys physical beauty, it is really "loving the shadow of God," so that "in this life we shall love God in all things so that in the next we may love all things in God . . . for living in this way we shall proceed to the point where we shall see both God and all things in God, and love both Him, and all things which are in Him."[14] We can notice the eschatological momentum here, drawing the contemplative onward to that fullness which is now perceptible but not yet within reach. For Traherne, in our exile from Eden the poignant impediment to this contemplative advance is often the sheer overwhelming presence of God's generosity in giving us a whole universe to appreciate and enjoy—being so familiar yet always beyond us, we forsake the vast goodness of sun, moon, stars, seas, and our fellow human beings for small, graspable trifles that we insist on possessing to our mortal impoverishment. In Ficino, our bewilderment is more directly attributable to our disordered and confused desires, unable to sense the full but hidden identity of what we truly long for:

> Hence it happens that the passion of a love is not extinguished by the sight or touch of any body. For he does not desire this or that body, but he admires, desires, and is amazed by the splendor of the celestial majesty shining through bodies. For this reason lovers do not know what they desire or seek, for they do not know God Himself, whose secret flavor infuses a certain very sweet perfume of Himself into His works. By which perfume we are certainly excited every day. The odor we certainly smell; the flavor we undoubtedly do not know . . . we rightly do not know what we are desiring and suffering.[15]

The passion of the lover not only misdirects the lover's own heart, but it does injury to the fellow creatures who are loved, for it fails to recognize in them the true identity betokened by the sweet perfume infused within the creatures by their Creator. The sensory excitement and allurement Ficino evokes here are intense, a wonderfully disturbing evocation of the lover's predicament—both panting after the enchanted fragrance of eternal life, yet bound the more within the musty confines of a love too small and limited.

For both Ficino and Traherne, of course, it is the redeeming presence of Christ, the eternal Truth incarnate, who in his dying and rising radiates ultimate meaning from within this constricted mis-perceiving, mis-loving world, and reorients the contemplative gaze. The cross, writes Traherne, is "the abyss of wonders, the centre of desires. . . . It is a Well of Life beneath in which we may see the face of Heaven above: and the only mirror, wherein all things appear in their proper colours: that is, sprinkled in the blood of our Lord and Saviour" (I.58–59). The very wounds of Christ, he says, are the portals by which alone humanity can regain a true contemplation of reality in God—though even they cannot let one adequately see again "the vast comprehensions of Thine eternal love" (I.64). Traherne thus describes the spiritual transformation and cleansing of the contemplative, who comes to see all things afresh by gazing within the mirror of the cross.

Ficino had often spoken of a similar healing and reharmonizing of the contemplative vision, using the metaphor of music—the ravishing beauty of the divine music "in the eternal mind of God," arousing the mind to a desire that burns free from earthly beauty: by hearing this celestial harmony "the soul receives the echoes of that incomparable music, by which it is led back to its rightful home, so that it may enjoy that true music again."[16] Interestingly, however, one of Ficino's most powerful accounts of such a cleansing ascent or restoration of the contemplative mind comes not in a general Christian Platonic pattern but in a more specifically Christian participation in the paschal mystery. Commenting on *The Divine Names*, Ficino observes that we need the whole apparatus of affirmations and negations in speaking of God only because our beings have not yet passed through the dying away of our fallen misperception of reality and into the full splendor of God's infinite truth; and this will happen just as the sun awakens seed in the womb of the earth when Christ's risen body will give birth to new humanity. The body, mind, and soul of Christ will recondition and shine forth within the human person, and the contemplative will rejoice in "the soul of Christ shining forth in our understanding," and God will at last "unite [our] mind to Himself" so that the mind will be "formed by God through God Himself."[17] In a sense, we might say that, for Ficino and Traherne, the beatific fulfillment of the contemplative vocation is fundamentally a paschal event, a transformation of the human capacity for intelligible vision through the death of the false knowing of reality. This happens, Ficino suggests, by means of a sharing in that ultimate knowing by the Father of the Son, which, in our world, takes place as the resurrection of Christ from the dead and Christ's new body the church in him.

I am suggesting here that the act by which the Father knows himself eternally in the begetting of the Son (and all the ways in which the creatures participate in existence by God's gift) is isomorphic with the act by which the Father acknowledges and vindicates his beloved Son in the resurrection, and this is isomorphic as well, with the act by which in beatitude God gives his own Word, the eternal Idea of himself, to be the form or idea by which the blessed see and know God. In other words, once again, the eternal divine self-knowing—within which takes place the infinite act of knowing of all the creatures in the Word (represented by the divine ideas)—is the ground and basis for both the truth and life of creatures and also the saving source of the contemplative's vision.

I have argued in this brief essay that one might begin to investigate the deep significance of the contemplation of God's beauty in the world by considering the approach of Ficino and Traherne. We have seen reasons for thinking that the very heart of this contemplative calling is a recovery, even now within this world, of that eternal divine knowing of all creatures within the Word. In the history of Christian thought, of course, the divine ideas have functioned both as elements in theological metaphysics (as exemplars or archetypes by which all creatures come to be what they are), and also as elements in theological epistemology (as the eternal reasons by which creaturely minds are illuminated and know the ultimate truth of things). There are also strong examples throughout the tradition of the divine ideas functioning as important features of various approaches to the doctrine of salvation.[18] In many ways, it is perhaps the mystical or contemplative role of the divine ideas that holds many of these various aspects of their career together. Contemplatives who behold and appreciate the real truth of creatures in the light of their divine reality in the Word are able to set alight within the world something of the creatures' purity and vivacity as that flows from their creative archetypes; and this action of the contemplative mind in a sense continues and fosters the creatures' own ascent to the redemptive intelligibility by which, in Christ, they are restored to genuine likeness to themselves as their Author had always intended them to be.

Ficino gives a particularly lovely expression of this co-inherence of the creatures' final destiny with the contemplative's own. Speaking of those who journey via the contemplative turn from the finite forms of things to their ultimate reality in God, he writes of the effect of this ascent on the contemplative as well. He says:

> Anyone who surrenders himself to God with love in this life will recover himself in God in the next life. Such a man will certainly return to his own Idea, the Idea by which he was created. There any defect in him will be corrected again; he will be united with his Idea forever. For the true man and the Idea of a man are the same. For this reason as long as we are in this life, separated from God, none of us is a true man, for we are separated from our own Idea or Form. To it, divine love and piety will lead us. Even though we may be dismembered and mutilated here, then, joined by love to our own Idea, we shall become whole men, so that we shall seem to have first worshipped God in things, in order later to worship things in God, and to worship things in God for this reason, in order to recover ourselves in Him above all.[19]

In tracing the contemplative's journey into God, Ficino makes wonderfully clear this great, redemptive surprise; for in learning to apprehend the divine truth of all the creatures, contemplatives are also drawn by divine love into the first and final truth of themselves as well.

Notes

1. Thomas Traherne, *Centuries, Poems, and Thanksgivings*, ed. H. M. Margoliouth, 2 vols. (Oxford: Oxford University Press, 1958), 1:14. All references to Traherne's *Centuries* will be taken from this edition and given hereafter parenthetically in the text by century and paragraph (which are uniform across editions); thus I.27.

2. John Henry Newman, *Fifteen Sermons Preached before the University of Oxford between A.D. 1826 and 1843,* ed. James David Earnest and Gerard Tracey, new ed. (Oxford: Oxford University Press, 2006), 138.

3. Thomas Aquinas, *Commentary on the Gospel of St John,* §136, trans. J. A. Weisheipl (Albany, NY: Magi Books, 1980), p. 75.

4. Bonaventure, *Collations on the Six Days,* XIII.12, in *The Works of Bonaventure, Cardinal, Seraphic Doctor, and Saint,* trans. José de Vinck, 5 vols. (Paterson, NJ: St. Anthony Guild Press, 1970), 5:190–91.

5. For a magisterial survey of Ficino's mystical thought and his teaching on contemplation, see Bernard McGinn, *The Varieties of Vernacular Mysticism (1350–1550),* vol. 5 of McGinn's *The Presence of God: A History of Western Christian Mysticism* (New York: Crossroad, 2012), 252–70.

6. For an introduction to the discovery of Traherne manuscripts and the new, much more significant Traherne that is emerging as a result, see the works of Denise Inge, *Thomas Traherne: Poetry and Prose* (London: SPCK, 2002); *Happiness and Holiness: Thomas Traherne and His Writings* (London: Canterbury, 2008); and *Wanting like a God: Desire and Freedom in Thomas Traherne* (London: SCM, 2009). On Traherne's link to Ficino, see Carol Marks Sicherman, "Traherne's Ficino Notebook," *Papers of the Bibliographical Society of America* 63 (Second Quarter, 1969): 73–81.

7. Michael J. B. Allen, "Marsilio Ficino on *Significatio,*" in *Midwest Studies in Philosophy* 26 (2002): 30–43, here 41.

8. Augustine of Hippo, *The Literal Meaning of Genesis,* 4.24.41, trans. John Hammond Taylor, 2 vols., Ancient Christian Writers 41–42 (New York: Paulist Press, 1982), 1:132. See also *The City of God* 11.29 on the angels' knowledge of creatures in the Word.

9. Marsilio Ficino, *The Philebus Commentary,* I.8, trans. Michael J. B. Allen (Berkeley: University of California Press, 1975), 124.

10. Marsilio Ficino, *Commentary on Plato's Symposium on Love,* Speech II, Chap. 5, trans. Sears Jayne, 2nd ref. ed. (Dallas: Spring, 1985), 51–52.

11. Thomas Aquinas, *The Disputed Questions on Truth,* q. 4, art. 8, in vol. 1, trans. Robert W. Mulligan (Indianapolis: Hackett, 1994), 198–99.

12. Lewis to his childhood friend Arthur Greaves, Letter 150, in *They Stand Together: The Letters of C. S. Lewis to Arthur Greaves (1914–1963),* ed. Walter Hooper (London: Collins, 1979), 386.

13. Louis Dupré, *Passsage to Modernity: An Essay in the Hermeneutics of Nature and Culture* (New Haven: Yale University Press, 1993), 49.

14. Ficino, *Commentary on Plato's Symposium,* Speech VI, Chap. 19, pp. 144–45.

15. Ibid., Speech II, Chap. 6, p. 52.

16. Ficino, *The Letters of Marsilio Ficino,* vol. 1, 7, trans. Language Department of the School of Economic Science (London: Shepheard-Walwyn, 1975), 45.

17. Ficino, *On Dionysius the Areopagite*, vol. 1, *Mystical Theology and The Divine Names*, Part I, trans. Michael J. B. Allen (Cambridge, MA: Harvard University Press, 2015), 137, 139.

18. For a brief introduction to the divine ideas tradition and its significance in Christian soteriology, see Mark A. McIntosh, "The Maker's Meaning: Divine Ideas and Salvation," *Modern Theology* 28 (2012): 365–84.

19. Ficino, *Commentary on the Symposium*, Speech VI, Chap. 19, p. 145.

Part II

Contemporary Issues
in Mystical Theology

9
When Mysticism Is Outlawed: The Case of Said Nursi

Margaret Benefiel

Said Nursi (1876–1960), arguably the most influential Muslim spiritual leader of the twentieth century, was born into a Kurdish family in the tiny village of Nurs in southeastern Turkey. Formed by Sufi spiritual teachings, a mystic himself, Nursi lived in tumultuous times, through the death throes of the Ottoman Empire, the Turkish War of Independence, and the establishment of the Republic of Turkey. Over his peripatetic lifetime, while in and out of prison and exile, Nursi wrote his voluminous *Risale-i-Nur* (Nursi 2006, 2008a, 2008b, 2010). This essay will argue that, in the crucible of the suppression and eventual outlawing of Sufism in Turkey, Said Nursi forged an innovative and far-reaching form of Islam, one that endures to this day.

The "Old Said" (1876–1899)

Born in 1876 in the days of the Ottoman Empire, Said Nursi was the fourth of seven children. His father, Mirza, also known as Sufi Mirza, was recognized for his piety in the Kurdish village of Nurs in what is now southeastern Turkey. The Naqshbandi Order of Sufism held sway over the religious atmosphere of the region, and several of Said Nursi's siblings developed an interest in religion. Said himself liked to go around and listen to the spiritual teachers of the area. Too small for a school, Nurs sent its children elsewhere for their education, and Said, following in the footsteps of his older brother, traveled with him to Tag, a two-hour journey by foot, for his first school experience at the age of nine, in

179

one of the religious schools of the province. A brilliant student, he also fought with another student and left soon thereafter. Repeating this pattern, he attended several schools, fought with other students, and stayed at each place only a short time, until 1891–92, when he studied for three months in Bayezit under Shaikh Muhammed Celali and completed the entire course of study then available. By age fifteen, Said Nursi had been recognized as a genius and a spiritual teacher.

After traveling to several cities and establishing himself by debating with the *ulama* (religious leaders) there, Said Nursi settled in Bitlis, staying at the governor's residence for two years. In Bitlis, Nursi continued to study and teach, memorizing around forty books and also a good part of the Qur'an. When he was nineteen or twenty, Nursi was invited to move to Van, because there were few *ulama* there; he accepted and there he commenced to teach for the next twelve years.

Middle Period (1899-1918)

For many of his twelve years in Van, Nursi stayed at the governor's residence, which became a center for discussions among government officials, teachers, and intellectuals. In these discussions, Nursi learned of the secularizing influences in Turkey, and he came to recognize that Islamic theology as it was being taught at the time could not answer the doubts and questions coming its way. He took it upon himself to learn the modern sciences and studied history, geography, mathematics, geology, physics, chemistry, astronomy, and philosophy. He formulated an approach to education that included teaching both science and religion, demonstrating that they did not conflict with each other, and he started working toward establishing a university in eastern Anatolia that would incorporate this approach.

During this time, Nursi found inspiration in nature, walking in the mountains, praying, and contemplating the "book of the universe" (Vahide 2005, 29). He developed his own form of mysticism, arguing that the Naqshbandi form of Sufism that had surrounded him in his childhood was not relevant to a world doubting the basic truths of Islam. The twentieth century, he argued, needed an innovative Islam that incorporated twentieth-century scientific knowledge, instead of an Islam that assumed that everyone believed and then led some into a more esoteric practice of the faith. The mysticism that Nursi practiced thrust him back out into the world to preach his message, instead of withdrawing him from the world, as the Sufi training of the time did. While Nursi maintained great respect for Sufism, his own mystical path took a different turn.

Nursi traveled to Istanbul in 1907 to procure support for his university. During this time, he established himself among the Istanbul *ulama* as a brilliant thinker and spiritual leader. Jealousies and political upheavals landed him in jail, and, upon his release, he headed back east to Van in 1910. In 1914, when the Ottoman Empire joined the Central Powers (Germany and Austria-Hungary) in World War I, Nursi enlisted in the army as a volunteer and was sent to fight the Russians in Erzurum. Captured in 1916, Nursi and others were taken by a circuitous route to a prison camp in Kosturma in northwestern Russia. Barely escaping with his life, Nursi found a way out of prison during the confusion of the Bolshevik Revolution in 1918.

Transitional Period (1918–1925)

After Nursi escaped his imprisonment in Russia and eventually made his way to Istanbul in June of 1918, he was met with a hero's welcome. Although he pleaded for rest after his two years of active duty in the war and his subsequent two and a half years of harsh imprisonment, he was appointed to the newly established Daru'l-Hikmeti'l-Islamiye, a learned Islamic council, in August of 1918. In his role on the council, Nursi opposed the secularizing influences of both the occupying British forces in Istanbul and the Nationalist resistance based in Anatolia, despite the anger and retribution directed toward him from both sides. Along with the British occupation after the war came attacks on Islam. Nursi wrote a terse response to a questionnaire on Islam from authorities in the Church of England, "Answer to a Scheming Cleric Who Wanted to Pour Scorn on Us":

Question: What does the religion of Muhammed consist of?

Answer: The Qur'an.

Question: What has it contributed to life and thought?

Answer: Divine unity and moderation.

Question: What is the remedy for man's troubles?

Answer: The prohibition of interest and usury and the obligatory payment of *zakat*.

Question: What does it say concerning the present upheavals?

Answer: Man has nought save that [for] which he strives (Qur'an 53:39). And those who amass gold and silver and do not spend it in the way of God; announce to them a most grievous punishment (Qur'an 9:34). (Nursi N.d ["Rumuz"], 85)

The British occupation eventually galvanized and reenergized the exhausted and defeated Turks to fight to take back their country, and the Turkish War of Independence began in 1920.

During this bitter time of occupation and war, Nursi underwent a profound spiritual transformation. Disillusioned with the philosophers and the path of reason alone, he returned to religion as the source of all truth. He later described this period in his life:

So I told myself that a way that even [the great philosophers] had been unable to take could not be made general, and I gave it up. . . . Then I had recourse to the way of Sufism and studied it. I saw that it was truly luminous and effulgent, but that it needed the greatest caution. Only the highest of the elite could take that way. So, saying that this cannot be the way for everyone at this time, either, I sought help from the Qur'an. And thanks be to God, the *Risale-i Nur* was bestowed on me, which is a safe, short way inspired by the Qur'an for the believers of the present time. (Sahiner 1979, 399; quoted in Vahide 2005, 167)

After the Turkish War of Independence (1920–22), Mustafa Kemal welcomed Nursi into deliberations about the new government. In 1922, Kemal invited Nursi to Ankara, which by then had become the seat of the new government, and Nursi was given a warm welcome by the Grand National Assembly. Nursi was not impressed, however. The secularism in the new government and lack of respect for Islam shocked and saddened him. He preached a fiery sermon about the necessity of prayer and devotion, and, as a result, sixty of the deputies renewed their daily prayer and a larger room needed to be found to accommodate them all. Nursi gave moving speeches about the necessity of a vibrant religion for a strong republic ("The foundation stones of the mighty revolution have to be firm" [Vahide 2005, 170]), and tried to convince the government to embrace Islam. In time, however, it became clear that, while Nursi saw the revitalization of Islam as the essential moral foundation of the new Turkish Republic, Kemal saw Islam as the cause of Turkey's "backwardness." The Kemalists sought to diminish the influence of religion in their efforts to modernize Turkey. Nursi, while supporting the concept of a secular government, continued to stress the importance of teaching religion alongside science, emphasizing that the two did not conflict with each other but rather needed each other to build a strong foundation for a modern Turkey. When Nursi felt that the differences between the Kemalist government and himself had become irreconcilable, he left Ankara in 1923 for Van in eastern Anatolia, giving up politics. The subsequent outlawing of the Sufi orders in 1925 was the last straw for Nursi. The "New Said" focused on the revitalization of Islam, eschewing politics, believing that it was through sincere religion that Turkey would be strengthened to survive in the modern era.

The "New Said" (1925–1948) and His Remaining Years

Now the persecutions of Nursi began in earnest. While Nursi continued to maintain that the Sufi path held no relevance for modern Turkey, he did continue to practice his own form of mysticism, a simple, direct nature mysticism. He would withdraw to the mountains or build a simple tree house and fast and pray for hours, immersed in nature, away from civilization. His students reported that he would stay in his tree house all night, lost in contemplation, and that the birds would come in the morning to join him in prayer. He became known for his piety, frugality, brilliance, wisdom, and compassion. He attracted numerous followers wherever he went. His band of followers, drawn by his devotion and wisdom, grew exponentially. As his influence increased, so did the number of his enemies.

In 1925, the Kemalist government forced Nursi into exile in the remote village of Barla, accusing him and his students of participating in the Shaikh Said Revolt, despite Nursi's repeated refusals to support it. During his eight and a half years in Barla, Nursi wrote more than half of his magnum opus, the *Risale-i Nur*. Nursi believed that the *Risale-i Nur* was given through him as divine revelation, to address the rampant unbelief of his day. For Nursi, above all, belief formed the foundation of society:

> The *Risale-i Nur* is not only repairing some minor damage or some small house; it is repairing vast damage and the all-embracing citadel that contains Islam, the stones of which are the size of mountains. And it is not striving to reform only a private heart and an individual conscience; it is striving to cure with the medicines of the Qur'an and belief . . . the collective heart and generally held ideas that have been breached in awesome fashion by the tools of corruption prepared and stored up over a thousand years. (Nursi 1960, 10)

The *Risale-i Nur* focused on making basic teachings of the Qur'an accessible to all. Demonstrating the bankruptcy of materialist philosophy, Nursi used a method of reflecting on the material world that sought its deeper meaning, using allegory as a "telescope" to bring distant truths into sharp focus, as well as using reason and logic. In this way, he argued for the existence of God, the unity of God, the resurrection of the dead, and the last judgment, among other things. He also wrote on practical matters, such as frugality and caring for the sick and elderly. In an age when mysticism had been outlawed, Nursi, rather than inviting people onto the mystical path that he followed, exhorted people to believe and to live lives of faithfulness in the midst of ordinary life. With the great threats of atheism and positivism looming, Nursi propagated a simple faith that would stem the tide of unbelief.

Nursi often contrasted the way of the *Risale-i Nur* with the way of Sufism. In the *Risale,* Nursi began with the material world and moved to knowledge of God through "reading the book of the universe." In the Sufism of his time, Nursi noted, the universe's existence was either denied or ignored, since the Sufis' journey to God was an inner journey, through the heart. Nursi integrated both mind and heart, using logic and reasoned argument and drawing on scientific principles, to link modern scientific awareness with the spiritual insights of the Qur'an. When he was later charged with teaching Sufism by the Eskisehir court, Nursi responded, "As I have written in numerous treatises, this is not the time of Sufism; it is the time to save belief. Many people enter paradise without following the Sufi path, but none enter it without belief. It is therefore the time to work for belief" (Nursi 1976, 199).

As Nursi's students hand-copied the *Risale-i Nur* and disseminated it widely, the authorities became nervous. Increased persecution and constant raids to confiscate copies of the *Risale-i Nur* made Nursi's life miserable. In 1935, he and thirty-one of his students were arrested and sent to prison in Eskisehir. Released a year later, Nursi was sent to Kastamonu to live under house arrest for the next seven and a half years, under constant surveillance and harassment. In 1943, he and his leading students were arrested and held in Denizli prison under appalling conditions. More exiles and imprisonments followed. Throughout his many imprisonments and exiles, Nursi was poisoned a number of times and barely survived. When in prison, Nursi continued his prayers and his teaching, so much so that hardened criminals were converted, began praying, and changed their ways. Nursi stressed prayer and surrender to God in his teaching. As it was said, "The prison became a mosque." Nursi's deep prayer sustained him, and he focused on serving God and his fellow human beings, even while in prison. The *Risale-i Nur* continued to grow and develop, copied by prisoners who had been converted, and smuggled out of the prisons by his followers. Nursi continued to emphasize both the importance of turning to God in the face of secularization and the harmony between religion and modern science.

Nursi's mystical religion provided him with strength and insight to endure prolonged persecution and work for the renewal of religious practice in a form compatible with modern science and secular government. Through his long years of exile and imprisonment, as he wrote the *Risale-i Nur* on scraps of paper, it was through the hard work of his followers' hand-copying that the text was disseminated (six hundred thousand handwritten copies of various parts of the text exist [Vahide 2005, 204]). Nursi persevered in his mission throughout his long life.

After the Turkish election of 1950, he lived to see a lifting of many of the restrictions on the practice of Islam. By 1956, the *Risale-i Nur* could be printed, something that increased its readership to hundreds of thousands (Vahide 2005, 305).

By the end of his life, through the *Risale-i Nur* and his other teachings, Said Nursi had influenced nearly a million people to see Islam in a new light. Instead of viewing Islam as the cause of Turkey's backwardness, they came to understand Islam as the new Turkey's source of strength. Instead of feeling embarrassed about their religion, Turkey's Muslims could hold their heads high and join the efforts to modernize Turkey, through prayer, surrender, and serving humanity.

The Nur Movement after Nursi's Death (1960–present)

After Nursi's death in 1960, his influence increased. The "Nur Movement" mushroomed. It also split. Interestingly, its impact increased with the divisions. According to *Risale* scholar Metin Karabasoglu, this occurred "probably because after each secession or division, each new part tried hard to compensate for the unintended consequences of the process of disintegration with new activities and initiatives" (2003, 283). One of the most successful splinter groups was led by Fethullah Gulen, whose Hizmet Movement now numbers ten to fifteen million followers, in 163 countries. The Hizmet Movement focuses on education (Agai 2002; Balci 2003), relying on Turkish businessmen to fund secondary schools and universities that fulfill Nursi's vision of promoting excellence in science while at the same time honoring Islam. Gulen has also expanded into other areas, promoting interreligious dialogue and peace education. A controversial figure because of his critique of the current Turkish government, Gulen succeeded in establishing schools worldwide (including charter schools in the United States); this, as well as his perceived reclusiveness, has raised many questions. He now lives in retirement in Pennsylvania. Recently, Gulen was the recipient of the 2015 Gandhi King Ikeda Award for Peace at Morehouse University in Atlanta, a prize that includes such past awardees as Nelson Mandela, Desmond Tutu, Mikhail Gorbachev, and Rosa Parks.

Conclusion

After mysticism was outlawed in Turkey, through the crucible of persecution and the practice of a clandestine mysticism, Said Nursi, motivated by a powerful drive, forged an innovative form of Islam based on prayer and the Qur'an, one compatible with modern science, which he believed could thrive in a secular republic. Through prayer, surrender, and service, Nursi insisted that Muslims could help build the new Turkey. As a result, the far-reaching, powerfully motivated Nur movement, in its various forms, endures and maintains substantial influence to this day (Agai 2002; Balci 2003; Yavuz 2003, 2013).

References

Abu-Rabi, I., ed. 2003. *Islam at the Crossroads*. Albany: State University of New York Press.

———, ed. 2008. *Spiritual Dimensions of Bediuzzaman Said Nursi's Risale-i Nur.* Albany: State University of New York Press.

Agai, B. 2002. "Fethullah Gulen and His Movement's Islamic Ethic of Education." *Critique: Critical Middle Eastern Studies* 11:27–47.

Balci, B. 2003. "Fethullah Gulen's Missionary Schools in Central Asia and Their Role in the Spreading of Turkism and Islam." *Religion, State, and Society* 31:151–77.

Dorroll, P. 2014. "The Turkish Understanding of Religion: Rethinking Tradition and Modernity in Contemporary Turkish Islamic Thought." *Journal of the American Academy of Religion* 82:1033–69.

Karabasoglu, M. 2003. "Text and Community: An Analysis of the *Risale-i Nur* Movement." In *Islam at the Crossroads,* ed. I. Abu-Rabi, 263–96. Albany: State University of New York Press.

Mardin, S. 1989. *Religion and Social Change in Modern Turkey: The Case of Bediuzzaman Said Nursi*. Albany: State University of New York Press.

Nursi, S. 2006. *The Words (Risale-i Nur Collection)*. Clifton, NJ: Tughra Books.

———. 2008a. *The Reasonings (Risale-i Nur Collection)*. Clifton, NJ: Tughra Books.

———. 2008b. *The Letters (Risale-i Nur Collection)*. Clifton, NJ: Tughra Books.

———. 2010. *The Rays: Reflections on Islamic Belief, Thought, Worship, and Action (Risale-i Nur Collection)*. Clifton, NJ: Tughra Books.

———. 1960. *Kastamonu Lahikasi*. Istanbul: Sinan Matbassi.

———. 1976. *Risale-i Nur Kulliyati Muellifi*. Istanbul: Sozler Yayinevi.

———. N.d. "Rumuz." In *Asar-i Bedi'iyye*.

Sahiner, N. 1979. *Said Nursi ve Nurculuk Hakkinda Aydinlar Konusuyor*. Istanbul: Yeni Asya Yayinlari.

Turner, C., and H. Horkuc. 2009. *Said Nursi*. London: Oxford University Press.

Vahide, S. 2005. *Islam in Modern Turkey: An Intellectual Biography of Bediuzzaman Said Nursi*. Albany: State University of New York Press.

Yavuz, M. H. 2003. *Islamic Political Identity in Turkey*. New York: Oxford University Press.

———. 2013. *Toward an Islamic Enlightenment*. New York: Oxford University Press.

10

Being as *Símbolo*: A Latino Reading of Dionysian Aesthetics

Peter Casarella

I. Theological Aesthetics in Latino/a Perspective

Latino/a theology has from its inception maintained a theological epistemology that grounds the reasonableness of Christian belief in forms of knowing that are grasped symbolically and that arise from rituals, performances, and icons. These symbols are oriented not just toward the good (moral action) and the true (foundational or fundamental theology) but also toward beauty (theological aesthetics). One important reason for proposing the program of theological aesthetics in precisely this fashion has to do with Latino/a theology's methodology from below, one that listens to the faith of the people as a prime source for theological reflection. As Orlando O. Espín has explained in *Faith of the People*, the cultural and religious symbols of *religiosidad popular*, or popular Catholicism, carry more weight than the application of the abstract

---

This essay is a form of mourning and celebration for one who passed much too early. John Jones first contacted me just after he finished his dissertation under Cyril O'Regan but before he began to work for Crossroad. At the time he was looking for contributions to a collection he was assembling on new approaches to the thought of Dionysius the Areopagite. Sadly, the book never came to fruition, but I offer this essay, belatedly and fondly, to a generous friend and brilliant theologian. John truly grasped the challenge we face when we, like "sculptures who set out to carve a stone," dare to "remove every obstacle to the pure view of the hidden image, and simply by this act of clearing aside . . . show up the beauty which is hidden" (MT II, 1025AB; see n. 26 below).

categories drawn from European and North American theology.[1] This is not a denigration of the European inheritance but is, rather, a search for a hitherto unexplored path to knowledge about God and the world. Moreover, the beauty of symbolic forms embedded within the practices of Latino/a believers is as important as the cry emanating from the poor for social justice. Beauty and justice thus became intertwined in Latino/a experience.

The perdurance of Latino/a theological aesthetics has been sharply (and unfairly) criticized as an elitist flight from the real socioeconomic struggles of the people, but in spite of that it does not seem to be fading.[2] Several authors have contributed to this development. Roberto Goizueta Jr. highlighted the distinctiveness of a Latino "theopoetic" in *Caminemos con Jesús.*[3] In *Jesus Our Companion* he continued to open up the aesthetic dimension of faith with an even more explicitly christological focus. Michelle Gonzalez Maldonado contributed to Latino theological aesthetics with her study of Sor Juana de la Cruz.[4] She shows that the complex question of gender and gender stereotypes cannot be separated from the perception of embodied beauty. I myself articulated a Latino theory of aesthetic expressiveness derived principally from works of art, popular devotions, a study of Mexican-American curatorship, and the aesthetics of Octavio Paz.[5] In my work I recognize that philosophical theories of art and the theological valorization of popular piety have usually been treated as opposed. It does not suffice to place religious works of art and the aesthetic dimensions of acts of devotion in separate domains. So I attempt to bridge the gap between theorizing about the phenomenon of religious art and attending to the poetic acts of devotion in Latino/a experience. The distinct perspectives are valid in the terms set out by certain scholars, but the most interesting aspect of each for a more ample theological aesthetics is their convergence. In sum, all three of these theologians—Goizueta, González, and myself—uphold theological aesthetics as a highly illuminating way (but not the only way) to articulate the faith of the people. There is no path to *teología en conjunto* (pastoral activity and reflection by the community) that bypasses the *via pulchritudinis* ("the way of beauty").[6]

The most philosophically elaborate defense of this philosophical dimension of Latino/a theology is Goizueta's 2004 essay on symbolic realism.[7] In this essay, the Latino/a symbol of faith stands at the crossroads of the separation of the physical from the spiritual in the advent of modernity. Here Goizueta returns to a theme in his work that had been present since the time of his comparative study of Enrique Dussel and Bernard Lonergan and that he has also articulated in terms of a new retrieval of the philosophical theology of Bartolomé de las Casas.[8] Utilizing Louis Dupré's genealogy of modernity alongside Rahner's theology of the symbol, Goizueta argues that Latino/a theology must recover some aspect of the premodern synthesis of nature and culture, that is, of sacramental beauty in material forms and the search for the absolute in a spirituality of the everyday. One-sided theological modernisms that fail to critique the Gnostic return in modernity serve the Latino/a people of God poorly.[9] This retrieval includes, but also goes beyond, recognizing that the roots of Latino/a piety are to be found in medieval and Baroque forms. It also includes reflecting on the current state of everyday piety:

> The God of Latino/a Catholics is one whose reality is inseparable from our everyday life and struggles. It is in the very warp and woof of everyday life, what Latino/a theologians have called *lo cotidiano* (the everyday), that God becomes known to us. For Latino/a Catholics, our faith is ultimately made credible by our everyday relationship with a God whom we can touch and embrace, a God with whom we can weep or laugh, a God who infuriates us and whom we infuriate, a God whose anguished countenance we can caress and whose pierced feet we can kiss.[10]

There are indeed resonances of what Dupré wistfully calls "the medieval synthesis" in contemporary Latino/a faith and experience. But the task of theologian is hardly one of attempting in vain to turn back the clocks. The present task is rather a search for a new synthesis that proclaims the sacramental worldview in *lo cotidiano* with the same fervor and audacity as was displayed by the mendicants, preachers, and confraternities who accompanied Columbus to the new world over five hundred years ago.[11] But that proclamation has the additional burden of having to speak to an entirely different world.

What about Dionysian aesthetics? Is there any connection between the aesthetics that has recently emerged from "the underside" of late modern U.S. history and the speculative thought of this nebulous figure from fifth- or sixth-century Byzantium? Some Latino/a theologians have already answered these questions in the affirmative. In *The Community of the Beautiful*, Alex García-Rivera set out to define the metaphysical breadth of Latino/a theology while still maintaining as his point of departure the concrete narratives of holy women and men in Latino/a popular piety. He lifts up local devotions ranging from Our Lady of Guadalupe to the daily struggles of working-class Peruvians and Mexicans whom he pastored as a Lutheran minister in Allentown, Pennsylvania.

How can the signs provided by these devotions lead to knowledge of the beautiful, the good, and the true? The first step, according to García-Rivera, is a reconstruction of the metaphysical breadth of the vision of form in terms of a fourfold dynamism of the human person as *capax Dei*. The second step comes by way of Charles Sanders Peirce and Josiah Royce and the development of an intercultural semiotic of the forms of *religiosidad popular*. The fourfold capacity for God is laid out as follows: (1) the recognition that grace is in some fashion intrinsic to human experience, that is, the critique of neoscholastic two-tiered theology of nature and grace set forth by Maurice Blondel and Karl Rahner; (2) the articulation of the analogy of being as defended by Erich Przywara and Hans Urs von Balthasar; (3) the engagement with the discourse of the human flesh of the incarnate Word as a point of entry to the symbolic realism of all knowledge of God; and (4) "seeing the form" (e.g., St. Francis's mystical experience of the crucified seraph) as the perception of radical difference through mystical anagogy.[12] Dionysian aesthetics enters in the third dimension and plays a crucial role in the entire movement because Dionysius alone accentuates the "dissimilar similarity" that makes possible an anagogical appropriation of difference (both Creator/creature and intracosmic difference).[13] García-Rivera saw more clearly than anyone else the twofold challenge of a Latino/a fundamental theology: first, locating the question of difference outside of a politics of identity and inside of an unfolding according to both reason and faith of how the palpable presence of the Absolute relates to everyday experience; and, second, the need, prior to articulating an intracultural and socially mediated semiotics of difference, to affirm "the radical objectivity of the form, at once accessible to reason and faith."[14] In both these respects, Dionysian aesthetics plays a pivotal and creative role.

Cecilia Gonzalez-Andrieu has broadened the argument for the Latino/a retrieval of Dionysian aesthetics in *A Bridge to Wonder*.[15] She begins with the experience of wonder in attending a live performance of *La Pastorela* in Luis Valdés's Teatro Campesino ("The Farmworker Theater").[16] The melding of popular religiosity with a shepherd's play written in a distinctively contemporary and Latino/a key opens the eyes of the viewer not just to the plight and worldview of immigrants, but to a far broader aesthetic lens for perceiving natural and social reality. The awakening to beauty in the *La Pastorela* "shocks" one into seeing the world in a new, postconsumerist way:

> As the experience of *La Pastorela* shows, it is the ability to recognize the truly beautiful in all its complexity that returns us to life. The gift of God we recognize in *La Pastorela* . . . would disappear if we come to believe what advertising all around us proclaims: that beauty is not inherently ours at all, but it is for sale.[17]

It is in this context that she cites the Areopagite on how beauty "bids all things to itself," a beckoning to primordial beauty that emerges from the midst of life.[18] As she puts it, the "ethics of life" follow from "the aesthetics of life."[19]

The second deployment of Dionysius in *A Bridge to Wonder* occurs in speaking about the theology of art. Given the priority of wonder as a total experience of reality, Gonzalez-Andrieu abjures the idea that she is a writing a book simply about the religious dimensions of art. Instead, she is investigating how the experience of a wondrous work of art opens up a dimension of reality that facilitates the imagining of a hope for salvation even in the presence of radical personal and social evil. She therefore adopts Erwin Panofsky's rather idealized praise for Dionysian aesthetics as the philosophical groundwork for the sacramental art and architecture of the scholastic period.[20] In any case, Gonzalez-Andrieu demonstrates convincingly that the Dionysian reflection on beauty in and beyond the world offers the contemporary theologian an ideal idiom not just for speaking to the sacred beauty of a work of art but also for penetrating its depth and discovering its ability to open up a new world of experience.

In the light of the above, it appears that there is a heavy dosage of Balthasarian formalism running through the veins of Latino/a theology.[21] In other words, the modern and contemporary eclipse of the concrete presence of the form of Christ, its palpability and ontological density, stands as the first roadblock to grasping the beauty of popular religion. García-Rivera adopts quite polemical language in defending Balthasar's breakthrough on form even while suggesting that the semiotics of G. M. Hopkins and C. S. Peirce provide a much-needed critique of Balthasarian formalism.[22] Why, one might then ask, is not recourse made to Karl Rahner's modern transcendental theology and especially his more anthropocentric notion of "being as symbol"? Given Rahner's importance in the development of the idea of a "World Church," is Rahnerian post-Heideggerian aesthetics of the symbol a better fit for Latino/a religiosity than the Balthasarian retrieval of ancient form?[23] I offer two initial comments. First, Latino/a theology begins with the faith of the people in its own community of believers. It is not indifferent to important debates deriving from the legacies of the perhaps the two greatest figures of the German-speaking Catholic world of the twentieth century, but critical reflection on the faith of the people need not necessarily lead to an adjudication of this question wholly in favor of one or the other of these two European influences on U.S. theology. Second, Rahner and von Balthasar theologized about the *phainein* ("appearing") of symbolic knowledge early in their careers, at which point they knew each other as collaborators rather than combatants.[24] Balthasar was still heavily indebted to the expressivism of Goethe, and Rahner was, like his equally prodigious brother Hugo, still exploring the theological significance of the symbols of the Fathers of the Church. It is quite possible, as Miguel Díaz has cogently argued, that the meaning of the symbol in U.S. Latino/a experience speaks to a Catholic sense of sacramentality that is already presupposed by both authors in this period when their visions still converged.[25]

In sum, the Dionysian moment in Latino/a theological aesthetics has in the first instance a negative force. The desire for an encounter with God and with the good through the mode of beauty cannot be reduced to an experience that is either wholly private or mainly subjective. The former is ruled out by the primordial presence of the symbolic and culturally mediated forms of *religiosidad popular*. The latter also does not accord with the weight placed on the *presence* of an expressive transcendental of being in a diverse array of radiant, concrete forms. This perception is not an opting for an objective aesthetics (Bernard Bosanquet, for instance) over a subjective, idealist one, because the aesthetic mediation of faith is still centered on the lifting up of the human heart in an upward movement of anagogy. Stated in positive terms, Latino/a aesthetics is an encounter with the epiphany of beauty that occurs in the culturally determined works of art and acts of devotion that are particular to a people. That encounter with the incarnate beauty of God transforms the believer into an adorer of the God who died for the sake of humanity and an agent of social transformation within a holy people, loyal to God (*santo pueblo, fiel a Dios*) who accompany the poor of Jesus Christ.

II. Reading the *Corpus Dionysiacum* "latinamente"

What is most mysterious about the *Corpus Dionysiacum* (CD) is neither the author's decision to write pseudonymously nor the inability of scholars to pin down his identity. What is most mysterious is the fact that certain key concepts that at first glance seem familiar, for example, "symbol," "hierarchy," and "mystical theology," have an original meaning within the CD that belies our own everyday understanding. The reading that follows seeks to highlight this anomaly. To read a text through a Latino/a lens is thus not at all an interpolation. It is a reading that allows the strangeness of the text to come to the fore. A Latino reading, therefore, has to highlight what is fundamentally other in the CD, an act that entails attending to philology and contextual research even where our knowledge of certain basic facts remains murky.

Let us begin by examining the concept of the symbol in the Dionysian synthesis. The model for symbolic manifestation lies in sacramental action, although it is found in the whole cosmos and not just in the actions of a liturgical presider. For Dionysius, the point and principal goal of every sacrament is to impart the mysteries of the deity to whom one is already initiated. In the "illumination" regarding baptism, for example, Dionysius writes:

No one could understand, let alone put into practice, the truths received from God if he did not have a divine beginning. Is it not the case that at the human level we must first begin to exist and then do what is appropriate to us? The nonexistent neither moves nor even begins to exist, whereas that which has some mode of being produces or experiences only that which is natural to it. This, it seems to me, is quite clear. So, therefore, let us behold the divine symbols which have to do with the divine birth and let no one who is uninitiated approach this spectacle.[26]

The illumination imparts insight that is more than moral exemplarity, although the performance of the latter is indeed a condition for the possibility of attaining illumination. As the above quotation illustrates, both the discipleship in a life of holiness and the beholding of the form are geared toward the experience of union with God.

In fact, René Roques has argued convincingly that philosophical realism and eucharistic symbolism are not at all opposed in Dionysius.[27] He makes this claim acknowledging that there is no reference in the CD to a real presence of Christ in the eucharistic elements, a chief focus of the high medieval West, and also in recognition of the infinite deferral of meaning in the Dionysian interpretation of sacramental presence:

The fact that the Eucharist prefigures and announces a fuller possession does not deprive it at all of its reality nor of its efficacy in the present moment. On the contrary, just as full possession [of a reality] cannot take place without the prefiguration of that which it already realizes, the inchoate reality of the image must not hamper the mind from stretching itself towards [ne doit pas entraver l'élan de l'intelligence vers] an ever more spiritual and complete possession.[28]

This statement accurately conveys the sense in which Dionysius stands at the beginning of a philosophical realism that is grounded in sacramental actions and thus remains resistant to the kind of modern bifurcations between material reality and spiritual meaning that Goizueta highlighted. The latter point is in fact anachronistic, since Dionysius could not foresee either the oppositions that developed in the Latin West and much less so a new form of Gnostic dualism in modernity. There is therefore a Humpty-Dumpty quality to invoking the Dionysian synthesis. We are reconstructing a sense of reality that is more original than that which we can presently imagine. The Dionysian prefiguration of a future Latino/a form of symbolic realism is nonetheless accessible to us and therefore highly instructive.

There is still a more direct form of symbolic manifestation in the CD. *Symbolic Theology* is the title given to a work by Dionysius that was either never written or was lost.[29] At first glance, it seems that Dionysius wants to maintain a sharp distinction between the content of *The Divine Names* and that of the *Symbolic Theology*. The latter concentrates on the material representations of the divinity that are found in scripture, and the former on the immaterial realities signified by names such as goodness, wisdom, and so on. The Ninth Letter addresses the contents of the *Symbolic Theology* in a much more synthetic fashion. Although his language is rather patronizing regarding those who have a "childish imagination regarding the sacred symbol," or worse still, "the contamination of the mob," Dionysius is actually trying to work out the relationship between religious symbols that in their literal sense seem shocking to the vast majority of believers and their hidden sense.[30] These divine attributes include the bosom of the Father, inebriation, and (in the Song of Songs) "passionate longings fit only for prostitutes."[31] Dionysius sees both the need to preserve the paradoxical symbols with all of their abrasiveness and to defend the use of demonstrative reason to clarify their "interior" meaning:

> Theological tradition has a dual aspect, the ineffable and mysterious on the one hand, the open and more evident on the other. The one resorts to symbolism and involves initiation. The other is philosophic and employs the method of demonstration. . . . Jesus himself speaks of God by means of parables, and passes on to us the mystery of his divine activity by using the symbolism of a table.[32]

For Latinos theological reflection arises from the symbols of popular piety (which are by no means divorced from the material symbols of Scripture). The Dionysian double standard regarding levels of understanding is rejected, but the need to correlate dual modes of a single divinely inspired discourse remains.

Eric Perl has shown that the notion of symbol is a structuring principle in the Dionysian philosophy of God that extends beyond the discrete task of scriptural exegesis or the interpretation of rituals.[33] The key idea of προβάλλειν in both the Ninth Letter and in *The Divine Names* refers to either a "presenting" or a "screening" of God.[34] To the degree that all creatures are symbolic representations of the divine, Perl then concludes that "every being is at once a presentation and concealment of God."[35] This means that being itself is a symbolic reality and that the dynamism of revealing and concealing is present in every display of reality. No symbol can then be taken as a fully present reality. Each symbol shares the mysteriousness of coming to presence that we might associate with a beautiful work of art. In Spanish, the sense that reality itself is an illusion that contains two sides is termed *desengaño*. Unlike modern dualism, the Spanish term preserves the duality of appearance qua appearance and appearance as inherently veiled. The *obras sacramentales* of the Spanish dramatist Pedro Calderón de la Barca also highlight this theme in a very Neoplatonic fashion.

In the medieval Latin tradition of interpretion, Dionysius's "symbolic theology" (not just the purported treatise but the very idea) came to be understood as a new form of knowing. This line of thought provoked scholastic thinkers to reflect on the nature and purpose of theology itself.[36] The birth of a high medieval theological aesthetics in the Latin West cannot be separated from the dissemination of Dionysian symbolic theology. Latino/a theologians likewise recognize that there is a distinctive *ars* ("craft") to symbolic theology. This form of theological discourse complements rather than replaces the scientific rigor of academic theology. The Latino/a theologian is attracted to and guided by the beauty of *religiosidad popular*, but cannot rest content with a subjective evocation of how pleasing it may seem to engage these exotic practices. Their theological content and social significance must be rigorously scrutinized without depriving them of the meaning that they hold in the lives of the people of God. For both the Dionysian theologian and the Latino/a theologian, one must attend carefully to the givenness of what is displayed (in scripture, in liturgical celebrations, in the cosmos) before one can reflect on its meaning. This is what García-Rivera means by "seeing the form."[37]

Dionysius writes as a Christian sacramental theologian inspired by Neoplatonism whose main concern in the *Symbolic Theology* is to explain how a God who takes up no space whatsoever can be depicted in spatial terms.[38] He is, at least implicitly, a theoretician of sacred topology.[39] Although his approach to the Neoplatonic and Stoic sources on finite knowledge of the cosmos is not uncritical, he still maintains in a Neoplatonic fashion that immaterial form can be known apart from its individuation in matter.[40] There is thus an interesting divergence between Dionysius and García-Rivera on the purpose of matter in the order of creation. Both philosophies of nature are realist, but the latter follows late scholastic theology and John Duns Scotus in particular by maintaining that matter individuates form and that a "formal distinction" can be maintained between common natures and their individuated appearances. For Dionysius, the process of giving expression to immaterial form through material symbols and sacramental activities is inexhaustible since it extends to the depth and breadth of the entire cosmos, but there is no distinction to be made, formal or real, between common natures and their individuated expression. *Haecceitas*, or "thisness," is for Scotus a composite of a specific nature and an individual difference, but is a foreign term in the Dionysian universe. The advantage of Scotistic *haecceitas* over Dionysian realism, according to García-Rivera, is that it valorizes material expression unequivocally and avoids the seemingly redundant supposition of an abstract presence of an immaterial nature for individuals that are differentiated materially.[41] Dionysian symbols, by contrast, remain screens that veil and unveil their immaterial natures.

What can Latino/a theologians learn from Dionysius's approach to sacraments? The liturgical actions described in *The Ecclesiastical Hierarchy* such as the synaxis (communion); blessing of the oils; the consecrations of bishops, priests, deacons, and monks; and funeral rites are not presented as celebrations on the streets. In fact, Dionysius, in contrast to his follower Maximus the Confessor, is indifferent to the church building.[42] What he says about "our most pious hierarchy" in *The Celestial Hierarchy* suggests a method for looking for layers of meaning beyond rote performance in the *fiesta* as such of liturgy.[43] Dionysius writes:

> Hence, any thinking person realizes that the appearances of beauty are signs of an invisible loveliness. The beautiful odors which strike the senses are representations of a conceptual diffusion. Material lights are images of the outpouring of an immaterial gift of light.

The thoroughness of sacred discipleship indicates the immense contemplative capacity of the mind. Order and rank here below are a sign of the harmonious ordering toward the divine realm. The reception of the most divine Eucharist is a symbol of participation in Jesus.[44]

The mind of the Latino/a sacramental theologian is called to contemplate the meaning of the materiality of sacred symbols and the ordering of liturgical actions in their totality as a form of grasping the call of the people to partake of the body of Christ. The *ritmo* of Latino/a liturgical discipleship is undoubtedly more dynamic in its conception of order, but the Latino/a process for discovering a human ordering of things, persons, and actions within the person of Christ is not radically distinct from the one described here by Dionysius.

What about *religiosidad popular*? At least one archeological study of the processions of the icon of the Virgin from the narthexes of Byzantine churches through the streets of Constantinople (the so-called *litai*) states that they display "mobile emotions" in the embodied city that can be seen (citing Robert Taft) as paralleling the progress of the soul charted liturgically in Dionysius's EH.[45] After the resolution of the iconoclast controversy, the Virgin was a wall of protection for the entire city of Constantinople. It is thus not inconceivable that the contemplation of liturgical actions could have been extended by Dionysian symbolic theologians to Byzantine stational liturgies.[46] This is, however, very speculative. The more important point is that a bridge can be built between the form of contemplation of liturgical actions in EH and the contemporary reflection on popular religion. The recognition of the need to build this bridge goes far beyond the needs of the Latino/a community in the United States. A carefully phrased admonition by Pope Benedict XVI to seminarians illustrates this point:

> I urge you to retain an appreciation for popular piety, which is different in every culture yet always remains very similar, for the human heart is ultimately one and the same. Certainly, popular piety tends towards the irrational, and can at times be somewhat superficial. Yet it would be quite wrong to dismiss it. Through that piety, the faith has entered human hearts and become part of the common

patrimony of sentiments and customs, shaping the life and emotions of the community. Popular piety is thus one of the Church's great treasures. The faith has taken on flesh and blood. Certainly popular piety always needs to be purified and refocused, yet it is worthy of our love and it truly makes us into the "People of God.[47]

Pope Benedict sees the connection between the anagogy of the soul and participation in public liturgies of a popular nature. Both need trimming. But the movement of the soul toward God is aided directly by reflecting upon this parallelism.

Latino/a theology is by its nature doxological. The offering of praise to God is not secondary to the task of theology. It is an essential element in the process of reflection. This suggests another lens for reading the CD. After introducing *The Mystical Theology* with a vibrant hymn to the most holy Trinity, in the next chapter Dionysius enjoins that we are:

> [T]o praise the Transcendent One in a transcending way, namely through the denial of all beings. We would be like sculptors who set out to carve a statue. They remove every obstacle to the pure view of the hidden image, and simply by this act of clearing aside they show up the beauty which is hidden.[48]

In other words, there is no distinction to be made between a charismatic style of worship as a mode of kataphaticism and the pull toward apophaticism. For the Dionysian theologian, the former leads directly to the latter. Dishing out praise for the revealed God and carving out a space for the ineffably Absolute One are one and the same movement of the human soul. This recognition makes the *via negativa* much more doxological than is often granted and makes the *via positiva* highly self-effacing. The same point is made by García-Rivera when he describes praise as an original human act.[49] To thank God *latinamente* has a rhythm and purpose that reflect the characteristically dialogical traits of the Latino/a soul. The person who speaks the word *¡Gracias!* before the divinity is by herself bidding to be spoken to and to learn to see a reason for praise in all that exists.[50]

One key contribution of Latino/a theology is the discovery of a new form of theopoetics.[51] The beauty of God is refracted in *el pueblo en marcha* rather than in an isolated, static *imago Dei*. Theopoetics is an aesthetic theology of finite freedom, and the building blocks for this dynamism are found in García-Rivera's fourfold elaboration of the *capax Dei*: the validity of grace as a human experience; the defense of the analogy of being; entering the flesh of Christ (individually and as a people) as the source of symbolic knowledge of God; and "seeing the form" as a form of mystical anagogy. In sum, the beauty of superabundant grace beckons the people of God to see and touch the wounds of Christ and thereby to be uplifted to partake of the divine being.

The upward movement of anagogy brings together some of these elements by dynamizing the Dionysian hierarchies.[52] The three powers of purification, illumination, and perfection are applied anagogically to finite human beings.[53] Accordingly, God lowers Godself to lure all beings through purification, illumination, and perfection into the incessant rhythm of the Godhead.[54] We are then lifted by God from the materiality of scripture into a new life in the divine splendor and with the divine goodness.[55] To this degree, one can speak of a theological anthropology within the synthesis based on the veiled and unveiling attraction to divine love. Anneliese Meise Wörmer is correct to see within this Dionysian anthropology a connection to his reading of Song of Songs 5:8.[56] Divine love draws human love to itself and beckons the human lover to move outside of herself:

> [God] is yearning on the move, simple, self-moved, self-acting, pre-existent in the Good, flowing out from the Good onto all that is and returning once again to the Good. In this divine yearning shows especially its unbeginning and unending nature traveling in an endless circle through the Good, from the Good, in the Good and to the Good, unerringly turning, ever on the same center, ever in the same direction, always proceeding, always remaining, always being restored to itself.[57]

The magnetism of unfathomable love does not break apart the hierarchical chain. On the contrary, it brings all the elements of the universe into unparalleled contact with God's rhythms. Human souls are in this cosmic ordering moved by the infinite Good through the mediation of the angelic beings. With that help, they are led to the source of all good things:

Next to these sacred and holy intelligent beings [the angels] are the [human] souls, together with all the good peculiar to these souls. These too derive their being from the transcendent Good. So therefore they have intelligence, immortality, existence. They can strive towards angelic life. By means of the angels as good leaders, they can be uplifted to the generous Source of all good things and, each according to his measure, they are able to have a share in the illuminations streaming out from that Source. They too, in their own fashion, possess the gift of exemplifying the Good.[58]

This is no modern notion of freedom as self-creation. Praxis, rather, is interpreted as a free contribution from within one's own state of being to and into a cosmic order whose activity, goodness, and beauty surpass the business of everyday life without measure. Divine generosity and goodness enter into the everyday through a free play of material symbols that are hidden sources of transcendent meaning and value.

García-Rivera praised the Dionysian synthesis for its aesthetic philosophy of being and placed it within a broader tradition of thinking about the analogy of being. In particular, he pointed to the interpretations of analogy by Erich Przywara and Hans Urs von Balthasar and extended these into a poetic being of signs inspired by Charles Sanders Peirce and Jan Mukarovsky.[59] His insights into the "different beauty" and the beauty of difference, help us to recognize that unity *in difference* is a characteristic on both the horizontal and vertical level of Dionysian metaphysics. Dionysius states:

We now grasp these things in the best way we can, and as they come to us, wrapped in the sacred veils of that love toward humanity with which scripture and hierarchical traditions cover the truths of the mind with things derived from the realm of the senses. And so it is that the Transcendent is clothed in the terms of Being, with shape and form on things which have neither, and numerous symbols are employed to convey the varied attributes of what is an imageless and supra-natural simplicity.[60]

That which is beyond being is clothed ontologically. Moreover, the "clothing" of material shapes and forms with a transcendence that is already present in their origin and end is itself a self-presentation of unity and difference. If all things were homogenous in this symbolic vision, then the ever-greater difference between God's love for humanity and the human response would also be lost. In this sense, the Dionysian synthesis hints at the idea of semiotic difference theologically even while opting for a more uniform ontology derived from Platonism.

What does the CD say about analogy and its relationship to the divine name τὸ Ἕτερον ("difference")? A key passage is found in DN book IX:

> But "difference" too is ascribed to God since he is providentially available to all things and becomes all things in all for the salvation of them all. Yet at the same time he remains within himself and in his one unceasing activity he never abandons his own true identity. With unswerving power he gives himself outward for the sake of the divinization of those who are returned to him. "Difference" means that the many visions of God differ in appearance from one another and this difference must be understood to indicate something other than what was outwardly manifested.[61]

God becomes all things in all things without ceasing to be absolutely different from the world. The difference between a God who melds with worldly being and the God of Dionysius who "never abandons his own true identity" indicates that the cosmos is a sign of embrace of the one who wants to bring all things into the grasp of his salvific will.[62] Only a God who is different in this absolute sense could offer genuine salvation. For this reason, too, no one true vision of God is reducible to another. The outward manifestations of God's difference are themselves different from one another. Without using the term "inculturation," Dionysius has laid out an intriguing foundation for linking analogy and cultural difference.

Latino/a theology is radically Christocentric and keeps the suffering, *mestizo* face of Christ in view at all times. This quasi-baroque element in Hispanic devotion seems at first glance far removed from the serene rhythms of Dionysian mystical ascent. On the other hand, the encounter with the person of Christ is of great importance to Dionysius's symbolic theology, especially in its sacramental dimensions. The hierarch in the synaxis "offers Christ to our view."[63] The Latin tradition of interpretation as found in Hugh of St. Victor and St. Bonaventure was eager to highlight this point and accentuate the spiritual language of the flesh.

The Third Lettter is particularly revealing in this regard, for here Dionysius emphasizes in a methodologically significant manner the way that Christ appears suddenly (ἐξαίφνης). This teaching presupposes a topic that constitutes the third hypothesis of Plato's *Parmenides*, but is based even more so on several instances in the Gospels and in the Acts of the Apostles when the adverb is attributed to Christ's appearance, or is used to describe how a result of his presence takes place.[64] Dionysius says:

> What comes into view, contrary to hope, from previous obscurity, is described as "sudden." As for the love of Christ for humanity, the Word of God, I believe, uses this term to hint that the transcendent has put aside its own hiddenness and has revealed itself to us by becoming a human being. But he is hidden even after this revelation, or, if I may speak in a more divine fashion, is hidden even amid the revelation. For this mystery of Jesus remains hidden and can be drawn out by no word or mind. What is to be said of it remains unsayable; what is to be understood of it remains unknowable.[65]

Christ's activity, in other words, arises all at once in the midst of the everyday. He is "the presence of 'the sudden.'"[66] It is not a mere extension in its form of love, or in its temporality of the worldly order of things. For Dionysius this means that "[i]t is on Jesus himself, our most divine altar, that there is achieved the divine consecration of intelligent beings. In him, as scripture says, 'we have access' to consecration and are mystically offered as a holocaust."[67] Latino/a theologians make a similar affirmation, especially in affirming real, symbolical presence in liturgy and life. But for Latino/as, the notion of Christ's "suddenness" extends to his *fiesta escandalosas* that are celebrated by the Mexican adherents to popular Catholicism in the streets of San Antonio. It extends likewise to the biblical admonition whereby divine hospitality exhorts welcoming those without documents into our community. Latino/as thus call Jesus Christ "the God of incredible surprises."[68]

A final point of convergence is the relationship between trinitarian communion and the communion shared and promoted by the people of

God. In the Dionysian synthesis the intimate bond of love shared by the persons of the Trinity overflows into the forms of communion intelligible in the world of finite beings. The connection to the people of God, however, arises in the Dionysian synthesis only indirectly, by virtue of an often overlooked monastic strand in Dionysian mysticism. The recognition of some form of ecclesial and social communion in any event accords with the rich emphasis on a distinctively trinitarian theology and ecclesiology of communion in Latino/a thought and experience.[69]

We must first pose a prior question: Can one legitimately maintain that a trinitarian hermeneutic can be found in the CD? It seems not only that one can make the assertion but that this often-suppressed dimension is an Ariadne's thread. As John N. Jones cogently articulated, the Holy Trinity for Dionysius is "the cause of all."[70] Jones argues that mystical theology is the core of Dionysius's theology, and Dionysian mystical theology must be read in a trinitarian manner if one is to understand it as a coherent whole. This means that there is a sense in which the revelation of God as Father, Son, and Holy Spirit is not only a conceptual framework undergirded by the possibility of a kataphatic affirmation, but also a more original, hermeneutic reality that transcends both apophasis and kataphasis.[71] For Jones, the key passage for unfolding the veiled Dionysian "trinitarian hermeneutics" thus reads:

> We learn from the sacred scriptures that the Father is the originating source of the Godhead and that the Son and the Spirit are, so to speak, divine offshoots, the flowering and transcendent lights of the divinity. But we can neither say nor understand how this could be so.[72]

The Trinity erupts as a valid affirmation of doctrinal truth regarding three distinct persons *by virtue of the unfathomable mystery of its divine revelation*. It does not come into the world as a truth to be assigned alongside other truths. As an assertion, it cannot be known by reason alone, and the source of its appearance in the world is not dependent on concepts or beings. The paternal Godhead and the so-called offshoots of Son and Spirit not only originate in this "superessential" manner but are revered and adored as such and therefore always as mysteries. The mystery of the Trinity is not therefore exhausted or made less sudden in its mode of appearance when it appears in the world. In DN IV, as we saw above, the triune God "is yearning on the move . . . traveling in an endless circle through the Good, from the Good, in the Good and to the Good, unerringly turning, ever on the same center, ever in the same direction, always proceeding, always remaining, always being restored to itself."[73] The overflow of goodness in the origin of the revelation of divine Tri-unity cannot be pinned down in words, concepts, or beings. But the love that flows over into this endless circle is indeed marked with palpable and adorable signs of this singular revelation.

What effect, then, does the communion of Father, Son, and Holy Spirit have on the church and the world? This question is not as novel as it might seem at first glance. John of Skythopolis, an influential seventh-century admirer of Dionysius and bishop in Palestine, glossed the Ninth Letter in terms of a kind of political theology. He added the notation "social" next to a section that speaks to how biblical authors

[I]n their consideration of a theme look at it sometimes in a social and legal perspective and sometimes purely and without any mixture with anything else. . . . Sometimes they rely on the laws governing visible things, sometimes on rules which govern invisible things.[74]

Here the commentator outlines a division of the sciences that would account for both politics (which is practical) and theological cosmology (which is contemplative and theological).[75] Theory and practice, so it appears, are kept apart.

Latino/a theology attempts to integrate the trinitarian hermeneutic that it shares with the Dionysian synthesis into ecclesial and social praxis in a more integrated fashion. Since the negation is not only *not* Unitarian but actually a radical affirmation of the offer of communion, the Latino/a theologian looks to what Alexander Golitzin names "the little Church" by reference to Syriac monastic sources of Dionysian sacramental synthesis.[76] Speaking of a possible parallel between Macarius and Dionysius, Golitzin writes:

But once more, the echoes of this same, peculiarly Christian (and perhaps monastic) "politics" seem to us to constitute part and parcel of the atmosphere of the CD as well. Both men look for the kingdom to come, and imitation of its eternity in the life of the Church (and monastery) here below.[77]

For Golitzin, the path for linking the microcosm of church, soul, and city proleptically to the macrocosmic hierarchies was already in place in monastic authors writing before Dionysius. The personal and aesthetic dimensions of the Dionysian synthesis were among the factors that led to its broader dissemination after the composition of the CD.

Dionysius never brings to the fore the biblical notion of the church as a people of God. But at the origin of his microcosmic spiritual theology is an inspiring vision of the church as a place of interrelationship—in other words, what Pope Francis calls a *cultura de encuentro*.[78] The relationships that develop in this culture depend on the eucharistic encounter with the superabundant love of God incarnate in the flesh of Christ. These relationships lie at the point of convergence of the church and the world. These are the relationships that form the essence of the church and offer a new model of society at the same time. They neither mirror nor deflect the structures of the world. At root they express the ineffable gift of trinitarian communion. This is the ecclesial and social force of Dionysian apophaticism. This is also the sense in which Dionysian theology can be deployed to reveal the radicality and urgency of promoting the church of the poor. The church of the poor suddenly comes into view when we remove—as "sculptors" of the Triune source of all cosmic, ecclesial, and social beings and as a prophetic witnesses to God's sudden epiphanies in the world—the false pretensions that have been grafted onto the gift of the church as a place of genuine communion.

III. Symbolic Truth, Cosmic Beauty, and the Church in the *Nican Mopohua*

The aesthetics of Dionysius the Areopagite has afforded Latino/a theologians one starting point for thinking about the question of divine beauty. This reclaiming of Dionysius accords with the development of a vital tradition of theological aesthetics within Latino/a theology and, of course, more widely as well. But the fundamental agreement between readers of the Latino/a experience and readers of the CD is hardly the result of a recent theological development. The founding document, as it were, of Latino/a theology is the *Nican Mophua* [NM], the Nahuatl account of how Our Lady of Guadalupe appeared to St. Juan Diego in Tepeyac in 1531.[79] This narrative offers a theology of divine beauty made manifest in the finite cosmos that brings together an indigenous conception of the symbolic manifestation of truth and a fervent Christian hope to build a church of and for the poor. We conclude by examining just a few aspects of the NM that seem to echo a Dionysian perspective.

The plot centers on the multiple appearances of a brown Virgin (*La Morenita*) to the indigenous Juan Diego at Tepeyac, the mountain upon which according to ancient custom the goddess Tonantzin was worshiped. In a nutshell, the Virgin implores Juan Diego to ask the local bishop to build a temple to her on this site. It takes three separate trips to accomplish this task, and each time the reader of the NM is made more aware of the unique manner of the disclosure of the truth of the message of Our Lady of Guadalupe.

In fact, the sacredness of time and place is accentuated in the NM. The event takes place ten years after the conquest of the city of Mexico, at which point, we are told, "Thus, faith started; it gave its first buds; and it flowered in the knowledge of the One through Whom We Live, the true God, Téotl."[80] The juxtaposition of the Christian phrase "the true God" with the Nahuatl name for God (*Téotl*) shows that the actuality of the event lies in the truth about God expressed through a name unknown to the Christians, echoing in this way the primordial experience of the CD as related by Paul in Acts 17:22–34. The focus on the evidential and ontological question of truth becomes even more pronounced during the first encounter of Juan Diego with the Virgin. We are told that "It was Saturday, when it was still night."[81] This phrase repeats "a classical Nahuatl expression for the moment in mythical time immediately before creation."[82] Juan Diego arrives at Tepeyac as the dawn arrives. What we are then told encapsulates the symbolic realism of the entire NM:

> He heard singing on the summit of the hill: as if different precious birds were singing and their songs would alternate, as if the hill was answering them. Their song was most pleasing and very enjoyable,

better than that of the *coyototol* [a bird that sings like a bell],[83] or of the *tzinizcan* or of the other precious birds that sing.[84]

This detail is no mere ornament. It cuts to the core of the message. Birds signify the mediation between the heavenly and the earthly, and the bird with a bell-like song indicates great fecundity.[85] Most importantly, the sudden appearance of song, much like the miraculous flowers that follow, indicates the primal entrance of the reader into the domain of truth.[86] Moreover, there are five references to song in this passage. According to Elizondo, "the number five indicates—in the Nahuatl mode of communication—that we are at the very center of creation, where heaven meets earth."[87] The beckoning of Juan Diego by the Virgin is steeped in this thoroughly indigenous but also quasi-Dionysian aesthetics of flower and song:

> His gaze was fixed on the summit of the hill, toward the direction which the sun arises: the beautiful celestial song was coming from there to here. . . . When he arrived in her presence, he marveled at her perfect beauty. Her clothing appeared like the sun, and it gave forth rays.[88]

Juan Diego is called by a lady who knows his name and speaks to him with his own idiom and from within the philosophical matrix of his own culture. But the Virgin is a messenger imbued with more than just openness to dialogue, tenderness, and intimacy. She draws him to her message by refracting a beauty that is assuredly not from the Conquistadores nor derived from anything worldly.

In Juan Diego's first trip to announce this disclosure to the bishop, he is summarily dismissed. In the second trip, he is granted an audience but told to provide evidence for the truth of his outlandish assertions. The subsequent encounter with the Virgin at Tepeyac is thus decisive in grasping the nature of evidential truth. Distracted by the agony of his dying uncle, Juan Diego tries to avoid this encounter. In promising Juan Diego that his uncle will not die of his present illness, La Morenita reveals through a dialogical process the maternal womb of protection that God will provide to the indigenous:

Listen and hear well in your heart, my most abandoned son: that which scares you and troubles you is nothing; do not let your countenance and heart be troubled. . . . Am I not here, your mother? Are you not under my shadow and my protection? Am I not your source of life? Are you not in the hollow of my mantle where I cross my arms? What else do you need?[89]

By pinpointing a significant but thoroughly quotidian detail, the Virgin unveils a plan that goes far beyond the uncle's recovery. The disclosure is an epiphany of a new cosmic and social reality that is grasped by the heart. There is nothing sentimental about knowledge of maternal protection that comes through this faculty. This is in fact a sober statement about God's design to overthrow the dominion of the oppressors. The confirmation of God's plan in the third encounter is the sudden appearance of "exquisite flowers from Castile, open and flowering" during the period (December 12) in Mexico "when the ice hardens upon the earth."[90] In the process of giving Juan Diego convincing evidence with which to persuade the bishop, the Virgin completes her revelation "in flower and song." This pairing is in fact a familiar one in Nahuatl culture, a *disfrasimo* that signifies a poem or artistic creation that conveys revealed truth.[91] Juan Diego describes to the bishop the hill of the encounter as transfixing his eyes: "It was the Flowering Earth."[92] The bishop is convinced by Juan Diego's sincerity, the miraculous flowers from Spain, and the image of the Virgin painted on Juan Diego's *tilma* (cloak).

What was the effect of this new theological aesthetics for Christianity? In the long run, the consequences were drastic, and the narrative with great elegance and simplicity makes this point. As Juan Diego unfolds the cloak with the image and flowers, the bishop "and all who accompanied him fell to their knees and were greatly astonished."[93] The bishop gives permission for a "hermitage" for the Virgin of Guadalupe to be built at Tepeyac. The image is transferred from the episcopal residence in the capital to this more remote region so that the Virgin can be venerated in this specific place where she asked to be venerated. She does not become a fixture in the bishop's residence or in the heart of colonial Catholicism. In her new dwelling, we are told, "The entire city was deeply moved; they came to see and admire her precious image as something divine; they came to pray to her. They admired very much how she had appeared as a divine marvel, because absolutely no one on earth had painted her precious image."[94]

Here we have the connection to the present devotion, today a literally global celebration on December 12 of each year. But the original insight is thoroughly in accord with the Dionysian idea of anagogy as propagated in the Latin Middle Ages, as Hispanist and art historian John F. Moffitt observes.[95] The message of evangelization carried by the Virgin *is* the painting. The miracle that appears on the *tilma* is "a painted Word."[96] The artifact moves the viewer at the new hermitage beyond itself, upwardly, to "the truth about truth itself."[97] It is not a merely social message; it is a truth about God. But therein lies also its significance for a new common life. Whereas the Protestant Reformation placed its emphasis on reform through the proclamation of an unadorned Word, the Guadalupan event proposes an equally stringent reform of the church based upon the anagogy of the painted word.[98] Seeing Christ through the lens of the encounter with the Virgin of Guadalupe is the true starting point for social and ecclesial transformation. While lacking the dialectical negation of Dionysian apophaticism, Nahuatl aesthetics is equally emphatic in its claim for a reversal in the understanding of reality, especially with regard to the question of human dignity. The event gives birth to an "anthropological reversal" that is decisive for the rest of the history of the Americas.[99]

Notes

1. Orlando O. Espín, *Faith of the People: Theological Reflections on Popular Catholicism* (Maryknoll, NY: Orbis Books, 1997), 71–77.

2. See Manuel J. Mejido, "A Critique of the 'Aesthetic Turn' in U.S. Latino Theology: A Dialogue with Roberto Goizueta and the Positing of a New Paradigm," *Journal of Hispanic/Latino Theology* 8.3 (February 2001): 18–48; and Manuel J. Mejido, "The Fundamental Problematic of U.S. Hispanic Theology," in *New Horizons in Hispanic Latino(a) Theology*, ed. Benjamín Valentín (Cleveland, OH: Pilgrim, 2003), 163–78. The Argentine Ivan Petrella supports this criticism in *The Future of Liberation Theology: An Argument and Manifesto* (London: SCM, 2006). A balanced and thoughtful response is found in Michelle González, "Response," *Journal of Feminist Studies in Religion* 22.2 (2006): 109–10; and González, *A Critical Introduction to Religion in the*

Americas: Bridging the Liberation Theology and Religious Studies Divide (New York: New York University Press, 2014), chap. 3, esp. 160 nn54, 55.

3. Roberto S. Goizueta, *Caminemos con Jesús: Toward a Hispanic/Latino Theology of Accompaniment* (Maryknoll, NY: Orbis Books, 1995).

4. Michelle A. Gonzalez, *Sor Juana: Beauty and Justice in the Americas* (Maryknoll, NY: Orbis Books, 2003).

5. See Peter Casarella, "Beauty and the Little Stories of Holiness: What Alejandro García-Rivera Taught Me," in *Diálogo* 16.2 (Fall 2013): 53–58; Casarella, "Art and U.S. Latina and Latino Religious Experience," in *Introduction to the U.S. Latina and Latino Religious Experience*, ed. Hector Avalos (Boston: Brill Academic, 2004), 143–69; Peter Casarella, "The Painted Word," *Journal of Hispanic/Latino Theology* 6 (November 1998): 18–42.

6. For the phrase *via pulchritudinis*, see Filippo Santoro, *Estética Teológica: A Força do Fascínio Cristão* (Petrópolis: Vozes, 2008); and the Apostolic Exhortation of Pope Francis *Evangelii Gaudium* (2013), 167, in which it is linked to a 2012 address of Pope Benedict, where it has a primarily homiletic role. Speaking at the meeting of CELAM (Consejo Episcopal Latinoamericano) in Aparecida, Brazil, Cardinal Paul Poupard stated, "Popular devotions as well as the so-called *via pulchritudinis* are excellent pastoral instruments for effectively grasping and expressing in a culturally sensitive manner the dimension of the ineffable in the everyday life of faith. [These instruments] are to be fully welcomed, thought through in their entirety, and lived faithfully." As a result, the Aparecida final document closely links beauty and goodness in God. The original text is accessible online at http://www.zenit.org/es/articles/intervencion-del-cardenal-paul-poupard-en-aparecida. This translation is my own.

7. Roberto S. Goizueta, "The Symbolic Realism of U.S. Popular Catholicism," *Theological Studies* 65 (2004): 255–74.

8. See Roberto Goizueta, "In Defense of Reason: Dichotomous Epistemology and Anthropology of Modernity and Postmodernity Oppressive to Hispanics," *Journal of Hispanic/Latino Theology* 3.3 (1996): 16–26; and Goizueta, "Bartolomé de las Casas, Modern Critic of Modernity: An Analysis of a Conversion," *Journal of Hispanic/Latino Theology* 3.4 (1996): 6–19.

9. Cyril O'Regan's *Gnostic Return in Modernity* (Albany: State University of New York Press, 2001) is fundamental to the argument being made here, even though it is not mentioned by Goizueta.

10. Goizueta, "Symbolic Realism of U.S. Popular Catholicism," 266.

11. In this sense, the agenda is not different from that of Louis Dupré in *Passage to Modernity: An Essay in the Hermeneutics of Nature and Culture* (New Haven: Yale University Press, 1993). Dupré's identity as a U.S. citizen with roots in a profoundly sacramental Flemish Catholic culture that is now part of a secularized, multilingual Belgium attunes him to the kinds of intercultural realities that Latino/as face.

12. Alejandro García-Rivera, *The Community of the Beautiful: A Theological Aesthetics* (Collegeville, MN: Liturgical Press, 1999), 74–90.

13. Ibid., 81.

14. Ibid., 90.

15. Cecilia González-Andrieu, *A Bridge to Wonder: Art as a Gospel to Beauty* (Waco, TX: Baylor University Press, 2012), 56.

16. On the name of the theater, see ibid., 176 n23.

17. Ibid., 33–34.

18. Ibid., 35.

19. Ibid.

20. Ibid., 177 n28. Panofsky's work provoked a negative reaction from more recent art historians. See, e.g., Peter Kidson, "Panofsky, Suger, and St. Denys," *Journal of Warburg and Courtauld Institutes* 50 (1987): 1–17. It would be interesting to pursue a critical study of material cultural and aesthetics through the lens of Latino/a theology, but this task falls outside the purview of this essay.

21. There are parallels in this respect between Latino/a theology and the so-called theology of the people that emerged in Argentina under the leadership of Lucio Gera and played an exemplary role in the thought of Jorge Mario Bergoglio. Gera, a student of Johann Auer in Bonn, was strongly influenced in his formulation of an Argentinian theology of and from the people by Romano Guardini and Hans Urs von Balthasar and seldom references Karl Rahner and transcendental theology.

22. Alejandro García-Rivera, *Community of the Beautiful*, 90, 146, 165–68.

23. It is now acknowledged that there are subterranean elements of Rahner's thought that bring theology and aesthetics closer together. See Peter Fritz, *Karl Rahner's Theological Aesthetics* (Washington, DC: Catholic University of America Press, 2014). I discuss Rahner's breakthrough on the *Weltkirche* in Peter Casarella, "Conversion and Witnessing: Intercultural Renewal in a World Church," *Proceedings of the Catholic Theological Society of America* 68 (2013): 1–17.

24. I personally do not believe that there was anything less than cordiality in their private exchanges, but we do have public exchanges like Balthasar's *The Moment of Christian Witness* (San Francisco: Ignatius, 1994) and Rahner's claim in a radio interview that Balthasar's theology of Holy Saturday broached neo-Gnosticism that indicate that there was a rift. See, e.g., Werner Löser, "Karl Rahner and Hans Urs von Balthasar," *America* 181 (October 19, 1999): 11–16.

25. Miguel H. Díaz, *On Being Human: U.S. Hispanic and Rahnerian Perspectives* (Maryknoll, NY: Orbis Books, 2001), 61–76.

26. EH II.1, 292BC; *Pseudo-Dionysius: The Complete Works*, trans. Colm Luibheid, translation collaboration by Paul Rorem, Classics of Western Spirituality (Mahwah, NJ: Paulist Press, 1987), 201. Abbreviations: DN = *The Divine Names*; MT = *The Mystical Theology*; CH = *The Celestial Hierarchy*;

EH = *The Ecclesiastical Hierarchy*; and Ep. I = First Letter. The translations that follow are taken from that of Luibheid/Rorem unless indicated otherwise.

27. René Roques, *L'univers dionysien: Structure hiérarchique du monde selon le Pseudo-Denys* (Paris: Aubier, 1954), 271.

28. Ibid.

29. There are numerous references to this work in the CD: DN I, 7–8 (597AB), XIII, 4 (984); MT III (1033AB); CH XV, 6 (336A), and Ep. IX (1104B).

30. Ep. IX (1105C).

31. Ep. IX (1105B); Ep. IX (1108A).

32. Ep. IX (1105D–1108A).

33. Eric D. Perl, *Theophany: The Neoplatonic Philosophy of Dionysius the Areopagite* (Albany: State University New York Press, 2007), 101–38.

34. See, e.g., Ep. IX (1108B, with reference to Rom. 1:20), which Rorem renders as "makes known the invisible things of God" and Perl as "presents the invisible things of God," and DN V.5 (820A) on the self-*presentation* of being before all other attributes to that which participates in it, a point rendered by Rorem more weakly as: "Whatever beings participate in these things must, before all else, participate in Being."

35. Perl, *Theophany*, 107.

36. I think especially of Albert the Great's reflections on the CD. See Henryk Anzulewicz, "Albertus Magnus über die *ars de symbolica theologia* de Dionysius Areopagita," *Teología y Vida* 51.3 (2010): 307–43. It is no coincidence that Alejandro García-Rivera makes Albert the prime dialogue partner with Sophia in his dialogue (modeled on Galileo's *Dialogue concerning the Two New Sciences*) about the presence of symbolic form: *Community of the Beautiful*, 65–73.

37. García-Rivera, *Community of the Beautiful*, 63–90.

38. See Paul Rorem, *Biblical and Liturgical Symbols within the Pseudo-Dionysian Synthesis*, Studies and Texts 71 (Toronto: Pontifical Institute for Mediaeval Studies, 1984), 69–73.

39. Robert Schreiter highlights the role of topology in the thought of García-Rivera in "Spaces Engaged and Transfigured: Alejandro García-Rivera's Journey from Little Stories to Cosmic Reconciliation," *Diálogo* 16.2 (Fall 2013): 43–47.

40. See DN IV.4–5 (697B–701A) in which he contrasts the physical (visible) and spiritual (invisible) meanings of "Sun" and "light." There is still a significant difference between the account of the opposition between the spiritual and the material that is found in Dionysius's Christian Neoplatonism and that of Valentinian Gnosticism. On this point, see Roques, *L'univers dionysien*, 53–59; and Perl, *Theophany*, 101–38.

41. This formulation leaves aside the question of the individuation of angelic natures.

42. Paul Rorem, *Pseudo-Dionysius: A Commentary on the Texts and an Introduction to Their Influence* (Oxford: Oxford University Press, 1993), 122.

43. CH I,3 (121C).

44. CH I,3 (121D–124A).

45. Vicky Manolopoulou, "Processing Emotion: Litanies in Byzantine Constantinople," in *Experiencing Byzantium: Papers of the 44th Spring Symposium of Byzantine Studies, Newcastle and Durham, Spring 2011*, ed. Claire Nesbitt and Mark Jackson (Surrey, England, and Burlington, VT: Ashgate, 2013), e-book, 153–72.

46. An in-depth treatment of the stational liturgies is found in Jon Baldovin, *The Urban Character of Christian Worship: The Origins, Development, and Meaning of Stational Liturgy*, Orientalia Christiana Analecta 228 (Rome: Pontificium Institutum Studiorum Orientalium, 1987). There still may be an implicitly urban dimension to the Dionysian synthesis. On the difference between the *republique platonicienne* and the *cité dionysienne*, see Roques, *L'univers dionysien*, 90.

47. Letter of His Holiness Benedict XVI to Seminarians, October 18, 2010, online at http://w2.vatican.va/content/benedict-xvi/en/letters/2010/documents/hf_ben-xvi_let_20101018_seminaristi.html.

48. MT II (1025AB).

49. García-Rivera, *Community of the Beautiful*, 19.

50. I have explored this latter theme in Peter Casarella, "Sacra ignorantia: Sobre la doxología filosófica del Cusano," in *Coincidência dos opostos e concórdia: Caminhos do pensamiento em Nicolau de Cusa*, ed. João Maria André and Mariano Alvarez Gómez (Coimbra: Faculdade de Letras, 2002), 51–65.

51. I discuss the history of this term in the foreword to Anne M. Carpenter, *Theopoetics: Hans Urs von Balthasar and the Risk of Art and Being* (Notre Dame, IN: University of Notre Dame Press, 2015).

52. Roques, *L'univers dionysien*, 204.

53. CH III (165C–168B) and EH VI (537ABC).

54. EH VI.3 (537BC): "The highest and most divine beings have the task, in proportion to the heavenly hierarchy, of purifying from all ignorance those heavenly ranks inferior to them, of bestowing upon them the fullness of divine enlightenments, and, finally, of perfecting them in the most luminous understanding of divine conceptions. For I have already stated, as discussed in the scriptures, that the ranks of heaven do not possess the exact same enlightened understanding of the sights of God. It is God himself who directly enlightens the primary ranks, through whose mediation he grants indirect enlightenment to the subordinate ranks, in proportion to capacity, and he does so by spreading among them the shining splendors of the divine beam."

55. DN I, 1 (588AB): "Let us therefore look as far upward as the light of sacred scripture will allow, and, in our reverent awe of what is divine, let us be drawn together toward the divine splendor. For, if we may trust the superlative wisdom and truth of scripture, the things of God are revealed to each mind in

proportion to its capacities; and the divine goodness is such that, out of concern for our salvation, it deals out the immeasurable and infinite in limited measures."

56. "I adjure you, Daughters of Jerusalem, if you find my lover, What shall you tell him? that I am sick with love." See Anneliese Meis Wörmer, *Antropología Teológica: Acercamientos a La Paradoja del Hombre,* 3rd updated ed. (Santiago de Chile: Ediciones Universidad Católica, 1992), 409–10.

57. DN IV, 14 (712CD–713A).

58. DN IV, 2 (696C).

59. García-Rivera, *Community of the Beautiful*, 78–82 and 164–68.

60. DN I, 4 (592B).

61. DN IX, 5 (912C–913D).

62. See Roques, *L'univers dionysien*, 59–64; and Alexander Golitzin, *Et Introibo ad Altare Dei: The Mystagogy of Dionysius Areopagita with Special Reference to Its Predecessors in the Eastern Christian Tradition* (Thessaloniki: Patriarchikon Idryma Paterikon Meleton, 1994), 86–88.

63. EH III.13 (444C). See also Roques, *L'univers dionysien*, 305–29.

64. Cf. Mark 13:6 ("he should come *suddenly* and find"), Luke 2:13 ("And *suddenly* there appeared"), Luke 9:39 ("seizes him, and he *suddenly* screams," a reference to a boy being freed through exorcism), Acts 9:3 (Damascus, and *suddenly* a light"), and Acts 2:26 ("light *suddenly* flashed").

65. Ep. III (1069B). See Golitzin, *Et Introibo ad Altare Dei*, 222–28.

66. Golitzin, *Et Introibo ad Altare Dei*, 222.

67. EH III.12 (484D).

68. Virgilio Elizondo, *A God of Incredible Surprises: Jesus of Galilee* (Lanham, MD: Rowman & Littlefield, 2004).

69. See, e.g., Sixto García, "A Hispanic Approach to Trinitarian Theology: The Dynamics of Celebration, Reflection, and Praxis," in *We Are a People! Initiatives in Hispanic American Theology*, ed. Roberto S. Goizueta (Minneapolis: Fortress, 1992), 107–32; Peter J. Casarella, "The Expression and Form of the Word: Trinitarian Hermeneutics and the Sacramentality of Language in the Theology of Hans Urs von Balthasar," *Renascence* 48 (Winter 1996): 111–35; and Roberto S. Goizueta, "The Church," in *In Our Own Voices: Latino/a Renditions of Theology*, ed. Benjamín Valentín (Maryknoll, NY: Orbis Books, 2010), 133–54.

70. This phrase is used in DN II, 7 (see below) and in MT III, 2 (1000ABC). The latter usage, as Jones admits, appears to have a non-trinitarian meaning, and the former a radically trinitarian one. See John N. Jones, "The Status of the Trinity in Dionysian Thought," *Journal of Religion* 80.4 (2000): 645–57.

71. For more details on this very subtle point, see John N. Jones, "The Logic of Dionysian Negative Theology," *Harvard Theological Review* 89.4 (1996): 355–71.

72. DN II, 7 (645B).

73. DN IV, 14 (712C). See Jones, "Status of the Trinity," 656.

74. Ep. IX.2 (1108BC).

75. See Paul Rorem and John C. Lamoreaux, *John of Skythopolis and the Dionysian Corpus: Annotating the Areopagite* (Oxford: Clarendon, 1998), 261.

76. Golitzin, *Et Introibo ad Altare Dei*, 371–92.

77. Ibid., 379.

78. See Pope Francis, *Evangelii Gaudium*, 8, 75, 220.

79. In addition to García-Rivera, *Community of the Beautiful*, 55–59, see also Roberto Goizueta, *Caminemos con Jesús: Toward a Hispanic/Latino Theology of Accompaniment* (Maryknoll, NY: Orbis Books, 1995); Virgil Elizondo, *Guadalupe: Mother of a New Creation* (Maryknoll, NY: Orbis Books, 1997); and Jeanette Rodríguez, *Our Lady of Guadalupe: Faith and Empowerment among Mexican-American Women* (Austin: University of Texas Press, 1993).

80. NM, #4. This citation and all subsequent ones are taken from the translation in Elizondo, *Guadalupe: Mother of a New Creation*.

81. NM, #7.

82. Elizondo, *Guadalupe*, 32.

83. See *The Story of Guadalupe: Luis Laso de la Vega's Huei tlamahuiçoltica of 1649*, ed. Lisa Sousa, Stafford Poole, C.M., and James Lockhart (Stanford: Stanford University Press, 1998), 62n1.

84. NM, #9.

85. Elizondo, *Guadalupe*, 6n5.

86. Ibid., 34–38.

87. Ibid., 35.

88. NM, ##12, 16–17.

89. NM, #76. For commentary, see Elizondo, *Guadalupe*, 16n20.

90. NM, #81.

91. See, e.g., Alfredo López Austin, "Disfrasismos, cosmovisión, e iconografía," in *Revista Española de Antropología Americana*, vol. extraordinario (2003), 143–60, here 146; and Elizondo, *Guadalupe*, 34–35.

92. NM, #105. As Elizondo notes, this is a Nahuatl expression for "the place where ultimate truth resides" (*Guadalupe*, 20n28).

93. NM, #108.

94. NM, ##123–24.

95. MT 2 (1025AB). See John F. Moffitt, *Our Lady of Guadalupe: The Painting, the Legend, and the Reality* (Jefferson, NC: McFarland, 2006), 28–38.

96. Elizondo, *Guadalupe*, 135.

97. Ibid., 116.

98. For a Protestant appreciation of the encounter that complicates the simple opposition just enumerated, see *American Magnificat: Protestants on Mary of Guadalupe*, ed. Maxwell Johnson (Collegeville, MN: Liturgical Press, 2010).

99. Ibid., 107–12.

11

In Christ: Theosis and the Preferential Option for the Poor

Roberto S. Goizueta

At the heart of the Christian kerygma is the conviction that in the cruci-fied and risen Christ God's love is fully manifest. As embodied in the per-son of Christ, God's love is made present and experienced as irreducibly universal and utterly gratuitous. Any attempt, therefore, to circumscribe or set preconditions for God's love will, de facto, involve some form of idolatry.

Alongside this central Christian belief, a more recent theological development has been the assertion that God loves certain persons pref-erentially, namely, the poor, the marginalized, and the excluded. While the roots of God's "preferential love for the poor" are ultimately bibli-cal, this theme has been articulated most systematically over the last fifty years by liberation theologians, as well as in official church documents, both Roman Catholic and Protestant. Despite the growing acceptance of this theme in Christian theology, many Christians continue to resist the very notion of a preferential option for the poor on the grounds that, of its very essence, God's love is extended to all persons equally and gratuitously.

In fact, these two principles—the universality and gratuity of God's love, and God's preferential love for the poor—are what Gustavo Gutiérrez has called the two major overarching themes in scripture. In this essay, I will argue that, while ostensibly contradictory, these are mutually co-implicit principles. I will suggest further that (1) our Western indi-vidualistic theological anthropology prevents us from fully appreciating the integral character of these two principles; (2) the notion of theosis,

219

or deification, developed most extensively in Eastern Christianity, can provide an antidote to such an individualistic anthropology; but only if (3) deification is understood as cruciform Christification; and (4) if the notion of cruciform Christification is itself read through the lens of a preferential option for the poor as not only an ethical but fundamentally a soteriological category. The work of Ignacio Ellacuría, Jon Sobrino, and Xavier Zubiri will be particularly helpful in articulating the relationship between theosis and the option for the poor. Ultimately, we will perceive the unity of God's universal, gratuitous love and God's preferential love for the poor only insofar as we live "in" Christ or, more precisely, in the crucified and risen Christ as he is today mediated by those whom Ellacuría and Sobrino have called "the crucified people."

The Individual and the Option for the Poor

In a modern Western individualistic context, the twin precepts of God's universal, gratuitous love and God's preferential love for the poor will be invariably perceived as mutually irreconcilable. As Alasdair McIntyre has observed, what defines individualism is not so much the absolutization of the autonomous individual as a presupposed dichotomy between the individual and the community.[1] The "relationship" between the individual and the community is thus always extrinsic and, as extrinsic, conflictual in the sense that the communal is always a limitation, if not an outright rejection, of the individual. Those relationships never in-form the self (literally, help form the self) but are always merely optional extensions of the self. In this light, universality and particularity will thus be perceived as incommensurable; to love one person, even if only "preferentially," will be perceived as implying, if not a hatred, at least a "less preferential" and thus a lesser love of an other. For Western individualism, the universal and the particular are always in conflict.[2]

The fundamental problem with individualism is not that it denies the value of relationships and community but that it assumes that these are extrinsic to the self, not a necessary dimension of the self that forms and, indeed, generates the self. Consequently, relationships can only be a zero-sum-game: if relationships depend on my choice, then to choose one option is necessarily to preclude another, different option.[3]

This problem surfaces not only among Western Christians who resist the option for the poor because it appears to undermine the universality and gratuity of God's love, but also, I would submit, among those of us who promote an option for the poor. In this latter case, an extrinsicist understanding of the relationships among individuals may unwittingly assume reductionist, conflictual presuppositions inherent in Western individualism. Liberation theologies have consistently and appropriately insisted that conflict and power are dimensions of human relationships that are ignored only at the peril of those who have no power. An equally destructive danger, however, is that of reducing human relationships to nothing but power relationships. Underlying the reduction of human relationships to power relationships is always an individualistic anthropology.

A proper understanding of the preferential option for the poor demands that we view relationships as intrinsic to the person; to be a person is to be in relationship, and relationships help define and form the person. More precisely, to be a person is to be loved and to love. By definition, then, a person is one who *receives* before he or she is one who *acts* or, much less, one who *thinks*. It is the experience of being loved unconditionally that ruptures the illusory autonomy and isolation of the individual. In so doing, that experience compels a response. The autonomous individual is incapable of responding to an other because, by definition, the individual's actions are always self-generated. As only extrinsically related to others, the individual cannot *inter*act with an other but only act *upon* an other.[4]

An interpretation of the option for the poor that presupposes an individualistic theological anthropology will thus posit such an option as "merely" one more option among many; it is the autonomous individual who, "free to choose," decides to enter into solidarity with the poor. What is obscured here is the fact that, regardless of whether we choose to enter into the lives of the poor, the poor are *already* an intrinsic part of our own lives, whether we like it or not. Thus, to opt for the poor is simply to acknowledge practically what is already true ontologically and in fact. Moreover, because the lives (and deaths) of the poor are already intrinsic dimensions of our own selves, love of the poor is not a limitation of self-love but the only authentic form of self-love. It is precisely this intrinsic connection that is obscured in any individualistic society.

So, for instance, our society is blinded to the causal link between urban homicide rates and suburban suicide rates, or between the rise of wealthy gated enclaves and the subsequent increase in rates of depression and addiction among the wealthy.[5]

The extrinsicism of such an individualistic anthropology affects more than just our understanding of human relationships, and the relationship between the poor and the non-poor; for Christians, it also ultimately affects our understanding of our relationship with Christ. To understand ourselves as individuals in "relationship" to Jesus Christ—*qua* individuals—is ultimately to preclude an experience of and encounter with the universality and gratuity of God's love as this is embodied in the person of Christ. That is, Christ is no more an individual than we are. Furthermore, such an understanding will necessarily pit love of Christ over against love of others. It is gratuitous love, however, that makes *persons* of individuals; it is God's gratuitous love as embodied in the crucified and risen Christ that ruptures my isolation by transforming my defensiveness vis-à-vis the other into a new receptivity and openness. That love defines and shapes my very being.

By definition, the autonomous individual is unable to receive, since receptivity implies an agent (an "other") antecedent to the individual. Such a contra-ceptive theological anthropology has destructive consequences not only for our relationships with others but also for our relationship with Jesus Christ. The very notion of grace presupposes a receptivity to the Other, who "has loved us first." That love defines me and empowers me to respond, to love back. Yet, by definition, the autonomous individual can only love what he or she "freely" *chooses* to love; the individual cannot conceive that, before he or she can choose, he or she has already been chosen.

Finally, if God has indeed "loved us first," it is not to limit our freedom but, on the contrary, to invite us into a relationship that, because it affirms who I indeed am as a being-in-relation, liberates me to love. If the individual is free to choose, the person is free to love. This notion of relationship as integral to and empowering of the self will always remain elusive as long as we remain beholden to Western individualism. For this reason, it might be helpful to look beyond the West for ways of conceiving the notion of relationship in general, and the relationship between persons and God in particular. One such helpful resource might be the theological notion of theosis that, while certainly present in Western Christianity, is "the central dogma of [Eastern] Orthodoxy."[6]

Theosis

The notion of the Christian life, or Christian discipleship, as a participation in God is central to Christian theology from the beginning.[7] Despite its influence in the West, however, this notion has been most fully developed in Eastern Christian mystical theology, in the doctrine of theosis. The roots of theosis are thoroughly biblical; the idea is implicit already in the Genesis account of men and women being created "in the image and likeness" of God. This theological anthropology is then assumed and asserted throughout the Hebrew Bible and Christian Scriptures. So, for example, Paul writes, "And we, who with unveiled faces all reflect the Lord's glory, are being transformed into this likeness (image) with ever-increasing glory, which comes from the Lord, who is the Spirit" (2 Cor. 3:18). In 1 John 3:2–3 we read, "Dear friends, now we are children of God, and what we will be has not yet been made known. But we know that when he appears, *we shall be like him*, for we shall see him as he is." In John's Gospel, the identity between the Father and the Son is portrayed as the same as that between the Father, the Son, and all believers:

> My prayer is not for them alone. I pray also for those who will believe in me through their message, that all of them may be one, Father, just as you are in me and I am in you. *May they also be in us* so that the world may believe that you have sent me. I have given them the glory that you gave me, that they may be one as we are one—I in them and you in me—so that they may be brought to complete unity. (John 17:20–23)

Similar language appears also in 2 Peter 1:3–4:

> His divine power has given us everything we need for life and godliness through our knowledge of him who called us by his own glory and goodness. Through these he has given us his very great and

precious promises, so that through them you may *participate in the divine nature* and escape the corruption in the world caused by evil desires.

Our destiny, *telos*, and salvation, therefore, are nothing less than a *participation* in the trinitarian life of God. Far from a principle drawn from a few biblical prooftexts, moreover, theosis is implicit in the entire biblical drama and in the central doctrines of creation and incarnation. As Jaroslav Pelikan observed in his study of Maximus the Confessor, deification is a discernible theme throughout the New Testament:

The purpose of the Lord's Prayer was to point to the mystery of deification. Baptism was "in the name of the life-giving and deifying Trinity." When the guests at the wedding in Cana of Galilee . . . said that their host had "kept the good wine until now," they were referring to the Word of God, saved for the last, by which men were made divine. When, in the Epistles of the same apostle John, "the Theologian," it was said that "it does not yet appear what we shall be," this was a reference to "the future deification of those who have now been made children of God." When the apostle Paul spoke of "the riches" of the saints, this, too meant deification.[8]

This soteriology underlies the doctrine of the incarnation itself, a point emphasized repeatedly by many patristic authors. Clement of Alexandria, for instance, writes, "[T]he Word of God became human, that you may learn . . . how humans may become God" (*Exhortation to the Heathen*, chap. 12). And again, "[T]o be incorruptible is to participate in divinity" (*Stromata* 5.10). And in Irenaeus's classic exposition of the principle: "The word of God, our Lord Jesus Christ . . . did through his transcendent love, become what we are, that he might bring us to be even what he is himself" (*Against Heresies* 5, preface).[9] In the self-emptying, kenotic love whereby God takes on human flesh in the person of Jesus Christ, who is crucified not only "for" us but especially "with" us, the divine nature embraces and assumes, thereby elevating our human nature, making us by adoption what Jesus Christ is by nature.

The great twentieth-century Orthodox theologian Vladimir Lossky likewise explains that theosis is implicit in the self-emptying love of God, the *exitus–reditus* manifested in the creation, incarnation, crucifixion, resurrection:

> The descent . . . of the divine person of Christ makes human persons capable of an ascent . . . in the Holy Spirit. It was necessary that the voluntary humiliation, the redemptive kenosis, of the Son of God should take place, so that fallen [persons] might accomplish their vocation of theosis, the deification of created beings by uncreated grace. . . . If this union has been accomplished in the divine person of the Son, who is God become [human], it is necessary that each human person, in turn, should become god by grace, or "a partaker of the divine nature," according to St. Peter's expression (II Peter 1:40).[10]

Our participation in divinity is made possible only through grace; salvation-as-deification is sheer gift: "Yet Eastern theology says very clearly that 'becoming god' does not mean an identification with God's divine nature (essence) but rather something experienced by adoption, by grace, and by imitation."[11] The differences between theosis and Hellenistic notions of deification and apotheosis are fundamental; the two key distinguishing characteristics of Christian theosis are that it is gratuitous and that it is kenotic:

> Although the Eastern Christian tradition has spoken of "becoming God/god," it has also made it clear that theosis does not mean that people become little gods; nor does it mean apotheosis, the unChristian notion of the post-mortem promotion of certain humans (heroes, emperors, etc.) to divinity. Rather, theosis means that humans become like God. The tradition of theosis in Christian theology after the New Testament begins with the famous dictum of Irenaeus, later developed by Athanasius: "God became what we are to make us what he is." Theosis is about divine intention and action, human transformation, and the telos of human existence — union with God.[12]

Neither can the Christian notion of theosis as participation in the trinitarian life be simply identified with the dissolution of the self. Indeed, as a response to the gratuitous, kenotic love of God the human person's participation in divine life is uniquely and peculiarly human; it is the fulfillment of the self. John Meyendorff writes:

> All things exist by participation in the Only Existing One, "but man has a particular way in which he participates in God, different from that of all other beings. He communicates with him *freely*, because he carries in himself the image of the Creator. Deification is precisely this free and conscious participation in the divine life, which is proper to man only. Because of that, the union with God mentioned by the Fathers never amounts to a disintegration of the human person into the divine infinite; but, on the contrary, it is the fulfillment of his free and personal destiny.[13]

This is a crucial distinction, since the "self" that is emptied in the process of theosis is the "false self," which must be relinquished so that we may find our "true self" in God, in Christ. Thus, Christian "self-emptying" is always a concomitant "filling" with the power of Christ that generates personhood and makes possible resistance to the disintegration of the true self.[14]

Cruciform Christification

For the Christian, participation in God is made possible and is mediated by life in Christ. It is the event of the incarnation in the person of Jesus Christ that makes deification possible. If what defines that event is its character as the absolutely gratuitous, self-emptying love of God, its defining characteristic is not only Christoformity but, more specifically, Cruciformity. No one is clearer about this than the apostle Paul himself. For Paul, to participate in divinity is to participate in the crucified Christ, that is, in the self-emptying God revealed on the cross. According to biblical scholar Michael Gorman, "Theosis is transformative participation in the kenotic, cruciform character of God through Spirit-enabled conformity to the incarnate, crucified, and resurrected/glorified Christ, who is the image of God."[15] For Paul, as Gorman notes, theosis is thus but the "actualization or embodiment of justification by faith."[16]

Focusing on the famous Pauline hymn in Philippians 2:6–11, Gorman demonstrates convincingly how that text is key evidence of a Pauline soteriology of deification. Gorman begins by suggesting that the first line of the hymn, "Though he was in the form of God," might also be translated as, "Because he was in the form of God." Hence, the self-emptying divine love embodied in the crucified Christ, as "the form of God," is not an exceptional form of God's love but is the very definition of that love:

> The story of Christ in [Phil.] 2:6-8 show us that kenosis—specifically cruciform kenosis, or cruciformity—is the essential attribute of God while at the same time, paradoxically, being the expression of divine freedom (parallel to Paul and his apostleship/kenosis/freedom, according to 1 Thessalonians 2 and 1 Corinthians 9). God, we must now say, is essentially kenotic, and indeed essentially cruciform. Kenosis, therefore, does not mean Christ's emptying himself of his divinity (or of anything else), but rather Christ's exercising his divinity, his equality with God.[17]

It is in this light that we must understand Paul's notion of *imitatio Christi*. In its deepest sense, to "imitate" Christ is not to perform the same acts that Christ performed (something we could never do on our own, in any case), but to participate in Christ's own kenotic activity in the world; it is to participate in the very death–resurrection dynamic of divine love described in the Philippians hymn. This is why Paul has such little interest in the specifics of Jesus's life and deeds beyond the fact of his crucifixion; to imitate Jesus is to be crucified with him and, thereby, to be raised with him. Here again, an individualistic rendering of "imitation" as an extrinsic relation between the imitator and the imitated fails to account for the truly radical character of Christian soteriology as a mutual indwelling and participation in the trinitarian life of God—and that perichoretic life is inherently cruciform. Douglas Campbell likewise distinguishes between imitation and participation:

> Just as Jesus faithfully endured suffering to the point of death and then received a triumphant and glorious resurrection, so too Christians who maintain their loyalty to God and to Christ until the end

receive a resurrection. Moreover, in so doing, God is not asking them to imitate Christ—perhaps an impossible task—so much as to inhabit or to indwell him. That is, any such endurance through duress is evidence that the Spirit of God is actively reshaping the Christian into the likeness of Christ, and that they are already part of the story, a story that will result in eschatological salvation! Consequently, such enduring fidelity is critical evidence that God is at work, incorporating the believer into the prototypical story of Christ. In essence, to be part of this first sequence, despite its difficulties, is to be guaranteed being part of its second: this is no mere imitatio Christi.[18]

A similar analysis is provided by David Litwa in his exegesis of 2 Corinthians 3:18: "And we, who with unveiled faces all reflect the Lord's glory, are being transformed into his image with ever-increasing glory, which comes from the Lord, who is the Spirit." Here, Paul speaks of our being transformed into Christ's image, who is himself the image of God; we become by grace what Christ is by nature: "Christ has a direct share in the Father's divinity, but humans an indirect share—through Christ. Thus the Son always has an entirely unique relation to divinity. Divinity is his proper possession. Humans only receive divinity through Christ. They only possess it as gift."[19]

To flesh out this understanding of theosis as cruciform Christification, Gorman and Litwa make two further points: (1) this process always has a communal, ecclesial dimension; and (2) it always has a social dimension. The church itself receives an eschatological call to participate in the cruciform life of Christ. And that participation necessarily implies a participation in the lives and struggles of the weak and powerless:

> The nature of theosis as we have seen it in Paul's letters is thoroughly communal as well as personal (without being private), and it is thoroughly horizontal ("ethical") as well as vertical ("spiritual"). For the justified to become, in Christ, the justice of God in the world could not be otherwise. Theosis, in other words, is a theopolitical reality as the church embodies, or actualizes, its justification in the world, bearing the image of the one true, holy, cruciform God among an array of other alleged deities and their

communities. By the power of the Spirit, the church lives a countercultural life of fidelity and love, generosity and justice, purity and promise-keeping, nonviolence and peacemaking. It is, in other words, a Spirit-infused, living exegesis of the cross; or better, a living exegesis of the Crucified, who is the image of God. The church inhabits this triune, cruciform God, who in turn inhabits the church. Thus the church's life story embodies and thereby proclaims the narrative identity and gracious saving power of the triune God whom Paul encountered and preached: the source of justification, holiness, and peace—theosis.[20]

Though not using the specific term, another theologian who also placed the notion of theosis at the very center of his understanding of Christian discipleship was Dietrich Bonhoeffer. For Bonhoeffer, Christian discipleship is ultimately not about imitating Christ but about becoming conformed to Christ through the power of grace in our lives:

> It is Christ's own form which seeks to manifest itself in us. Christ does not cease working in us until he has changed us into Christ's own image. Our goal is to be shaped into the entire form of the incarnate, the crucified, and the transfigured one.[21]

Thus, one does not "follow" Christ in the same sense as one would follow some other role model, for the very following of Christ is itself already made possible by Christ himself, whose life we do not simply emulate but in which we participate. And this participation is necessarily cruciform; to live in Christ is to be crucified with Christ.

Finally, theosis has not only ecclesial and social dimensions but also a cosmic dimension. Paul explicitly draws the connection between human deification and cosmic deification:

> The Spirit himself testifies with our spirit that we are God's children. Now if we are children, then we are heirs—heirs of God and co-heirs with Christ, if indeed we share in his sufferings in order that we may also share in his glory. I consider that our present sufferings are not worth comparing with the glory that will be revealed in us. For the creation waits in eager expectation for the

children of God to be revealed. For the creation was subjected to frustration, not by its own choice, but by the will of the one who subjected it, in hope that the creation itself will be liberated from its bondage to decay and brought into the freedom and glory of the children of God. We know that the whole creation has been groaning as in the pains of childbirth right up to the present time. Not only so, but we ourselves, who have the firstfruits of the Spirit, groan inwardly as we wait eagerly for our adoption to sonship, the redemption of our bodies. For in this hope we were saved. But hope that is seen is no hope at all. Who hopes for what they already have? But if we hope for what we do not yet have, we wait for it patiently. (Rom. 8:16–25)

Just as we are destined to become heirs of God and co-heirs with the crucified and risen Christ, so too is creation itself destined to share in "the freedom and glory of the children of God." Just as those who have been crucified with Christ will also share in his own resurrection, so too will the creation, which "was subjected to frustration" and is thus "groaning as in the pains of childbirth." This is anything but an individualistic redemption, glorification, or salvation!

God's self-emptying love ultimately embraces all of creation. Indeed, creation is itself the primordial act of kenotic love, representing the foundational divine act of "othering" wherein God effaces Godself in order that an "other" may come into existence. As Simone Weil among others argues so powerfully, "creation is an act, not of expansion on God's part, but of abdication. God in creation, by allowing the existence of other creatures, refuses to be everything."[22] Thus, the self-emptying love embodied in the incarnation and crucifixion is already implicit in the divine act of creation, which is itself cruciform. Likewise, the ultimate transformation and glorification of Christ in his resurrection are also implicit in the divine act of creation. It is not just we who die and are raised with Christ and in Christ, but so too all of creation.

Among contemporary thinkers, few have articulated a nondualistic (not nondual) understanding of the relationship between Creator and creation as systematically and rigorously as Ignacio Ellacuría (who himself is profoundly influenced by the Spanish philosopher Xavier Zubiri). According to Ellacuría:

Creation can be seen as the taking-form *ad extra* of the Trinitarian life itself, . . . an act of communication and self-giving by the divine life itself. . . . This taking-form and self-communication has degrees and limits, so that each thing, within its own limits, is a limited way of being God. . . . God's communication, the taking-form *ad extra* of the divine life, has gone through a long process that has been oriented toward the taking-form of that divine life in the human nature of Jesus, and ultimately toward the "return" of all creation to its original source.[23]

Robert Lassalle-Klein has suggested that Ellacuría, as well as his fellow Jesuit Jon Sobrino, locates theosis (or, in Zubiri's word, *deiformación*) at the very center of the Christian faith.[24]

At the core of Xavier Zubiri's philosophical thought is a sustained analysis of the word "in" as a corrective to extrinsicist understandings of the relationship between Creator and creation. For Zubiri, transcendence is always transcendence "in": "Real things are real 'in' God. . . . Things are not only real in God but in the person which God is. . . . Now, things are real 'in' God, in God as a person, and God is in them constituting them formally. But God is 'in' them as something transcendent."[25]

This notion of "transcendence *in*" will be very influential in the thought of Sobrino and, especially, Ellacuría, who holds that "[t]he total unity of a single history, of God in humanity and humanity in God . . . affirms the dual unity of God *in* humanity and humanity *in* God."[26] To denote God's act of transcending "in," Zubiri and Ellacuría use the term *plasmación*.[27] In his analysis of Ellacuría's soteriology, Michael Lee notes, "Critical components of this [soteriology] lie in presenting transcendence as something 'in,' not 'away,' adopting the concept of *plasmación*, and describing human existence as participation in the Trinitarian life of God *ad extra*."[28]

This mutual indwelling between Creator and creation implies that human praxis is a participation in divine praxis. Yet, as we have seen in our discussion of the cruciform character of theosis, such participation presupposes and demands a particular kind of praxis; after all, there is such a thing as sin. Unless we are able to specify what kind of praxis is, in fact, a participation in the trinitarian life of God, our notion of theosis will remain susceptible to idealistic and individualistic distortions. Theology will end up legitimizing human praxis that is, in fact, idolatrous because it reduces the God who transcends "in" to a god who transcends "away from" (hence objectifying God and reducing the relationship between creation and Creator to an extrinsic "relationship"). Such a reductionist, dualistic understanding of relationality will inevitably also be individualistic, since relationships between persons—or between persons and God—will themselves be conceived of extrinsically, that is, between autonomous objects. In order to safeguard against this danger, we must now consider once again the preferential option for the poor, though this time in the light of our prior discussion of theosis or, more specifically, cruciform Christification. If, in his study of the Pauline letters, Gorman insisted that theosis is also a "theopolitical reality," the preferential option for the poor will safeguard the cruciform, liberative character of that reality by pointing to a particular locus as the privileged place wherein we participate in God's own cruciform, liberative praxis in history. That privileged locus is what Ellacuría and Sobrino have called "the crucified people."

The Preferential Option for the Poor

Despite the insistence that theosis always has a social, ecclesial, and even cosmic dimension, the process of theosis as cruciform Christification remains itself susceptible to an individualistic, privatized interpretation unless it is read through the lens of a preferential option for the poor. That is, the safeguard against an individualistic, privatized understanding of our participation in the life of the crucified and risen Christ is our preferential identification with those whom Ellacuría and Sobrino have called the crucified people, in whom Christ continues to be crucified today. To paraphrase the words of Sobrino, there is no theosis outside the poor, for they are the privileged locus of Christ's activity in history (cf. Matt. 25:31–46).[29]

We cannot live in Christ unless we live in those places and among those persons in whom Christ said he would be found. To be crucified with

Christ is not an abstract idea but a practical program. This is not to canonize the poor. As Gustavo Gutiérrez never tires of reminding us, God loves the poor preferentially not because *they* are good, but because *God* is good.[30] Because God's love is indeed universal and gratuitous, it will be encountered first among the unloved, abandoned, and excluded—as the confirmation and safeguard of its universality and gratuity. Because God, as Mystery, is incomprehensible, God will be encountered first in those lives that themselves "make no sense," are incomprehensible—among the powerless in a power-hungry world, among the insecure in a world obsessed with security, among the vulnerable in a world that glorifies invulnerability. Because God, as Mystery, does not "belong" in and cannot be confined within the borders of our world, God will be encountered first among those who themselves "do not belong" in and are thus excluded from our world. If God is indeed revealed in our world, it can only be as—in Zubiri's term—"*transcendence in.*" The outcast, crucified God will be revealed to us among the outcast, crucified people, who are the privileged mediators of transcendence in history. In this way, God's preferential option for the poor guarantees the gratuity and universality of God's love; it safeguards Mystery.

Because the preferential option for the poor is ultimately God's—and not ours—theosis as deification will itself presuppose and demand such an option. Conversely, and precisely because the preferential option for the poor is a theocentric option, a Christian, nonindividualistic understanding of theosis will be grounded in an understanding of that praxis as a real (not just metaphorical) participation in the trinitarian divine life made fully manifest in the crucified and risen Christ.[31]

An appreciation of this intrinsic relationship between the option for the poor and deification would also help to underscore the cosmic dimension of the former, that is, the intrinsic relationship between the liberation of the poor and the liberation of creation. Because deification ultimately involves all of creation, when that process is mediated by a solidarity with the poor, such solidarity implies a participation in God's own praxis of drawing all creation into God's trinitarian life. If liberation is ultimately God's own praxis, in which we are invited to participate, then the liberation of the poor implies the liberation of all creation: "The creation itself will be liberated from its bondage to decay and brought into the freedom and glory of the children of God" (Rom. 8:21).

Ellacuría and Sobrino have emphasized this intrinsic connection between theosis and the preferential option for the poor. In the words of Lassalle-Klein, "The Greek fathers describe this dynamic as *theosis*, which Ellacuría and Sobrino apply to the option for the poor where the disciple is drawn into a transformative encounter with the divine mystery of the inner life of God."[32] The Christian reality of theosis is what guarantees the historicity of salvation: "For Ellacuría it is the dynamics of theosis (or what Zubiri calls *deiformación*) that explains the human capacity to historicize transcendence by entering into a historical relationship with the divine."[33] This historical relationship is, in turn, mediated (not effected) by the crucified people, through whom the crucified and risen Christ continues to liberate and save in the world today.

The Christian tradition of theosis thus has radical sociohistorical implications as the theological ground and warrant for a preferential option for the poor, which is itself always a theocentric option. Otherwise, such a practical option devolves into but one among many "options" that an individual is "free to choose" and which has no necessary or intrinsic relationship to the Source of our liberative praxis. Jesus Christ would then be only a model or exemplar, not the one in and through whom our praxis is made possible. Conversely, the preferential option for the poor has equally profound implications for the Christian tradition of theosis, as the sociohistorical mediation of the crucified and risen Christ's salvific activity in the world. To participate in Christ's salvific work, in the kenotic trinitarian life of God, is to participate in Christ's ongoing crucifixion in history, alongside the crucified people.[34] The cross locates theosis, and the option for the poor historicizes that location. When—in the words of Ellacuría and Sobrino—we "take the crucified people down from the cross," we become participants in Christ's ongoing resurrection in history, a resurrection that—precisely as historical—will forever bear the wounds of crucifixion. Moreover, as the final assurance that we are indeed invited and empowered to participate in God's self-emptying love on the cross, Christ's resurrection reveals the utterly gratuitous, unmerited, and universal character of God's love. It is thus that the dynamic process of theosis, or deification, reveals the integral relationship between God's universal, gratuitous love and God's preferential love for the poor. In the person of the crucified and risen Christ, God invites us to participate in a love that is gratuitous and universal precisely because it accords a privileged place to the outcasts, the excluded, the crucified people.

NOTES

1. Alasdair MacIntyre, "Durkheim"s Call to Order," *New York Review of Books*, March 7, 1974, 26.

2. For an extended elaboration of my understanding of "liberal individualism" in relation to the various ways of understanding that term, see chap. 3 of my *Caminemos con Jesús: Toward a Hispanic/Latino Theology of Accompaniment* (Maryknoll, NY: Orbis Books, 1995), 47–76.

3. Ibid.

4. See my discussion of human action in ibid., 77–131.

5. Roberto S. Goizueta, *Christ Our Companion: Toward a Theological Aesthetics of Liberation* (Maryknoll, NY: Orbis Books, 2009), 15–18.

6. I. Bria quoted in Emil Bartos, *Deification in Eastern Orthodox Theology* (Eugene, OR: Wipf and Stock, 1999), 7. See also Norman Russell, *The Doctrine of Deification in the Greek Patristic Tradition,* Oxford Early Christian Studies (New York: Oxford University Press, 2004).

7. For an overview, see Cynthia Peters Anderson, *Reclaiming Participation: Christ as God's Life for All* (Minneapolis: Fortress, 2014). Despite the inevitable concerns about idolatry or theological arrogance, the notion of participation-as-deification is implicit, for instance, in the Western Christian anthropological and soteriological emphasis on knowledge as participation (with not only biblical and patristic but also Aristotelian roots). In addition to the entire mystical tradition in the West, the most obvious example here is the Angelic Doctor Thomas Aquinas himself:
"Now the gift of grace surpasses every capability of created nature, since it is nothing short of a partaking of the Divine Nature, which exceeds every other nature. And thus it is impossible that any creature should cause grace. For it is as necessary that God alone should deify, bestowing a partaking of the Divine Nature by a participated likeness, as it is impossible that anything save fire should enkindle" (*Summa theologiae*, Ia–IIae, q. 112, a. 1, resp.). In her book, Anderson also looks especially to Hans Urs von Balthasar as a twentieth-century proponent of deification (pp. 147–210).

8. Jaroslav Pelikan, quoted in Veli-Matti Karkkainen, *One with God: Salvation as Deification and Justification,* Unitas Books (Collegeville, MN: Liturgical Press, 2004), 19.

9. Quoted in Karkkainen, *One with God*, 26.

10. Vladimir Lossky, *In the Image and Likeness of God* (Crestwood, NY: St. Vladimir's Seminary Press, 1974), 97–98.

11. Bartos, *Deification in Eastern Orthodox Theology*, 7.

12. Michael J. Gorman, *Inhabiting the Cruciform God: Kenosis, Justification, and Theosis in Paul's Narrative Soteriology* (Grand Rapids: Eerdmans, 2009), 4–5.

13. John Meyendorff, *Christ in Eastern Christian Thought* (Crestwood, NY: St. Vladimir's Seminary Press, 1975), 128–29.

14. On the notions of the true and false self, see Thomas Merton, *New Seeds of Contemplation* (New York: New Directions, 2007). In an ongoing debate concerning the Christian doctrine of self-emptying, or kenosis, feminist theologians have alerted us to the history and dangers of distorting that doctrine for oppressive purposes. Here see esp. Daphne Hampson, "On Power and Gender," *Modern Theology* 4.3 (1988): 234–50; Sarah Coakley, "Kenosis and Subversion: On the Repression of 'Vulnerability' in Christian Feminist Writing," in *Swallowing a Fishbone? Feminist Theologians Debate Christianity*, ed. Daphne Hampson (London: SPCK, 1996), 82–111; Coakley, "Kenosis: Theological Meanings and Gender Connotation," in *The Work of Love: Creation as Kenosis*, ed. John Polkinghorne (Grand Rapids: Eerdmans, 2001), 192–210; Anna Mercedes, *Power For: Feminism and Christ's Self-Giving* (London: T&T Clark, 2011); Aristotle Papanikolaou, "Person, Kenosis, and Abuse: Hans Urs von Balthasar and Feminist Theologies in Conversation," *Modern Theology* 19.1 (2003): 41–65; Annie Selak, "Constructing a Comprehensive Feminist Understanding of *Kenosis*: Jon Sobrino in Conversation with the Feminist *Kenosis* Debate (paper presented at Boston College, Systematic Theology Colloquium, March 20, 2015). Selak presents a very helpful summary of the *status quaestionis* and makes an important contribution to a critical retrieval of kenosis, drawing on the work not only of Coakley, Mercedes, and Papanikolaou, but also of Jon Sobrino. In this way, her project of critical retrieval of kenosis, using the groundbreaking work of the Jesuit theologian, is analogous to my own attempt to retrieve theosis in the light of Sobrino's work.

15. Gorman, *Inhabiting the Cruciform God*, 7.

16. Ibid., 125.

17. Ibid., 27–28.

18. Douglas Campbell, quoted in ibid., 167–68.

19. M. David Litwa, "2 Corinthians 3:18 and Its Implications for *Theosis*," *Journal of Theological Interpretation* 2 (2008): 129.

20. Gorman, *Inhabiting the Cruciform God*, 172.

21. Dietrich Bonhoeffer, in *Dietrich Bonhoeffer Works*, vol. 4, *Discipleship* (Minneapolis: Fortress, 2001), 284–85; also quoted in Gorman, *Inhabiting the Cruciform God*, 169.

22. J. P. Little, "Simone Weil's Concept of Decreation," in *Simone Weil's*

Philosophy of Culture, ed. Richard H. Bell (New York: Cambridge University Press, 1993), 27. See also Polkinghorne, *The Work of Love: Creation as Kenosis*.

23. Ignacio Ellacuría, "The Historicity of Christian Salvation," in *Ignacio Ellacuría: Essays on History, Liberation, and Salvation*, ed. Michael E. Lee (Maryknoll, NY: Orbis Books, 2013), 151; see also Robert Lassalle-Klein, *Blood and Ink: Ignacio Ellacuría, Jon Sobrino, and the Jesuit Martyrs of the University of Central America* (Maryknoll, NY: Orbis Books, 2014), 300.

24. Lassalle-Klein, *Blood and Ink*, 300–313, 332–43.

25. Xavier Zubiri, *Man and God* (Lanham, MD: University Press of America, 2009), 140–42.

26. Ignacio Ellacuría, quoted in Michael E. Lee, *Bearing the Weight of Salvation: The Soteriology of Ignacio Ellacuría* (New York: Herder & Herder, 2009), 38.

27. Of the unusual word *plasmación*, Kevin Burke writes, "[T]he verb *plasmar* means to 'mold, shape, form or give concrete form to something,' or even 'to represent' (as in 'give visible form to' something), but the nominatives, 'form' and 'shape' are too weak to translate *plasmació*" (*The Ground beneath the Cross: The Theology of Ignacio Ellacuría* [Washington, DC: Georgetown University Press, 2000]), 173n53.

28. Ibid., 58.

29. See Jon Sobrino, *No Salvation outside the Poor: Prophetic-Utopian Essays* (Maryknoll, NY: Orbis Books, 2008).

30. See, e.g., Gustavo Gutiérrez, *On Job: God-Talk and the Sufferings of the Innocent* (Maryknoll, NY: Orbis Books, 1987), xiii; see also Goizueta, *Christ Our Companion*, 104–8.

31. It bears repeating that this is in no way to "canonize" the poor for, as Gustavo Gutiérrez insists, the poor themselves are called to make an option for the poor and resist the oppressive forces of the dominant culture.

32. Lassalle-Klein, *Blood and Ink*, 282.

33. Ibid., 301.

34. The paradigm of such participation in Christ's ongoing crucifixion in history is the experience of martyrdom. For Sobrino, that participation "is strikingly emblemized by the blood-stained pages of Jürgen Moltmann's *The Crucified God*—a subject of his 1975 dissertation on Jürgen Moltmann—which fell from the bookshelf of his room into the blood of Juan Ramón Moreno on the morning of November 16, 1989 [when Moreno, five other Jesuits, and two women were murdered by Salvadoran security forces]" (Lassalle-Klein, *Blood and Ink*, 310). In that book, the German theologian writes that the martyrs "do not merely imitate the sufferings of Christ and bear witness to it by doing the same, but take part in and fulfill the continuing sufferings of Christ. They are drawn into the mystery of the suffering of Christ and come to participate in him" (*The Crucified God* [Minneapolis: Fortress, 1993], 57).

12
The Christocentric Mystagogy of Joseph Ratzinger/Benedict XVI

Robert P. Imbelli

A Christological Vision

In the preface to a small volume of Christological essays and meditations, first published in 1984, then Joseph Cardinal Ratzinger spoke of his effort "to consider Christology more from the aspect of its spiritual appropriation" than he had previously done. He goes on to muse that only from the viewpoint of such an endeavor do "the classic formulas of Chalcedon appear in the proper perspective."[1] Then, in the book's opening essay, "Taking Bearings in Christology," he presents seven theses that lay the foundation for his position. For my purposes two of the theses have particular import.

Thesis 3 states, "Since the center of the person of Jesus is prayer, it is essential to participate in his prayer if we are to know and understand him."[2] Let us dwell for a bit on this concise assertion. For, embodied within it, is an entire spiritual-theological vision.

For Joseph Ratzinger/Benedict XVI the distinctive identity of Jesus is his relationship to the Father, the one whom he calls *"Abba."* Thus, the crucial Christological category is that Jesus is "the Son." In the first volume of *Jesus of Nazareth*, Benedict writes:

> The term "Son" along with its correlate "Father (Abba)" gives us a true glimpse into the inner being of Jesus—indeed, into the inner being of God himself. Jesus' prayer is the true origin of the term

238

"the Son." It has no prehistory, just as the Son himself is "new," even though Moses and the prophets prefigure him.[3]

A number of features of Benedict's Christology emerge from this statement. First is his stress on the uniqueness and originality of Jesus: his "newness." One is reminded of the splendid confession of St. Irenaeus: *Omnem novitatem attulit, semetipsum afferens,* "Christ brought all newness by bringing himself."[4] This conviction underlies all Benedict's preaching and teaching.

The second feature adumbrated in the above quotation is developed at greater length in Benedict's now classic lectures of summer 1967 at Tübingen, published as *Introduction to Christianity.* Here he sets forth a relational approach to Christology, as reframing, not contradicting, the more static two-natures Christology of the tradition. Indeed, he posits here and elsewhere a relational understanding of reality to complement the more "substantive" understanding of classical metaphysics. He writes:

> What we have already discovered in our reflections on the Triune God appears again here at the end of a different train of reasoning: he who does not cling to himself but is pure relatedness coincides in this with the absolute and thus becomes Lord. The Lord before whom the universe bows is the slaughtered Lamb, the symbol of existence that is pure act, pure "for." The cosmic liturgy, the adoring homage of the universe, centers round this Lamb (Rev. 5).[5]

The relatedness that constitutes Jesus's identity is twofold. It is inseparably relatedness to God and to God's people, those for whom Jesus has been sent. He is the one whose being is completely given to the Father (*pros ton theon,* John 1:1) and given for the sake of the many (*hyper pollōn,* Mark 14:24).

The prayer of Jesus, canonically summed up in the seventeenth chapter of the Fourth Gospel, offers precious testimony to the essence of the prayer of Jesus. He prays to the Father, the Source from whom he has received all—mission, disciples, life itself. At the same time, he does not intend to reserve his prayer-relation to himself alone. The teaching of the "Our Father" provides ample evidence of his desire that others participate in his intimate knowledge and love of the Father. Jesus's experience of prayer, though unique, is also inclusive. He wishes to incorporate others into this dynamism of communication "so that with Jesus and in him they can say 'Abba' to God just as he does."[6] Indeed, only in this way will they truly know him and themselves: filii in Filio.

This "knowledge by participation"—this affective knowledge of both head and heart—is integral to Ratzinger's "spiritual Christology." To use Cardinal Newman's categories: it moves beyond a merely "notional" apprehension to achieve a "real" apprehension of who Jesus is and of the new Way that he inaugurates and embodies for his disciples. It shows clearly the inseparability of theology and spirituality. The recovery of this intimate nexus between theology and spirituality was a key element in the program of ressourcement (the return to the sources: the New Testament and the Fathers) that flowered in the 1940s and 1950s, especially in France. A recent writer comments, "First of all, returning to the Fathers meant asserting the unity between dogmatic theology and the living experience of the mystery of Christ in the Church; in brief, the unity between thought and life."[7] The seminarian and young theologian Joseph Ratzinger drank deeply from this wellspring.

The fourth thesis that Ratzinger articulates in Behold the Pierced One can now be introduced:

> Sharing in Jesus' praying involves communion with all his brethren. Fellowship with the person of Jesus, which proceeds from participation in his prayer, thus constitutes that all-embracing fellowship that Paul calls "the Body of Christ." So the Church—the "Body of Christ"—is the true subject of our knowledge of Jesus. In the Church's memory the past is present because Christ is present and lives in her.[8]

What the then Cardinal Ratzinger expounds so succinctly in this assertion, dating from the early 1980s, had characterized his theology from an early date and continued to mark his writings as pope. A decisive influence in this regard was the eminent Jesuit theologian and later cardinal, Henri de Lubac, a pioneer among the ressourcement theologians.

In his informative personal memoir, Milestones, Joseph Ratzinger recalls how, in 1949, a young prefect of studies at the seminary where he was studying introduced him to de Lubac's masterwork, *Catholicism*. He writes, "This book was for me a key reading event." And he goes on to explain, "It gave me not only a new and deeper connection with the thought of the Fathers, but also a new way of thinking about theology and faith as such."[9] He specifies further:

> De Lubac was leading his readers out of a narrowly individualistic and moralistic mode of faith and into the freedom of an essentially social faith, conceived and lived as a "we"—a faith that, precisely as such and according to its nature, was also hope, affecting history as a whole, and not only the promise of a private blissfulness to individuals. I then looked around for other works by de Lubac and derived special profit from his book *Corpus Mysticum*, in which a new understanding of Church and Eucharist opened up to me.[10]

We have here an entire ecclesial vision *in nuce*. This essentially communal and corporate understanding of church remained paramount for Ratzinger throughout his theological work and received dramatic expression in his encyclical of 2007 on Christian hope, *Spe Salvi*.

In the encyclical, Pope Benedict once again credits de Lubac with helping lead Catholic theology from a narrowly individualistic focus to a more expansive communal and social understanding of faith's nature and implications. (It is noteworthy that the original subtitle in French of *Catholicism* was "The Social Aspects of the Dogma.")[11] Benedict concludes the encyclical with an almost lyrical utterance:

> Our hope is always essentially also hope for others; only thus is it truly hope for me too. As Christians we should never limit ourselves to asking: how can I save myself? We should also ask: what can I do in order that others may be saved and that for them too the star of hope may rise? Then I will have done my utmost for my own personal salvation as well.[12]

In beginning to explore Benedict XVI's Christological vision, it has quickly become apparent that it opens organically into ecclesiology, into an understanding of church. One knowledgeable commentator writes, "for Ratzinger ecclesiology is essentially Christology."[13] This foundationally Christological approach secures for the church its distinctive identity as the body of Christ. Even more, it expands the understanding of the mystery of Christ to include inseparably his ecclesial body. Here too de Lubac's influence is clear.

I dwelt above on Ratzinger's admission of his debt to de Lubac's *Catholicism*. But Ratzinger also asserted that he "derived special profit" from another of de Lubac's works, *Corpus Mysticum*. In this work, the French theologian recovered the intimate link among three facets of the Mystery of Christ—what might be called Christ's "tripartite body." There is the risen and ascended body of Christ, the body of Christ, the Eucharist, and the body of Christ, the church. The profound organic connection among the three was a given of patristic and medieval theology but had become neglected in subsequent centuries, as a one-sided emphasis on the institutional aspects of church emerged in reaction to the Protestant Reformation. For both de Lubac and Ratzinger, this interconnection among the three dimensions of the Mystery of Jesus Christ is fundamental to Christian identity and mission. They urged that its recovery was imperative.

One can hear explicit echoes of de Lubac in Benedict XVI's Apostolic Exhortation *Sacramentum Caritatis*, which he wrote subsequent to the 2005 Synod of Bishops devoted to the Eucharist. Benedict teaches, "Christian antiquity used the same words, *Corpus Christi*, to designate Christ's body born of the Virgin Mary, his Eucharistic body, and his ecclesial body. This clear datum of the tradition helps us to appreciate the inseparability of Christ and the Church."[14] At the same time, though the relation between Christ and the church is intimate, they are in no way commensurate. Christ remains the head upon whom the church is dependent for its very life. As Benedict says, "The Eucharist is Christ who gives himself to us and continually builds us up as his body. . . . the Church's ability to [celebrate] the Eucharist is completely rooted in Christ's self-gift to her. . . . For all eternity he remains the one who loves us first."[15]

One finds a similar sounding of the Mystery of Christ and church in a concept dear to St. Augustine, which Ratzinger has appropriated and employed throughout his theological ministry, that of the *Christus Totus*: the Whole Christ. In an essay dating from 1961, the young theologian wrote, "Following Christ . . . demands over and over again the personal risk of searching for him, of walking with him, but at the same time it means ceasing to build a wall around oneself, giving oneself over into the unity of 'the Whole Christ,' the *totus Christus*, as Augustine beautifully puts it."[16]

Forty-six years later, the elderly pontiff dedicated a section of *Sacramentum Caritatis* to "*Christus Totus in Capite et Corpore*" ("The Whole Christ in Head and Body"). Here Benedict celebrates anew Christ's action in the Eucharist. Through our reception of his body and blood, "Christ assimilates us to himself," thus creating a profound unity between believers and the Lord—the *totus Christus*. So intimate is this union that Ratzinger quotes approvingly St. Augustine: "One should not believe that Christ is in the Head, but not in the body; rather Christ is complete in the Head and in the body" (*Sacramentum Caritatis* 36).

Benedict's spiritual Christology is, therefore, far removed from any trace of "Christomonism"—the unique focus on the individual Jesus Christ. For the Whole Christ embraces both the head and the members, whose free assent is required for the building up of the body in holiness and truth. Indeed, as we shall see, an eschatological dynamic pervades Ratzinger's ecclesial vision. He joyfully proclaims, with the Letter to the Colossians, "The Mystery is this: Christ in you, the hope of glory" (Col. 1:27). A Mystery truly present, but whose fulfillment is yet to come.

The Dimming of the Vision

The oft-told tale has it that Joseph Ratzinger, the young "progressive" theologian who played a significant role at the Second Vatican Council, in the years immediately following the council turned "conservative." He, so the story continues, reacted against the events associated with 1968—indeed, was so traumatized by them, that he left the University of Tübingen (where his colleague was Hans Küng) and accepted the chair of dogmatic theology at Regensburg. Of course, some of the bare facts may indeed be correct, but their interpretation leaves out the heart of the matter.

A case can be made that what often transpired theologically after the council was a falling away from the council's robust Christocentric vision, clearly and cogently presented in all four of the conciliar "Constitutions." Such was Ratzinger's discernment of the situation at Tübingen.

A sort of "Christological amnesia" seems to have afflicted some in the theological community.[17] So, for example, in much of the discussion and disputes regarding intraecclesial issues that ensued after the council, sometimes lost to sight was the fact that the title of the "Dogmatic Constitution on the Church," *Lumen Gentium*, referred not to the church but to Christ himself, who alone is the "Light of the Nations." So too, in many of the conflicts raging around *participatio actuosa* in the liturgy, much less heed was accorded that radical "active participation" to which *Sacrosanctum Concilium* summoned believers: their wholehearted participation in Christ's paschal mystery.

Perhaps even more symptomatic of this widespread Christological neglect was the scarce notice given to the Christological foundations of *Gaudium et Spes*, the council's "Pastoral Constitution on the Church in the Modern World." *Gaudium et Spes* made clear that the church's commitment to scrutinize the "signs of the times" was to transpire "in the light of the Gospel" (GS 4), which, of course, means in the light of Christ, who, "by his cross and resurrection, liberates humanity from the power of the Evil One and transforms it according to God's purpose" (GS 2).

Ratzinger had made a significant contribution toward establishing the Christological foundations of *Gaudium et Spes*. It can be discerned most particularly in the composing of the new paragraph 10, which, after much discussion in the council was added to the previous drafts of the document.[18] It is noteworthy that the paragraph in question is strategically placed at the end of the "Introduction" of *Gaudium et Spes* and thus sets the theological context and direction for what follows. The second part of that paragraph is so crucial it is worth quoting in full.

It is the Church's belief that Christ, who died and was raised for everyone, offers to the human race through his Spirit the light and strength to respond to its highest calling; and that no other name under heaven is given to people for them to be saved. It likewise believes that the key and the focus and culmination of all human history are to be found in its Lord and master. The Church also affirms that underlying so many changes there are some things that do not change and are founded upon Christ, who is the same yesterday and today and forever (Heb. 13:8). It is accordingly in the light of Christ, who is the image of the invisible God and first-born of all creation (Col. 1:15), that the Council proposes to elucidate the mystery of humankind and, in addressing all people, to contribute to discovering a solution to the outstanding questions of our day.[19]

I maintain that Joseph Ratzinger, during his years as university theologian and, later, as prefect of the Congregation for the Doctrine of the Faith, and then as pope, sought faithfully and courageously to affirm and further this Christocentric conciliar vision.

As early as 1968, in the preface to *Introduction to Christianity*, he lamented, "The question of the real content and meaning of the Christian faith is enveloped today in a greater fog of uncertainty than at almost any earlier period in history." Yet he did not counsel the return to a merely rote repetition of fixed formulas. Rather, he sought in the book to "*understand faith afresh* as something that makes possible true humanity in the world of today."[20] Throughout his theological and pastoral ministry Ratzinger has consistently sought to promote a personal appropriation of the church's faith, centered in the good news of Jesus Christ. His "no" to a specious *aggiornamento* is always in function of a "yes" to a faithful and creative appropriation of the gospel.

An important essay, "Christocentrism in Preaching," bears further witness to the author's commitment to a radical and creative engagement with the kerygma. He is forthright in his critique:

Perhaps nothing in recent decades . . . has done more harm to preaching than the loss of credibility it incurred by merely handing on formulas that were no longer the living intellectual property of those who were proclaiming them. This is probably the only way to comprehend the abrupt change in the Church during the post-conciliar period, in which emphatically delivered dogmatic formulas were suddenly replaced by the same emphasis on secular slogans. . . . The first duty of the preacher is not to be on the look-out for foreign models and to expect relevance from them, but, rather, to start by becoming personally a hearer of the Word and welcoming its reality.[21]

Ratzinger's commitment to *ressourcement*—the return to the sources of the faith—has been, at its most profound, a *re-Sourcement*: a return to the unique Source who is the living Lord, Jesus Christ.

A particularly poignant indication of his concern regarding what I have called "the dimming of vision" is found in Benedict's volumes on Jesus. In the foreword to volume 1, he discusses a growing gap between the presumed "Jesus of history" and the "Christ of the Church's faith." He attributes this, in good measure, to a one-sided reliance in biblical studies on the historical-critical approach. For him this inevitably relegates Jesus to being a figure of the distant past. The result is to dismantle the faith and to leave Christian faith and spirituality bereft of its distinctive object. In his words, "Intimate friendship with Jesus, on which everything depends, is in danger of clutching at thin air."[22] Benedict's response, of course, is not to ignore the historical-critical approach (which is fully justified by an incarnational faith), but to complement it by bringing to bear a "Christological hermeneutic" that discerns the unity of scripture and its consummation in Jesus Christ. In effect, such is the understanding that animated the Second Vatican Council and that came to explicit expression in its Dogmatic Constitution on Divine Revelation, *Dei Verbum* (DV).[23]

In the foreword to volume 2 of his trilogy *Jesus of Nazareth*, Benedict explicitly associates his work with *Dei Verbum*. It represents his own attempt to put into practice the methodological principles elaborated in section 12 of the Constitution—a task that "unfortunately has scarcely been attempted thus far."[24] For him, the issue here is not "academic" in some rarefied sense but preeminently spiritual and pastoral, because friendship with the living Jesus lies at the center of what it means to be a disciple, whether in the first or the twenty-first century. In this vein, Benedict summoned the Synod of Bishops in 2008 to meditate on "the Word of God in the life and Mission of the Church." And, in the rich Apostolic Exhortation he composed to disseminate the fruits of the Synod, he wrote, "I encourage all the faithful to renew their personal and communal encounter with Christ, the word of life made visible, and to become his heralds, so that the gift of divine life—communion—can spread ever more fully throughout the world."[25]

Throughout his many years of theological and pastoral service to the church, Joseph Ratzinger has made it clear that any declension from

Catholic faith is not due to the documents of Vatican II. He has repeatedly affirmed that the council's texts "are wholly in continuity with the faith." Indeed, "the true inheritance of the Council lies in its texts" and every abuse of the faith must be resisted "precisely if one wants to uphold the will of the Council."[26] The challenge, then, is to interpret authentically and to appropriate faithfully the council's Christ-centered vision.

In the homily at the Mass marking the fiftieth anniversary of the opening of the council, he reiterated once again this persuasion:

> I believe that the most important thing, especially on such a significant occasion as this, is to revive in the whole Church . . . that yearning to announce Christ again to contemporary man. But, so that this interior thrust towards the new evangelization neither remain just an idea nor be lost in confusion, it needs to be built on a concrete and precise basis, and this basis is the documents of the Second Vatican Council, the place where it found expression. This is why I have often insisted on the need to return, as it were, to the "letter" of the Council—that is to its texts—also to draw from them its authentic spirit, and why I have repeated that the true legacy of Vatican II is to be found in them.[27]

The Christ whom the council proclaimed is "the goal of human history, the point around whom the desires of history and civilization turn, the center of the human race, and the fulfillment of all human aspirations" (GS 45). Even after fifty years, the "reception" of the council, which at heart is the reception of Jesus Christ, in the full height and breadth of his mystery, has only begun—in truth, it is always only beginning.

Intrinsic to the conciliar confession is that there is no "Third Age of the Spirit" which surpasses Christ, as some have maintained either explicitly or by implication. Joseph Ratzinger, in his second dissertation (the *Habilitationsschrift*), which allowed him to teach at university, explored the theology of history of St. Bonaventure, who was general of the Franciscan Order at a time of great tension and upheaval in the Western church.[28] Important for our purpose is what he learned from his study of Bonaventure and applied to the challenges of the present. According to Ratzinger, St. Bonaventure underscored the intimate and inseparable connection between Christ and the Holy Spirit:

The Word revealed in history is definitive, but it is inexhaustible, and it unceasingly discloses new depths. In this sense, the Holy Spirit, as the interpreter of Christ, speaks with his word to every age and shows it that this word always has something new to say. Unlike Joachim of Fiore, Bonaventure doesn't project the Holy Spirit into a future period, but it's always the age of the Holy Spirit. The age of Christ is the age of the Holy Spirit.[29]

Christian faith does not move beyond Christ but seeks to follow the risen Christ, who ever goes before (see Mark 16:7; Matt. 28:7). And the Holy Spirit is no anonymous spirit, but the Spirit of Christ, who leads believers into the full truth of him who is the way, the truth, and the life (John 14:6).

The late William Harmless (like John Jones, a fine student of Christian spirituality and mysticism, who left us at far too young an age) wrote of St. Bonaventure:

One expects Christian mystics to center on Christ. Not all do, in fact. But it is hard to name a mystical theology more self-consciously Christ-centered than Bonaventure's. He often speaks of Christ as the *medium*. . . . In his *Collations on the Six Days* he insists: "The beginning is best made from the center (medium), that is, from Christ. For he himself is the mediator between God and humankind, holding the central position in all things. . . . Therefore it is necessary to start from Christ if one wants to reach Christian wisdom."[30]

I contend that it is hard to name a contemporary Catholic theologian whose theology and spirituality are "more self-consciously Christ-centered" than Joseph Ratzinger, who manifests thereby his great debt to Bonaventure.

That debt strikingly appears in what he learned from Bonaventure concerning a deeper understanding of "revelation." In his *Memoirs*, Ratzinger recounts this lesson:

Where there is no one to perceive "revelation," no re-*vel*-ation has occurred, because no *veil* has been removed. By definition, revelation requires a someone who apprehends it. These insights, gained through my reading of Bonaventure, were later on very important for me during the conciliar discussion on revelation, Scripture, and tradition. Because, if Bonaventure is right, then revelation precedes Scripture and becomes deposited in Scripture, but is not simply identical with it. This in turn means that revelation is always something greater than what is merely written down.[31]

It will come as no surprise that one of the examiners of the *Habilitationsschrift*, in which Ratzinger set forth his findings, feared that Ratzinger was flirting perilously close to "subjectivism" here. The compromise reached was to omit the part on Bonaventure's view of revelation from the thesis. The complete study was only published many years later.[32]

For Ratzinger, however, the need for "subjective appropriation" does not preclude but presumes revelation's "objective content." The initiative is ever God's. Mystery precedes mysticism.[33] The crucial contribution of *Dei Verbum* was to free our understanding of revelation from a too narrow focus on "propositions" and to situate it within an overarching "personalist" context. After all, revelation is the loving initiative of the tri-personal God and finds its consummation in the person of Jesus Christ, "who is both mediator and fullness of all revelation" (DV 2). This Christ-centered personalism is at the heart of Benedict's "spiritual Christology," indeed, of his Christ-centered mystagogy. The challenge we face is not that of a new revelation. The council clearly teaches that in Christ the new and definitive covenant has been established (DV 4). What is always required, however, is the personal and communal appropriation of that covenant, the ever-new experiential realization of the Mystery.

Rekindling the Vision

Among the writings that had a decisive influence on the young Joseph Ratzinger were those of John Henry Newman (whom, Ratzinger, as Pope Benedict XVI, had the joy of beatifying in 2010). Newman's motto as cardinal was *cor ad cor loquitur*: "Heart speaks to heart." It well captures Newman's intense sense that the heart of faith and of human life is found in interpersonal encounter and relationship. In the *Grammar of Assent,* Newman famously stated his conviction that "persons influence us, voices melt us, looks subdue us, actions inflame us."[34] Wondrously, the center of Christian faith is the joyful revelation of the incarnation of God in the person of Jesus Christ and the invitation extended to us to enter into life-giving relation with him. The heart of God personally addresses the heart of the beloved creature.

In the first of his three encyclicals, *Deus Caritas Est*, Benedict XVI expressed the essence of his pastoral program: "Being Christian is not the result of an ethical choice or a lofty idea, but the encounter with an event, a person, which gives life a new horizon and a decisive direction."[35] Clearly for Benedict, mysticism, understood as personal encounter with the living Jesus, not moralism, stands at the heart of the gospel.

For this reason, both as cardinal and later as pope, Joseph Ratzinger supported the "ecclesial movements" such as Focolare, Communion and Liberation, and the Neo-Catechumenate. He sees them as fostering and supporting this personal encounter with Christ, this passage from a notional to a vivid apprehension of Christ and assent to his Way. His homily at the funeral Mass for Monsignor Luigi Giussani, the founder of Communion and Liberation, offers moving insight into both his appreciation of the witness of Giussani and also his conviction of the mystagogic importance of the ecclesial movements. Pope Benedict said:

> Fr. Giussani kept the gaze of his life, of his heart, always fixed on Christ. It was in this way that he understood that Christianity is not an intellectual system, a collection of dogmas, or moralism. Christianity is instead an encounter, a love story; it is an event. This love affair with Christ, this love story that was the whole of Giussani's life, was at the same time quite far removed from any superficial enthusiasm or vague romanticism. Seeing Christ, Giussani truly knew that to encounter Christ means to follow him. This encounter is a road, a journey, a journey that also passes—as we heard in the psalm—through the "valley of darkness.[36]

From a historical point of view, the emergence of ecclesial movements is by no means unprecedented. Monasticism in the early church began as such a movement, as did the early Franciscan movement of the Middle Ages. However, ecclesial movements assume a new urgency today when in so many instances the surrounding culture is indifferent or even hostile to Christian faith. Ecclesial communities catechize their members in the language and experience of faith, a language foreign to the secular culture's vastly different catechumenate. They provide a contemporary mystagogy in settings too often devoid of any sense of mystery.

Ratzinger recognizes that at times tensions can arise between these new communities and established institutions, such as geographic parishes, but he is convinced that the ecclesial movements are works of the Spirit and that, as they mature, such tensions will lessen.[37] They serve as crucial vehicles for rekindling a Christocentric vision in the church today. And, though, of course, not all are called to become members of these movements, the creative interaction between these movements and the more established organisms of the church can vivify both. There is one Christian Way, who is Christ himself; but there are myriad personal paths on the Way.

Permeating the writings and homilies of Joseph Ratzinger, as I have suggested, is a profound sense of the *novum* that is the Way of Christ or, even more exactly, the *novus* who is Christ himself, the "new Adam," who has become, through his paschal mystery, the giver of the Spirit. There follows upon this realization a sense of the profound transformation to which Christ summons believers. "Newness and transformation" are the leitmotifs, the thematic principles, of a new mystagogy capable of "singing a new song for the Lord."[38] In *The Spirit of the Liturgy*, Ratzinger writes, "The man who believes in the Resurrection of Christ really does know what definitive salvation is. He realizes that Christians, who find themselves in the 'New Covenant,' now sing an altogether new song, which is truly and definitively new in virtue of the wholly new thing that has taken place in the Resurrection of Christ."[39]

Therefore, "active participation" in the liturgy entails so much more than external activities. It calls worshipers to realize in our very bodies an intimate participation in the paschal mystery of Christ, whereby we are truly reborn to newness of life. In one of his most pregnant formulations of the transformation to which liturgy impels, Ratzinger writes with fervor:

> The Eucharist is never an event involving just two, a dialogue between Christ and me. Eucharistic Communion is aimed at a complete reshaping of my own life. It breaks up man's entire self and creates a new "we." Communion with Christ is necessarily

also communication with all who belong to him: therein I myself become part of the new bread that he is creating by the resubstantiation of the whole of earthly reality.[40]

This vision of "newness and transformation" is a distinguishing feature of the mystagogy of Pope Benedict. Late in his pontificate, in one of the catecheses delivered in Saint Peter's Square, he again sounds the theme:

> The dialogue that God establishes with each one of us, and we with him in prayer, always includes a "with"; it is impossible to pray to God in an individualistic manner. In liturgical prayer, especially the Eucharist, and formed by the liturgy in every prayer, we do not only speak as individuals but on the contrary enter into the "we" of the Church that prays. And we must transform our "I," entering into this "we."

So rich is this reflection of the aging pope, so recapitulative of his *mystagogy*, that it merits quoting at length. Benedict goes on:

> [I]t is the "total Christ," the whole Community, the Body of Christ united with her Head, that is celebrating. Thus the liturgy is not a sort of "self-manifestation" of a community; it means instead coming out of merely "being ourselves," being closed in on ourselves, and having access to the great banquet, entering into the great living community in which God himself nourishes us. The liturgy implies universality and this universal character must enter ever anew into the awareness of all. The Christian liturgy is the worship of the universal temple which is the Risen Christ, whose arms are outstretched on the Cross to draw everyone into the embrace of God's eternal love. It is the worship of a wide-open heaven. It is never solely the event of a single community with its place in time and space. It is important that every Christian feel and be truly integrated into this universal "we" . . . the Body of Christ which is the Church.

And he concludes:

So, the Liturgy is not the memory of past events, but is the living presence of the Paschal Mystery of Christ who transcends and unites times and places. If in the celebration the centrality of Christ did not emerge, we would not have Christian liturgy, totally dependent on the Lord and sustained by his creative presence. God acts through Christ and we can act only through and in him. The conviction must grow within us every day that the liturgy is not our or my "doing" but rather is an action of God in us and with us.[41]

Joseph Ratzinger's mystagogy seeks to foster, in season and out of season, this conviction that the Christian's deepest identity and most authentic freedom is to be a living member of the Body of Christ. It strives to help believers take on more fully "the mind of Christ" (Phil. 2:5), to know affectively "the love of Christ which surpasses knowledge" (Eph. 3:19), to experience personally "the Lord Jesus who loved me and gave himself for me" (Gal. 2:20).

One can call his vision "mystical" in the same sense that the apostle Paul's vision of the intimate union of Christ and Christians is mystical. Exegeting the famous passage in Galatians where Paul declares that all believers are one in Christ (Gal. 3:28), Ratzinger boldly states, "You have become a new, singular subject together with Christ."[42] Far from this being some private mysticism of "Jesus and me," it is essentially personal and ecclesial—indeed, Christic. "The new subject is much rather 'Christ' himself, and the Church is nothing but the space of this new unitary subject."[43] Here, in another formulation, is the Augustinian notion of the *totus Christus* that so captivated the young theologian, Joseph Ratzinger.

This is not "mysticism" in any esoteric sense. It is the personal appropriation and realization of the Christo-logic of baptism. It is the ever more intimate indwelling of Christ in the believing community effected by the Eucharist. It is a mysticism of the saving presence of the risen Christ, who, through his Eucharistic body, builds up his ecclesial body. De Lubac's insight into the threefold body of Christ continues to serve as foundation for Ratzinger's systematic exploration.

Yet the Eucharistic presence of Christ is not static and fixed; it is certainly not reified. It is the presence of him who is ever coming. In what is perhaps his most systematic work, *Eschatology*, Ratzinger writes, "The Eucharist is at once the joyful proclamation of the Lord's presence and a supplication to the already present Lord that he may come since, paradoxically, even as the One who is present he remains the One who is to come."[44] Thus, the celebration of Christ's real presence does not preclude an acknowledgment of absence. The lack is not in the risen and ascended Christ but in believers who are not yet fully incorporated into Christ. As the Australian theologian Anthony Kelly has recently expressed it, "It is not Christ who has become disembodied, but we human beings are not yet fully embodied in him as we are destined to be."[45] He is absent in the measure that we have not yet been fully transformed in Christ.

In this light we can see the true import of Ratzinger's proposal to recover a sense of the liturgy celebrated *ad Orientem*: toward the East. This has nothing to do with "turning one's back to the people," but with the recovery of an eschatological sense of the people of God on pilgrimage toward the Lord who comes to sanctify and transform his people.[46] He has made it abundantly clear that facing the "geographic East" is much less crucial than facing the "spiritual East." Placing a cross upon the altar of sacrifice is the symbolic expression that we are not our own but the Lord's, and of our ardent desire for his return. It is the realization that truly to appropriate Christ is to be disappropriated of self and appropriated by him. It is the recognition enshrined in St. Paul's exhortation to the Corinthians: "Do you not know that your body is a Temple of the Holy Spirit? . . . You are not your own; you were bought with a price. So glorify God in your body" (1 Cor. 6:19–20). Writing of St. Paul in *The Spirit of the Liturgy*, Ratzinger comments,

> The Apostle does not want to discard his body, he does not want to be bodiless. He is not interested in any flight of the soul from "the prison of the body," as envisaged by the Pythagorean tradition taken up by Plato. He does not want flight but transformation. He hopes for resurrection.[47]

Though sometimes misleadingly labeled a "Platonist," Ratzinger has an acute sense of what I call "somatic relationality." We have already seen his emphasis on the communal and corporate dimensions of such a bodily and relational vision. Let us briefly consider two other dimensions of his somatic sensibility: the sensory and the ecological.

Part of the thrust of Ratzinger's mystagogical catechesis is to renew the tradition of the "spiritual senses" so prominent in the Fathers of the Church and his well-loved Bonaventure. He speaks, apropos of the journey of transformation, of becoming increasingly conformed to Christ: "The senses are not to be discarded, but they should be expanded to their widest capacity."[48] In a culture in which even our physical senses are often atrophied and in which images are reduced to advertising devices and to "selfies," he seeks to recover and promote a sacramental sense of the image as icon.

> The image of Christ and the images of the saints are not photographs. Their whole point is to lead us beyond what can be apprehended at the merely material level, to awaken new senses in us, and to teach us a new kind of seeing, which perceives the Invisible in the visible. The sacredness of the image consists precisely in the fact that it comes from an interior vision and thus leads us to such an interior vision. It must be a fruit of contemplation, of an encounter in faith with the new reality of the risen Christ, and so it leads us in turn into an interior gazing, an encounter in prayer with the Lord.[49]

The Eucharist itself is the living icon of Christ, the sacrament of love. Hence, the training of the spiritual senses culminates in discerning the Eucharistic presence of Christ and to realize more fully his call to transformation and action, to a "Eucharistic form of life." In part 3 of *Sacramentum Caritatis*, Benedict speaks at length about "The Eucharistic Form of the Christian Life" and discusses its implications for social justice and for environmental concerns. These are not "add-ons," but are ingredient to a Eucharistic faith and spirituality and to our constitutive "somatic relationality."[50] To rekindle so radical a Christological vision requires not merely eyes of flesh, but Spirit-fueled eyes of fire. Vatican II has summoned the church to nothing less.

Conclusion

In an essay written just after the Second Vatican Council, Karl Rahner (who had collaborated with Ratzinger in responding to the conciliar drafts on behalf of the German bishops)[51] famously prophesied, "The devout Christian of the future will either be a 'mystic'—one who has 'experienced something'—or will cease to be anything at all."[52] Ratzinger himself has cited Rahner's dictum, but he demurs somewhat, opining, "I would not ask for so much. . . . We always remain just as weak as ever, which means that we will not all become mystics." He then goes on, however, to concede what Rahner, perhaps, really intended. "But Rahner is correct in that Christianity will be doomed to suffocation if we don't learn something of interiorization, in which faith sinks personally into the depth of one's own life and in that depth sustains and illuminates."[53]

I have maintained in this essay that Ratzinger's pastoral-theological intent, throughout his ministry, has been to foster such spiritual "interiorization." In a real sense, not only his splendid homilies but even his more technical theological writings have a definite mystagogic purpose: to lead into a new realization and personal appropriation of the Mystery of human salvation through and in Jesus Christ.

I think that what differentiates Ratzinger's approach from that of Rahner is his more concentrated focus on and appeal to the distinctive particularity of Christian identity. In a respectful but incisive critique of Rahner's theology, he faults Rahner for not giving due weight in his post-conciliar thought to the *novum* of the gospel and to the radical conversion and transformation to which it summons. He thinks that Rahner risks sacrificing the particularity of Christianity to his universal, transcendental concern. Thus, Ratzinger poses a series of pointed questions to Rahner's approach: "Is it true that Christianity adds nothing to the universal but merely makes it known? . . . Does not Christianity become meaningless when it is reinstated in the universal, whereas what we really want is the new, the other, the saving trans-formation [*Ver-änderung*]?"[54]

However accurate these challenges may be as an assessment of the shortcomings of Rahner's own theological investigations, a recent highly appreciative study of Rahner suggests that some of Rahner's epigones do indeed merit such indictment. Peter Joseph Fritz writes rather trenchantly:

They evacuated [Rahner's] richly textured theology of Mystery of its dogmatic substance, making it into an excuse not to study dogma or Christian history. This led to many popular appropriations of

Rahner that fled not only from him, but often also from Catholicism, into vapid spiritualities that were wrongly called "mysticism" because no mystery remained.[55]

The inseparable perichoresis of the Christian Mystery with Christian spirituality and mysticism is the very hallmark of Ratzinger's Christ-centered vision and mystagogy. Christian mysticism is always bodily—the body transformed in the tri-form body of Christ.

In the same work in which his critique of Rahner appears, Ratzinger discloses the foundation of his own theological approach. It lies not in universal human intentionality and aspiration but in the unique particularity of the resurrection of Jesus Christ. He writes:

> All Christian theology, if it is to be true to its origins, must be first and foremost a theology of Resurrection. It must be a theology of Resurrection before it is a theology of the justification of the sinner; it must be a theology of Resurrection before it is a theology of the metaphysical Sonship of God. It can be a theology of the Cross, but only as and within the framework of a theology of Resurrection. Its first and primordial statement is the good tidings that the power of death, the one constant of history, has in a single instance been broken by the power of God and that history has thus been imbued with an entirely new hope. In other words, the core of the gospel consists in the good tidings of the Resurrection and, thus, in the good tidings of God's action, which precedes all human doing.[56]

Since it is the risen, living Christ who is present in the Eucharistic celebration and faith of the church, it comes as no surprise to hear Benedict XVI proclaim:

> The Sacrament of the Altar is always at the heart of the Church's life: thanks to the Eucharist, the Church is reborn ever anew! The more lively the Eucharistic faith of the people of God, the deeper is its sharing in ecclesial life in steadfast commitment to the mission entrusted by Christ to his disciples. The Church's very history bears witness to this. Every great reform has in some way been linked to the rediscovery of belief in the Lord's Eucharistic presence among his people. (*Sacramentum Caritatis*, 6)

In light of the above, let me close with a Benedictine variant on the Rahnerian "prophecy." The Catholic Christian of the future will be a Eucharistic mystic—someone who encounters the living Christ in the Eucharist and experiences there her or his deepest identity to be a member of Christ's body—or will cease to be anything at all.[57]

Notes

1. Joseph Ratzinger, *Behold the Pierced One: An Approach to a Spiritual Christology*, trans. Graham Harrison (San Francisco: Ignatius Press, 1986), 9.

2. Ibid., 25.

3. Joseph Ratzinger/Pope Benedict XVI, *Jesus of Nazareth*, vol. 1, *From the Baptism in the Jordan to the Transfiguration*, trans. Adrian J. Walker (New York: Doubleday, 2007), 344.

4. Irenaeus of Lyons, *Adversus Haereses* 4.34.1 (*PG* 7:1083). This affirmation of Irenaeus is cited by Pope Francis in his Apostolic Exhortation *Evangelii Gaudium*, 11, available at http://w2.vatican.va/content/francesco/ en/apost_exhortations/documents/papa-francesco_esortazione-ap_20131124_ evangelii-gaudium.html.

5. Joseph Ratzinger, *Introduction to Christianity*, trans. J. R. Foster (San Francisco: Ignatius Press, 2004), 221.

6. Ibid., 225.

7. Paolo Prosperi, "The Birth of *Sources Chrétiennes* and the Return to the Fathers," *Communio* 39.4 (2012): 643.

8. Ratzinger, *Behold the Pierced One*, 27.

9. Joseph Ratzinger, *Milestones: Memoirs 1927–1977*, trans. Erasmo Leiva-Merikakis (San Francisco: Ignatius Press, 1998), 98.

10. Ibid.

11. The English translation modified the French subtitle: Henri de Lubac, *Catholicism: Christ and the Common Destiny of Man*, trans. Lancelot Sheppard and Sister Elizabeth Englund (San Francisco: Ignatius Press, 1988). This edition contains a foreword by Cardinal Ratzinger testifying again to the book's profound importance for him personally, as well as for Catholic theology: "[De Lubac] shows how the idea of community and universality, rooted in the Trinitarian concept of God, permeates and shapes all the individual elements of faith's content. The idea of the Catholic, the all-embracing, the inner unity of I and Thou and We, does not constitute one chapter of theology among others. It is the key that opens the door to the proper understanding of the whole" (11).

12. Benedict XVI, Encyclical Letter, *Spe Salvi*, 48, available at http:// w2.vatican.va/content/benedict-xvi/en/encyclicals/documents/hf_ben-xvi_ enc_20071130_spe-salvi.html.

13. Emery de Gaál, *The Theology of Benedict XVI: The Christocentric Shift* (New York: Palgrave Macmillan, 2010), 65.

14. Benedict XVI, Apostolic Exhortation, *Sacramentum Caritatis*, 15, available at http://w2.vatican.va/content/benedict-xvi/en/apost_exhortations/documents/hf_ben-xvi_exh_20070222_sacramentum-caritatis.html.

15. Ibid., 14.

16. Joseph Ratzinger, "Christocentrism in Preaching," in idem, *Dogma and Preaching: Applying Christian Doctrine to Daily Life*, trans. Michael J. Miller and Matthew O'Connell (San Francisco: Ignatius Press, 2011), 44.

17. I have argued the case more fully in Robert P. Imbelli, *Rekindling the Christic Imagination: Theological Meditations for the New Evangelization* (Collegeville MN: Liturgical Press, 2013). See especially "Preface" and "Introduction."

18. See the illuminating treatment by Jared Wicks S.J., "Six Texts by Professor Joseph Ratzinger as *Peritus* before and during Vatican Council II," *Gregorianum* 89 (2008): 233–311.

19. Vatican Council II, *Gaudium et Spes,* in *Decrees of the Ecumenical Councils,* vol. 2, *Trent to Vatican II*, ed. Norman P. Tanner S.J. (Washington, DC: Georgetown University Press, 1990), 1074–75.

20. Ratzinger, *Introduction to Christianity*, 31–32 (emphasis mine). This classic of twentieth-century Catholic theology has been reprinted twenty-four times and been translated into seventeen languages.

21. Ratzinger, *Dogma and Preaching*, 57.

22. Ratzinger, *Jesus of Nazareth*, 1: xii.

23. In the preface to *Rekindling the Christic Imagination*, I suggest that a measure of the loss of a Christocentric vision in some quarters after the council may be found in the not so benign neglect of *Dei Verbum*.

24. Benedict XVI, *Jesus of Nazareth*, vol. 2, *Holy Week: From the Entrance into Jerusalem to the Resurrection*, trans. Philip J. Whitmore (San Francisco: Ignatius Press, 2011), xv.

25. Benedict XVI, Apostolic Exhortation, *Verbum Domini*, 2, available at http://w2.vatican.va/content/benedict-xvi/en/apost_exhortations/documents/hf_ben-xvi_exh_20100930_verbum-domini.html. One notices the similarity of this purpose to that of Pope Francis in his own Apostolic Exhortation following the 2012 Synod on Evangelization, *Evangelii Gaudium*.

26. Joseph Cardinal Ratzinger, *Salt of the Earth: The Church at the End of the Millennium*, an interview with Peter Seewald, trans. Adrian Walker (San Francisco: Ignatius Press, 1997), 76–77.

27. Benedict XVI, "Homily for the Opening of the Year of Faith" (October 11, 2012), available at http://w2.vatican.va/content/benedict-xvi/en/homilies/2012/documents/hf_ben-xvi_hom_20121011_anno-fede.html.

28. The second part of the original dissertation has been published in English as *The Theology of History in St. Bonaventure*, trans. Zachary Hayes

O.F.M. (Chicago: Franciscan Herald Press, 1989). Ratzinger recounts the drama connected with the writing and defense of the dissertation in *Milestones*, 104–13. The complete work has now been published as *Offenbarung und Heilsgeschichte nach der Lehre des heiligen Bonaventure*, in Joseph Ratzinger, *Gesammelte Schriften, Bd. 2* (Freiburg: Herder, 2009).

29. Ratzinger, *Salt of the Earth*, 62–63.

30. William Harmless S.J. *Mystics* (New York: Oxford University Press, 2008), 102.

31. Ratzinger, *Milestones*, 108–9.

32. See n. 28. Ratzinger recounts the epochal rejection of the original schema on Divine Revelation at Vatican II and the eventual emergence of *Dei Verbum* with its much deeper understanding of revelation (*Milestones*, 124–29). As a young theologian he played an important role in the process.

33. See the important article by Henri de Lubac, "Mysticism and Mystery," in *Theological Fragments*, trans. Rebecca Howell Balinski (San Francisco: Ignatius Press, 1989), 35–69.

34. Cited by John F. Crosby in his fine study *The Personalism of John Henry Newman* (Washington, DC: Catholic University of America Press, 2014), 48.

35. Benedict XVI, Encyclical Letter, *Deus Caritas Est*, 1, available at http://w2.vatican.va/content/benedict-xvi/en/encyclicals/documents/hf_ben-xvi_enc_20051225_deus-caritas-est.html. It is significant that Pope Francis quotes these words of Benedict at the beginning of *Evangelii Gaudium*, remarking, "I never tire of repeating these words of Benedict XVI which take us to the very heart of the Gospel."

36. Cardinal Ratzinger's homily for Monsignor Giussani is available at http://www.communio-icr.com/articles/view/funeral-homily-for-msgr.-luigi-giussani.

37. See the essays gathered in Joseph Ratzinger, *New Outpourings of the Spirit: Movements in the Church*, trans. Michael Miller and Henry Taylor (San Francisco: Ignatius Press, 2007).

38. I evoke here the title of the book by Joseph Ratzinger, *A New Song for the Lord: Faith in Christ and Liturgy Today*, trans. Martha M. Matesich (New York: Herder, 1997). Part 1, "Jesus Christ, Center of Faith and Foundation of Our Hope," makes clear that our understanding and practice of liturgy depends on the prior question of who we confess Jesus Christ to be. Ratzinger writes, "the criteria of liturgical renewal ultimately culminate in one question: Who do people say the Son of Man is? (Mt. 16:14f.). Hence, this first section seems to me to be imperative for placing liturgical questions in the right context" (x).

39. Joseph Ratzinger, *The Spirit of the Liturgy*, trans. John Saward (San Francisco: Ignatius Press, 2000), 138.

40. Joseph Ratzinger, *Pilgrim Fellowship of Faith: The Church as Communion*, trans. Henry Taylor (San Francisco: Ignatius Press, 2005), 78.

41. Benedict XVI, Audience, October 3, 2012, available at http://

w2.vatican.va/content/benedict-xvi/en/audiences/2012/documents/hf_ben-xvi_aud_20121003.html.

42. Joseph Ratzinger, "The Spiritual Basis and Ecclesial Identity of Theology," in *The Nature and Mission of Theology*, trans. Adrian Walker (San Francisco: Ignatius Press, 1995), 52. To appreciate the force of his exegesis one must recall that Paul's Greek for "one in Christ Jesus" is not "one thing" but the much more radical "one person."

43. Ibid., 54.

44. Joseph Ratzinger, *Eschatology: Death and Eternal Life*, trans. Michael Waldstein (Washington, DC: Catholic University of America Press, 1988), 6.

45. Anthony J. Kelly, *Upward: Faith, Church, and the Ascension of Christ* (Collegeville, MN: Liturgical Press, 2014), 94.

46. The eschatological vision of chapter 7 of *Lumen Gentium*, "The Eschatological Character of the Pilgrim Church and Its Union with the Heavenly Church," has been seriously neglected. For a helpful study, see Thomas P. Rausch S.J., *Eschatology, Liturgy, and Christology: Toward Recovering an Eschatological Imagination* (Collegeville, MN: Liturgical Press, 2012).

47. Ratzinger, *Spirit of the Liturgy*, 218. The entire last section of the book is devoted to "The Body and the Liturgy."

48. Ibid., 123.

49. Ibid., 133. There is currently an important rediscovery of the tradition of the spiritual senses in theology. See the fine essays in *The Spiritual Senses: Perceiving God in Western Christianity*, ed. Paul Gavrilyuk and Sarah Coakley (Cambridge: Cambridge University Press, 2013), especially, for our purpose, the essay by Gregory La Nave, "Bonaventure."

50. I have sought to develop further this perspective in terms of a "Christological ontology and epistemology." See Robert P. Imbelli, "The Heart Has Its Reasons: Giving an Account of the Hope That Is in Us," in *Handing on the Faith*, College Theology Society Annual Volume 59, ed. Matthew Lewis Sutton and William L. Portier (Maryknoll, NY: Orbis Books, 2014), 21–42.

51. Ratzinger speaks briefly of their collaboration and differences in *Milestones*, 128–29.

52. Karl Rahner, "Christian Living Formerly and Today," in *Theological Investigations*, vol. 7, trans. David Bourke (New York: Herder, 1971), 15.

53. Ratzinger, *Salt of the Earth*, 267.

54. Joseph Ratzinger, *Principles of Catholic Theology: Building Stones for a Fundamental Theology*, trans. Sister Mary Frances McCarthy (San Francisco: Ignatius Press, 1987), 166.

55. Peter Joseph Fritz, *Karl Rahner's Theological Aesthetics* (Washington, DC: Catholic University of America Press, 2014), 265.

56. Ratzinger, *Principles of Catholic Theology*, 184–85.

57. At the conclusion of this essay I would like to pay tribute to the late Frans Jozef van Beeck, S.J., whose insightful book *Catholic Identity after Vatican II: Three Types of Faith in the One Church* (New Orleans: Loyola University Press, 1985) has not received the close attention it deserves. He writes, "In the mystical dimension of this Sacrament [the Eucharist] the Church comes to full actuality, as do those Christians who have found there both themselves and God" (66). Joseph Ratzinger would be in full accord.

13

Contemplative Ecology: A Mystical Horizon for the Twenty-First Century

Diarmuid O'Murchu MSC

John Jones, as a devoted and dedicated editor, may seem an unlikely adherent of apophatic mysticism, with a special interest in Dionysius the Areopagite. In his daily life John immersed himself in the duties and responsibilities as an editor, bringing to his work the expediency and efficiency that many associate with secular progress. Undoubtedly, those who knew John more intimately would be quick to point out that there were other dimensions to his life, rarely noticed by a mere external observer, and among those were John the deeply spiritual person and the mystic at heart.

The kind of language used by Dionysius suggests that mysticism describes a quality of absorption into God that requires departure from the earthly realm as popularly associated with the enclosed or monastic life. The apophatic tradition, with its strong emphasis on the God who is discovered in darkness, beyond the descriptive power of human language, suggests all the more strongly a quality of radical separation from earthly life and human concern.

Many studies throughout the twentieth century clearly indicate that this is a reductionistic view of mysticism and that great mystics such as Meister Eckhart and Hildegard of Bingen, John of the Cross, and Teresa of Avila were deeply immersed in the world of their time while also exemplifying in their lives an exceptional quality of holiness. In a similar vein, we note the remarkable mystical synthesis achieved by devotees like the late Bede Griffiths and many others, who espoused a more multifaith integration in their pursuit of mystical wisdom. This quality of mysticism suggests a degree of integration—what today we might call an *Integral Spirituality*[1] —that escapes the average Christian, and can be so subtle in people like John Jones that it goes largely unobserved.

In this reflective tribute to John, I wish to suggest that this subtle fascination with Holy Mystery is much more prevalent in the twenty-first century than is generally recognized. The darkness and the light intermingle in ways that mystics have long known, but at various historical moments the prevailing philosophical and theological wisdom was unable to discern the deeper integration. With advances in both sacred and secular (scientific) learning we are rediscovering afresh a quality of mystical wisdom largely hidden from human view. One articulation that may have a particular relevance for the twenty-first century is that of *contemplative ecology*, the topic I wish to explore in the present essay.

Contemplative Ecology

My primary resource here is Douglas Christie's book *The Blue Sapphire of the Mind: Notes for a Contemplative Ecology* (2013). Christie is Professor of Theological Studies at Loyola Marymount University and co-director of the Casa de la Mateada Program in Córdoba, Argentina. He is a specialist in the study of Evagrius of Pontus (345–399 C.E.) and has devoted much of his life to exploring the integration of monastic spirituality with the pressing ecological and cultural concerns of the present time. His work has been described as a vision of cosmic wholeness.

Christie captures a unique feature of our time when he observes that our culture is characterized by "the diverse and wide-ranging desire emerging within contemporary culture to identify our deepest feeling for the natural world as part of a spiritual longing."[2] Despite the apparent secularism, hedonism, consumerism, and fragmentation of our age—or perhaps because of these destructive forces—there also prevails a deep spiritual hunger, one not focused on escape into divine absorption but one that seeks to rediscover within the natural world itself the deep imprint of the sacred impulse. Rediscovering this natural mysticism and relocating it personally and collectively will not just be in monastic enclosures or sacred places away from the world, but more deeply integrated with the natural world itself. Thus, writes Christie:

> It seems to me that if the idea of contemplative ecology is to gain purchase on our imaginations and contribute something significant to our way of living in the world, it will of necessity have to find its way into the places where we are most vulnerable, especially in relation to the natural world. . . . The contemplative's "daily attentiveness, alertness, and eagerness of the senses turned outward" help rescue the world from oblivion, even as the contemplative is saved by the simple beauty of the world, by the recognition that the fabric is whole and we are woven deeply into it.[3]

Engage rather than *Escape* is the key word to describe the envisaged synthesis. And the engagement has anthropological, ecological, and cultural ramifications. The human *qua* human can only attain its full incarnational realization through the living earth itself. We are earthlings in the very heart of our being, an ancient spiritual intuition long suppressed and ignored but re-entering the spiritual and theological consciousness of our time, thanks to new insights from the social sciences particularly.[4] Our earthiness is our primary sacredness; therein we encounter and engage with the living vitality of divine creativity. This brings us to the ecological dimension, stretching our spirits far beyond the urgent and pressing issues of our time—global warming, pollution, earth erosion, threatened species—to wrestle with the profound sacredness of the living earth itself. In science it is known as the *Gaia Theory*.[5] Culturally, therefore, the emerging mystical consciousness seeks to address the fragmentation and alienation that haunt existence at the deepest level and, through sustained practice, to come to realize a different, more integrated way of being in the world.[6]

Contemplative ecology, therefore, seeks to develop an understanding of spiritual practice that places the well-being of the natural world at the center of its concerns, and an approach to ecology that understands the work of cultivating contemplative awareness as critical and necessary to its full meaning. Christie envisions a synthesis that overcomes what he calls "the corrosive dichotomies that have prevented us from seeing the world as whole."[7] We need to outgrow the dualistic split between sacred and secular, body and soul, matter and spirit. More significantly—and controversially—we need to reclaim the living earth itself as our primary sacred space, the mystical indwelling for the twenty-first century.

Much of Christie's concern is how to reintegrate contemplative/ monastic wisdom—so long associated with the reclusive nature of traditional monastic life—with the newly unfolding mystical earth-centered consciousness of the twenty-first century. A careful and more discerning examination of the historical record suggests that monastic communities have consistently borne witness to, and continue to contribute significantly to, the project of cultural, social, and even political renewal. Monastic communities in the past and present retain a close affiliation with the living soil, imbued with a deep love for God's creation. We detect such sentiments in these words of the great monastic visionary Thomas Merton: "Contemplation is the highest expression of our intellectual and spiritual life. It is spontaneous awe at the sacredness of life, of being. It is gratitude for life, for awareness and for being. It is a vivid realization of the fact that life and being in us proceed from an invisible, transcendent and infinitely abundant source."[8] To which Christie can truthfully add, "Contemplative prayer has always been understood as being rooted in an attention that is at once focussed and capacious."[9]

Abram's Sensuous Spirituality

Attempts at understanding mysticism's appeal in the twentieth and twenty-first centuries echo afresh the apophatic sentiment in tracing mystical elements even within nonreligious contexts. One notes this in the work of the British postmodern theologian Don Cupitt, in the American scientist John Horgan, as well as in the works of the religious philosopher Jeffrey John Kripal.[10] But one of its finest and most integrated articulations comes from the philosopher and naturalist David Abram, perhaps best known to readers for the inspiring book *The Spell of the Sensuous* (1996). In this essay I will draw more extensively from his more recent work, *Becoming Animal: An Earthly Cosmology* (2010).[11]

Abram is founder and creative director of the Alliance for Wild Ethics (AWE). Throughout the 1980s he spent a considerable period of time living and studying with traditional, indigenous magic practitioners in Sri

Lanka, Indonesia, and Nepal. For extensive time spans, over many years, Abram has roamed and explored the natural environment, sometimes sitting still for several hours observing a bird, an animal's stance, or a flower's texture. Endowed with an acute sensitivity to the natural environment, with highly developed perceptual and auditory skills, Abram detects the magic of spirit-power to a degree achieved by few human beings. Although he rarely uses religious language, the mystical depth of his wisdom and insight is indisputable.

Over many centuries our animality was considered the great enemy of our spiritual growth and development. For Abram, the animal is the sensuous carnality that grounds us inescapably in the divinely imbued web of planetary co-evolution. Our animal embodied coexistence is the doorway to the mystery of God's creation. In Abram's own words,

> An eternity we thought was elsewhere now calls out to us from every cleft in every stone, from every cloud and clump of dirt. To lend our ears to the dripping glaciers—to come awake to the voices of silence—is to be turned inside out, discovering to our astonishment that the wholeness and holiness we'd been dreaming our way toward has been holding us all along; that the secret and sacred One that moves behind all the many traditions is none other than this animate immensity that enfolds us, this spherical eternity, glimpsed at last in its unfathomable wholeness and complexity, in its sensitivity and its sentience.[12]

Rather than describe for the reader Abram's mystical immersion (or absorption) in carnal sacredness of the human and earth bodies, I quote at length his resume of his spiritual pilgrimage:

> The mass turn towards formal religion by citizens of industrial nations in the last half century, the swelling membership in fundamentalist creeds of every kind, the myriad new shapes of belief that adorn the spiritual marketplace, all give evidence that the human craving for relation with that which exceeds us is as strong as ever. Nonetheless, given the ancestral impulse toward otherness at the core of this craving, it is not likely to be finally sated by any God made in our image, anymore than it can be satisfied by our

human-made technologies. A much older and deeper accord is at stake here, an alliance as intimate as the breath, and one as easily overlooked by the intellect. When we speak of the human animal's spontaneous interchange with the animate landscape, we acknowledge a felt relation to the mysterious that was active long before any formal or priestly religions. The instinctive rapport with an enigmatic cosmos at once both nourishing and dangerous lies at the ancient heart of all that we have come to call "the sacred."[13]

Beyond the nostalgia for an idyllic past that Abram is likely to be accused of is a depth of engagement with the urgent human and ecological quandaries of our time. With an awe-inspiring transparency, Abram walks the talk! Precisely for that reason he has intuitions into our common future that are deeply imbued with an empowering spirituality. The hope for the future he claims rests not in the triumph of any single set of beliefs, but in knowing and appropriating anew a felt mystery that underlies all our doctrines and belief systems. Beneath all our beliefs is a corporeal trust in providence: the human body's implicit faith in the steady sustenance of the air and the renewal of light awakening every dawn, its faith in mountains and rivers and the enduring support of the ground, in the silent germination of seeds and the cyclic return of the seasons. For Abram, there are no priests needed for such a faith, no intermediaries or experts necessary to affect our contact with the sacred, since—carnally immersed as we are in the thick of this breathing planet—we each have our own intimate access to the big mystery.

Mysticism and Relationality

These reflections would be incomplete without alluding to the pioneering work of Father Thomas Berry, priest and geologist, who died in 2009. Berry is best known for his cosmic spirituality, arising more from a lifelong intellectual pursuit as distinct from the naturalist trail pursued by David Abram. These two visionaries have a great deal in common. In what many regard as his best-known work, *The Dream of the Earth,* Berry writes,

It is especially important in this discussion to recognize the unity of the total process, from that first unimaginable moment of cosmic emergence through all its subsequent forms of expression until the present. This unbreakable bond of relatedness that makes of the whole a universe becomes increasingly apparent to scientific observation, although this bond ultimately escapes scientific formulation or understanding. In virtue of this relatedness, everything is intimately present to everything else in the universe. Nothing is completely itself without everything else. This relatedness is both spatial and temporal. However distant in space or time, the bond of unity is functionally there. The universe is a communion and a community. We ourselves are that communion become conscious of itself.[14]

This is the same underlying unity that has enamoured and fascinated mystics over many millennia. For Berry, however, the realization of this unifying force does not awaken a desire to escape from this vale of tears, seeking to be more fully at one with the One who is the source of this unity. To the contrary, the relational wholeness, so vividly portrayed by Berry, invites us into a deeper more engaging adventure, *as earthlings*, born of the earth, a dream of the earth, earthiness becoming conscious of itself, and of its divinely endowed grandeur. For Berry, humans are uniquely the creatures in whom the universe reflects on and celebrates itself in a special mode of conscious self-awareness. Through this consciousness we find our role in the ongoing adventure of evolution, in what Berry describes in another book as *The Great Work*.[15]

In our totality we are born of the earth. Our spirituality itself is earth-derived. If there is no spirituality in the earth, then there is no spirituality in ourselves. The natural world itself is our primary language as it is our primary scripture, our primordial awakening to the mysteries of existence. Berry advocates that we might consider putting all our written scriptures on the shelf for twenty years until we learn what we are being told by the unmediated experience of the world about us, sacred in its deepest essence.

The reader will recognize the resonances with the visionary optimism of the Jesuit priest and paleontologist Pierre Teilhard de Chardin, whose pioneering evolutionary wisdom is currently enjoying a revival thanks to the scholarly synthesis developed by the Franciscan sister, Senior Fellow in Science and Religion at Georgetown University, Ilia Delio.[16] In the early decades of the twentieth century, Teilhard developed an earth-centered, evolutionary thrust, deeply imbued with spiritual animation. Far ahead of his time, his vision won the favor of neither scientists nor theologians. One wonders, however, if the mystical consciousness of the time lacked the spiritual coherence necessary for the fuller flowering of his ambitious dream. It looks like the spiritual and mystical soil of the twenty-first century is more conducive to the fertilization of his audacious vision, and Ilia Delio is among the scholars leading the revitalization of his seminal ideas.

From Apophatic to Pleroma

I began these reflections alluding to John Jones's fascination with Dionysius the Areopagite. In his *Mystical Theology*, chapter 1, Dionysius claims that Moses, having ascended Mount Sinai, passes through the sensible and intelligible contemplation of God and then enters the darkness above the mountain's peak. After that, Dionysius leaves the relation between Moses and the darkness highly obscure. Although he speaks only of Moses' "union" with the ineffable, invisible, unknowable Godhead, he insists that in this life we can never abandon the kataphatic aspect, based on the theophanic nature of creation itself. The Lutheran medieval church historian Paul Rorem informs us that "far from compartmentalizing his method into 'affirmative theology,' 'negative theology,' and 'symbolic theology,' the Pseudo-Dionysius seeks to hold together affirmation and negation, similarity and dissimilarity, as a dialectical way of understanding the many symbols of his tradition."[17]

The apophatic mystical wisdom favors the God who transcends all external expression and human elaboration, a God whose reality cannot be encapsulated in words and is best apprehended and comprehended in the dark silence of unknowing. Certainly, there are many in our noisy turbulent world who find this an attractive ideal. By the same token, the spirituality of "kenosis" carries a strong appeal for those who seek divine bliss after they have emptied out all the cares and preoccupations of our frenetic, boisterous culture. For many such devotees it is not a pursuit of salvific escape—from sin, temptation, and distraction—but a desire to encounter and serve the God whose enduring love and fidelity will forever transcend all the constructs and theories of the human mind.

It seems to me that the mystical consciousness of the twenty-first century is veering in another significant direction, briefly described in the reflections of this essay. However, as indicated above in the quotation from Paul Rorem, this should not be viewed as a negation of Dionysius, but rather as an expansion of his mystical vision. A Dionysius of the twenty-first century is likely to view the mountain peak through more expansive horizons: ecological, evolutionary, cosmic. The apophatic gives way to the pleroma, honoring rather than negating the intuitive wisdom of Dionysius himself.

The kataphatic should be viewed as complementary, rather than opposed to the apophatic. It is characterized by knowing rather than unknowing, fullness rather than emptiness, illumination (enlightenment) rather than darkness, engagement rather than abandonment. In our time, it may be described as a mysticism of the "pleroma," a growing awareness, even among scientists, of a mysterious intensity that characterizes the whole of creation, a fullness, rather than an emptiness, in what many cosmologists now consider to be a *multiverse* without beginning or end.

In this expansive context, our primary interest is in the God who inhabits all, and whose mysterious, empowering presence is most visibly at work in the physical creation itself. Before that radiant fullness the human may well fall silent, and words are often lacking to express the overpowering radiance of Holy Presence. On the other hand, we can learn from our indigenous peoples across Planet Earth whose silence before the great mystery—which they call the Great Spirit[18]—awakens not any kind of passivity (or unknowing) but a conscience to relate rightly, wisely, and lovingly. In their care for the living earth, our First Nations (indigenous) earthlings know that they are in solidarity with Holy Mystery. Theirs is the kind of mysticism that David Abram knows from first-hand experience. It is the contemplative inscape described so elegantly by Douglas Christie, and it is the theological horizon that so lured the Jesuit Teilhard de Chardin along with contemporary exponents like the late Thomas Berry. Is it not the same earthly-heavenly bliss that has intrigued and pursued mystics in every generation and across all the great religious traditions? A resource of incalculable value that it seems will morph into a range of expressions, as new spiritual needs arise. Amid so much turmoil and paradox in our troubled world, it looks like the pursuit of Holy Mystery continues undiminished.

Notes

1. See Ken Wilbur, *An Integral Spirituality: A Startling New Role for Religion in the Modern and Postmodern World* (New York: Random House, 2007).

2. Douglas Christie, *The Blue Sapphire of the Mind: Notes for a Contemplative Ecology* (New York: Oxford University Press, 2013), 3.

3. Ibid., 23, 56.

4. See Graeme Barker, *The Agricultural Revolution in Prehistory: Why Did Foragers Become Farmers* (Oxford: Oxford University Press, 2009); and Diarmuid O'Murchu, *Ancestral Grace: Meeting God in Our Human Story* (Maryknoll, NY: Orbis Books, 2012).

5. See James Lovelock, *Gaia: A New Look at Life on Earth* (Oxford: Oxford University Press, 1979).

6. Christie, *Blue Sapphire of the Mind*, 36.

7. Ibid., 161.

8. Thomas Merton, *New Seeds of Contemplation* (London: Burns & Oates, 1961), 1.

9. Christie, *Blue Sapphire of the Mind*, 176.

10. See Don Cupitt, *Mysticism after Modernity* (Oxford: Blackwell, 1998); John Horgan, *Rational Mysticism: Dispatches from the Border between Science and Spirituality* (Boston: Houghton Mifflin, 2003); and Jeffrey John Kripal, *Roads of Excess, Palaces of Wisdom: Eroticism and Reflexivity in the Study of Mysticism* (Chicago: University of Chicago Press, 2001); idem, *Mutants and Mystics: Science Fiction, Superhero Comics, and the Paranormal,* (Chicago: University of Chicago Press, 2011).

11. David Abram, *The Spell of the Sensuous: Perception and Language in a More-than-Human World* (New York: Vintage Books, 1996); idem, *Becoming Animal: An Earthly Cosmology* (New York: Vintage Books, 2010).

12. Abram, *Becoming Animal*, 181.

13. Ibid., 290.

14. Thomas Berry, *The Dream of the Earth* (San Francisco: Sierra Club Books, 1988), 91.

15. Thomas Berry, *The Great Work* (New York: Bell Tower, 2000).

16. See Ilia Delio, *The Emergent Christ: Exploring the Meaning of Catholic in an Evolutionary Universe* (Maryknoll, NY: Orbis Books, 2011); eadem, *The Unbearable Wholeness of Being: God, Evolution, and the Power of Love* (Maryknoll, NY: Orbis Books, 2013); eadem, *From Teilhard to Omega:*

Co-creating an Unfinished Universe (Maryknoll, NY: Orbis Books, 2014).

17. Paul Rorem, "The Uplifting Spirituality of Pseudo-Dionysius," in *Christian Spirituality I: Origins to the Twelfth Century,* ed. Bernard McGinn, John Meyendorf, and Jean Leclercq (New York: Crossroad, 1987), 132-51, here 136.

18. Diarmuid O'Murchu, *In the Beginning Was the Spirit: Science, Religion, and Indigenous Spirituality* (Maryknoll, NY: Orbis Books, 2012).

BIBLIOGRAPHY

Abram, David. *The Spell of the Sensuous: Perception and Language in a More-than-Human World.* New York: Vintage Books, 1996.

———. *Becoming Animal: An Earthly Cosmology.* New York: Vintage Books, 2010.

Barker, Graeme. *The Agricultural Revolution in Prehistory: Why Did Foragers Become Farmers?* Oxford: Oxford University Press, 2009.

Berry, Thomas. *The Dream of the Earth.* San Francisco: Sierra Club Books, 1988.

———. *The Great Work.* New York: Bell Tower, 2000.

Christie, Douglas. *The Blue Sapphire of the Mind: Notes for a Contemplative Ecology.* New York: Oxford University Press, 2013.

Cupitt, Don. *Mysticism after Modernity.* Oxford: Blackwell, 1998.

Delio, Ilia. *The Emergent Christ: Exploring the Meaning of Catholic in an Evolutionary Universe.* Maryknoll, NY: Orbis Books, 2011.

———. *From Teilhard to Omega: Co-creating an Unfinished Universe.* Maryknoll, NY: Orbis Books, 2014.

———. *The Unbearable Wholeness of Being: God, Evolution, and the Power of Love.* Maryknoll, NY: Orbis Books, 2013.

Horgan, John. *Rational Mysticism: Dispatches from the Border between Science and Spirituality.* Boston: Houghton Mifflin, 2003.

Kripal, Jeffrey John. *Mutants and Mystics: Science Fiction, Superhero Comics, and the Paranormal.* Chicago: University of Chicago Press, 2011.

———. *Roads of Excess, Palaces of Wisdom: Eroticism and Reflexivity in the Study of Mysticism.* Chicago: University of Chicago Press, 2001.

Lovelock, James. *Gaia: A New Look at Life on Earth*. Oxford: Oxford University Press, 1979.

Merton, Thomas. *New Seeds of Contemplation*. London: Burns & Oates, 1961.

O'Murchu, Diarmuid. *Ancestral Grace: Meeting God in our Human Story*. Maryknoll, NY: Orbis Books, 2008.

———. *In the Beginning Was the Spirit: Science, Religion, and Indigenous Spirituality*. Maryknoll, NY: Orbis Books, 2012.

Rorem, Paul. "The Uplifting Spirituality of Pseudo-Dionysius." In *Christian Spirituality I: Origins to the Twelfth Century*, edited by Bernard McGinn, John Meyendorf, and Jean Leclercq, 132–51. New York: Crossroad, 1987.

Wilber, Ken. *An Integral Spirituality: A Startling New Role for Religion in the Modern and Postmodern World*. New York: Random House, 2007.

Earlier Volumes from
The Presence of God: A History of
Western Christian Mysticism Series

Volume 1
The Foundations of Mysticism
Origins to the Fifth Century
Paperback, 516 pages, 978-0-8245-1404-4

Volume 2
The Growth of Mysticism
Gregory the Great Through the 12th Century
Paperback, 648 pages, 978-0-8245-1628-4

Volume 3
The Flowering of Mysticism
Men and Women in the New Mysticism: 1200-1350
Paperback, 542 pages, 978-0-8245-1743-4

Volume 4
The Harvest of Mysticism in Medieval Germany
Paperback, 768 pages, 978-0-8245-1245-9

Volume 5
The Varieties of Vernacular Mysticism
1350–1550
Paperback, 736 pages, 978-0-8245-4392-1

Please support your local bookstore or order
directly from the publisher at
www.crossroadpublishing.com.

To request a catalog or inquire about
quantity orders, e-mail sales@crossroadpublishing.com.

The Crossroad Publishing Company

The Presence of God: A History of Western Christian Mysticism Series continued . . .

Volume 6, Part 1
Mysticism in the Reformation
1500–1650
Hardcover, 350 pages, 978-0-8245-2230-8

Coming Winter 2017

Volume 6, Part 2
Mysticism in the Golden Age of Spain
1500–1650
Hardcover, 496 pages, 978-0-8245-0090-0

Please support your local bookstore or order directly from the publisher at www.crossroadpublishing.com.

To request a catalog or inquire about quantity orders, e-mail sales@crossroadpublishing.com.

The Crossroad Publishing Company

Additional Reading

Bernard McGinn and Patricia Ferris McGinn
Early Christian Mystics
The Divine Vision of the Spiritual Masters

The McGinns are uniquely qualified to introduce us to the rich
tradition of the mystics in this accessible book on the insights of
the great early Christian mystics and how we can apply that
wisdom to our lives today.

Paperback, 256 pages, 978-0-8245-2106-6

Bernard McGinn
The Mystical Thought of Meister Eckhart
The Man from Whom God Hid Nothing

"Without doubt, this will long stand as the best comprehensive introduction to Eckhart's thought in any language."
—Oliver Davies, *The Eckhart Review*

Paperback, 320 pages, 978-0-8245-1996-4

Bernard McGinn
Doctors of the Church
Thirty-Three Men and Women Who Shaped Christianity

Written by one of the great authorities on Catholic wisdom, this user-
friendly resource is designed as a general introduction to the thirty-three
remarkable individuals who shaped the understanding of the Church's
faith. After a brief account of the concept and development of the office
of *doctor ecclesiae*, sketches of the lives and teachings of the influential
doctors are presented in chronological order. A list of major translations
of each doctor's writings for further reading is also included.

Paperback, 280 pages, 978-0-8245-2549-1

*Please support your local bookstore or order
directly from the publisher at www.crossroadpublishing.com.*

*To request a catalog or inquire about
quantity orders, e-mail sales@crossroadpublishing.com.*

 The Crossroad Publishing Company